CRUEL AND UNUSUAL PUNISHMENT

A Memoir
of the
Psychological Realities
of Federal Prison

PAUL SMITH

WILDBLUE
PRESS

WILDBLUEPRESS.COM

CRUEL AND UNUSUAL PUNISHMENT published by:
WILDBLUE PRESS
P.O. Box 102440
Denver, Colorado 80250

Publisher Disclaimer: Any opinions, statements of fact or fiction, descriptions, dialogue, and citations found in this book were provided by the author, and are solely those of the author. The publisher makes no claim as to their veracity or accuracy, and assumes no liability for the content.

WILDBLUE PRESS is registered at the U.S. Patent and Trademark Offices.

ISBN 978-1-964730-75-2 Hardcover
ISBN 978-1-964730-76-9 Trade Paperback
ISBN 978-1-964730-74-5 eBook

Cover design © 2025 WildBlue Press. All rights reserved.

Interior Formatting and Book Cover Design by Elijah Toten
www.totencreative.com

CRUEL AND UNUSUAL PUNISHMENT

CONTENTS

DISCLAIMER

This book contains strong language, including explicit terms and slurs, that reflect the raw realities and culture of prison life. These words are not used to condone hate or discrimination, but to accurately portray the environment, experiences, and dialogue encountered during the author's time incarcerated.

CHAPTER ONE: THE SAVAGE

Out of the wilderness emerged a twelve-year-old boy. Disheveled blond hair, wild blue eyes, sunburned forehead, hands cupped together holding wild raspberries. I was miles from the nearest town and light years from civilization. I lived mostly in the "here and now," often focused on that moment, that hour, or that day. I thought about events and situations that would likely occur in the future, such as my birthday or going back to school in the fall, and that occurred in the past, like the death of my pet crow. But those thoughts came and went, never lingering long.

I was a smart boy, and in some ways gifted. I felt and understood deeply the rhythms of my environment, the different life cycles, the rotating signs of the seasons, all the sensational changes and what those changes meant. Looking into the sky, then closing my eyes, turning my face toward the sun, it was easy to verify I was facing northeast and the time was getting close to five p.m. I enjoyed the sun on my face, so I would stand for a few moments more. I could judge direction from the position of the sun, smell and course of the wind, and/or moss on a tree, but over time, I developed a deep sense of my physical global position, looking for certain signs to simply verify what I already sensed and knew.

Now my stomach growled, again. Not having eaten since breakfast, I felt both strong hunger and thirst, which had been ignored for hours, but now became distracting. I was intensely focused on an important task. But I often, involuntarily, panned my surroundings looking for things to eat. I could satiate my body easily; I knew what type of plant life were safe to eat and which were poisonous. If I had time to hunt, I could catch frogs, snare rabbits, or spear fish, and make a meal over an open fire. I also knew the location of clean and safe water springs; the closest was two hundred yards due south from my location. I could picture that place in my mind, along with the aluminum ladle left hanging from a tree nearby. I also knew that drinking water from any random creek or stream could make you sick, that sometimes you should boil the water first. If I desired, I could stay outdoors for weeks and be just fine, which I had done twice earlier that summer with friends. I could even keep camp in the wintertime, which was no easy feat for anyone, especially a half-grown child. Even one capable, competent, and thriving, and never lost in my world.

But outside my world, I struggled in lacking "know how" in many social, cultural, and civil situations and interactions in the "civilized" world. Some people considered me rude, maybe barbaric, and certainly unsophisticated. I simply did not know many common social manners and etiquettes like table manners, common pleasantries, and courting a beautiful girl. During the recent school year, one of my teachers laughed at the way I looked when I entered the classroom. My clothes were a mixture of discordant patterns and colors, and my hair was scraggly. I did not know what fashion meant, how to color coordinate my clothes or style my hair. I wore clothes based on the weather and styled my hair by the wind. I was not intentionally rude to anyone.

While in the cafeteria at school, a teacher walking by observed me eating and commented, "Do we eat like that at home?" I was pulling bites of meat from a fork instead of cutting the meat into smaller pieces. I was told spitting was a bad habit, but did not know why and could not think of a good reason, so I spit. I would never spit on someone unless I was angry. I often urinated, and defecated, outside, not unlike most people do when camping outdoors. I had no understanding about current fads, fashions, or modern trends.

I despised and feared civilization with its so-called advancements and progressive ideas but knew civilization was coming, that in adulthood I would live way out there, light years away, and I dreaded it. To me, civilization was nothing more than a prescribed and forced life full of rules and requirements about how to act and what to think. *Why would anyone choose to live in such a system?*

I stuffed the raspberries into my mouth, scanned (through sight, sound, and smell) the surrounding area, and moved slowly. I was tracking one of the family dogs, a bitch who was unleashed and roaming. The dog was a purebred bloodhound, an impressive and mean hunter, but undisciplined. I did not like the dog because she would often growl and nip at my ankles, sometimes very hard, drawing blood. I had reached an impasse with the dog, and I had had enough. I was going to make deep corrections and establish dominance by force. I understood the animal way—that dominant behavior, which I observed in many animal species, is the quality that opens the door for preferential access to food, shelter, mating, and anything else needed (or desired).

On the edge of a field, I knelt and observed. The dog was where I thought she would be, rooting around in the garbage dump. I was downwind from her and hidden by tall grass. I picked up a nearby stick, plenty sufficient for the job at hand; it would second as a Lord's scepter until I carved a new one. I moved slowly around the edge of the field to about fifty feet from the dog. My plan was to distract her by throwing a piece of bark, go in for the capture, then discipline her firmly with the stick. But once I cocked my arm back to throw the bark, I made a slight rustle, and the dog noticed and started running towards me. Dropping the royal scepter, I tore off into an open field, running like a spooked rabbit toward the farm. I was fast, truly fast. But that dog caught up with me after two hundred feet and took me down by the ankle.

I let out a strong scream; the pain was so intense, I felt that I was going to puke or pass out. Then, enraged, grabbing the dog by an ear and yanking downward hard, I jabbed her in the eye with my thumb, then bit her neck, sinking my teeth down into the flesh. Side to side my head swung violently. I could feel the flesh give way under the fur. And then came the taste of blood—warm, salty, metallic—and, what seemed simultaneously, a strong mesmerism toward the savage and feral. The dog, yelping deep cries, was desperately digging her hind legs into my stomach trying to break free. I had never heard a cry like that before. I let go; no more was needed. The dog ran towards the farm, looking back a few times to confirm she was at a safe distance.

So, it was done. Through teeth, jab, blood, and pain, a law had been communicated deeply and remembered. That dog would never bite me again—I knew this, and the dog learned this. I was pack leader from that day forward. My blood pressure went down. I spit dog hair out of my mouth and headed home. Soon I would think of other things.

As I was walking, the sound of the dinner bell rang. *Mother must have dinner ready. I hope it's venison or fish… I hope she did not make liver again... Why make liver and onions when no one likes them? I hate liver, so does everyone else, and I don't like feeling hungry.* I started to jog, but then hunger pushed me into a full run, and I sprinted for fun because I was fast. And the feelings of liberty and power dominated me suddenly and strongly, almost overwhelming me.

CHAPTER TWO: THE CIVILIZED

The year was 1983. When I completed high school, I had two immediate options for my future: go to work or join the military. These two options, set long before I was born, were more like family expectations. "When you are eighteen, you are out of the house," my parents would say repeatedly, most often while upset with me for one or more of many reasons: misbehaving, being defiant, forgetting to put out the trash, or cleaning up after myself. I was not singled out; each of my five siblings were told the same. I imagined my father was told the same by his parents, and the same for my grandfather. I did not become upset when I heard this. I was excited about the idea of establishing my own independent life.

I decided to go to college, a decision that surprised those around me. This decision was not encouraged by my parents, or even my teachers or guidance counselor. They viewed me as average and ordinary, and certainly not having the aptitude for college. But they never told me that, nor sat down with me to discuss plans. I was utterly unprepared. I had not thought about college until three months prior to graduating high school. I had no college fund. My grades were below average. Even my family history and culture were against it; no one in my family—not parents, grandparents, aunts, uncles, or cousins—went to college. The family was of an enduring hardcore working class, employed as general laborers and in the trades. Most were union members.

There was one brave exception. My older brother went to college. This brother was entering his third year and doing well. I was proud of him. And because this brother introduced the idea, I decided I, too, would go to college.

Once I made up my mind to go, the idea became like an obsession. I fantasized about being a professional and becoming rich. I was not sure what area of academic study I would pursue but had no doubt I would succeed.

Over the summer, I completed an enrollment application and financial aid forms. Three weeks later, I was accepted into the only college that I applied to—Ferris State University in Big Rapids, Michigan, the same college attended by my older brother. After discussions with my college advisor, I selected computer sciences as a major.

Summer ended, and so did my childhood. I packed all my clothes and personal documents into one gigantic luggage bag, a graduation gift from my parents. I had five hundred and seventy-five dollars in my pocket from a summer job. I owned an old Ford Ranger and a .32 Marlin deer rifle. I hugged my parents, said goodbye, and walked out the door. As I approached my rickety truck, I stopped and looked up into the sky with a smile on my face as images of success flooded my mind. Then I said in a quiet but firm tone, "It's time to take big bites out of life." With that, I jumped into my truck and left.

This was a critical point in my life. This decision deviated significantly from what was expected of me, from how I had been raised, and from what I was taught to believe about myself.

I was simply not prepared for the world out there, so-called civilization, and certainly not for academia, complex social situations, or city life: I lacked greatly in social sophistication and tactfulness. Had never experienced, for more than a few days, any significant cultural diversity, metropolitan living, or variety in social interaction. Had never been to a museum, art exhibit, public library, or zoo.

Because of my lack of preparation, insufficient worldly experiences, little if any support from family, and life's random acts of harshness, I would suffer greatly. This was a certainty, and I was obligated to accept it. Life did not and would not ask for my opinion or permission.

Perhaps I would have been spared from intense agony if only someone had told me, or God had revealed to me, a simple truth: I was an ordinary man. Average, common, undistinguished, unremarkable. And if told I was ordinary, I might have surrendered to an ordinary working-class life. That would have been my safest path, certainly, even though that path would have likely led to suffocation and quiet desperation, which is hell, but a lesser version. But no one told me I was ordinary. So, against all the odds, I aimed for the stars.

***

But logical consequences occurred. I suffered intensely through my first couple years of adulthood culminating in grossly mismanaged finances and failure to balance my lifestyle, especially educational studies and social and recreation needs. I skipped class for girls, often had no income, and was in deep debt. Then I became chronically stressed and alarmed, suffering greatly from anxiety, depression, and poor sleep. I also began to drink alcohol frequently and heavily, which gave me some immediate relief but exacerbated my suffering over time.

I was barely surviving.

It was simple math… my narrow wisdom, knowledge, and resources were far less than what life required, including the many changes in lifestyle, routines, social interactions, recreation, financial, and more.

It was obvious I lacked an adequate understanding of the ways and rhythms of the world out there. For me, that world was like a foreign country, with a different language, customs, and beliefs. I was unaware of many obvious and common things, like fashion, technology, modern music, fads, political issues, and social trends. Also, I was completely oblivious of the subtleties in that world; the interpretation and meaning of those subtleties required a sophistication I simply did not have.

My lack of understanding was not the main problem. Far worse was my ineffective and outdated approach to life. I often reacted to novel situations instinctively, with intuition or quick thinking, which caused many errors. Instinctive reaction or even intuition may work in the heat of battle or when fighting a dog, but not as a general life approach. I needed, when time allowed, to observe, ponder, and respond rationally. But that would require patience, something often lacking in a young man, and especially so in a savage.

After barely completing my second year of college, I needed significant change. I was not thriving. It felt as if I was further away from my goals than when I first left home. I needed progress, and some successes. I began to think about the military, which had been an option whispered to me throughout my youth. Military service was a family tradition; my father, grandfathers, uncles, older brothers, and cousins had served. My occasional thoughts of the military quickly became a rumination, almost an obsession, as the real threats of homelessness became imminent. A week prior to this decision, I went to the Catholic Social Services food bank. I was beyond desperate.

One week after the initial thought, I enlisted in the US Navy. I had not given up on college or furthering my formal education. I was told that in exchange for a three-year enlistment, the federal government would pay my college tuition through the GI Bill. Yes, indeed, I would go back to school once I fulfilled my enlistment. Three years in the military would allow me to recoup, reflect, and prepare for my return. Within six weeks after making my decision to enlist, I was headed for Great Lakes boot camp in Chicago.

My decision to enlist proved to be a good one. I was assigned to a frigate in the 7th Fleet, in San Diego, California. The military was a profound change, a life of structure and discipline, which was what I desperately needed. I was told how to look, speak, and act, and to follow routines. When dressed in formal attire and inspection ready, I was sharp and impressive. I gave respect to officers and superiors, saluted when required, and used formal language and the appropriate military jargon. When among the enlisted, expectations and standards were relaxed. Cuss words were not encouraged by officers, as they were so-called gentlemen or gentlewomen. But when among themselves, the enlisted were experts at swearing and tough talk.

I experienced some successes, including being promoted three times. My thoughts were maturing. I became more reflective, more worldly, and began to develop a deeper understanding of life and the way things are.

However, I also began to discover a relationship between awareness and depression. Sometimes I disagreed with or disliked the raw realities of life. Sometimes I did not accept the things I could not change: I wanted to grow a full beard but couldn't. I wanted a girlfriend who looked like a Victoria's Secret model... to be an Olympic downhill skier... to be an eagle with the ability to fly.

But the more I understood life, the laws of nature (physical, biological, psychological), the more I felt depressed and viewed it as a heavy burden. I certainly felt happiness, joy, love, and excitement, but never had I experienced a long state of these positive emotions. Rather, I often experienced extended states of stress, anxiety, and depression.

Though I could not articulate it in words, I began to understand that life establishes law and truth, and without my consent. This bothered the hell out of me. So, on occasion, in an act of rebellion, I picked a fight with life. I would throw everything I had at it, starting with my most developed defenses, which always failed, and then regressing back to my most primitive toe-to-toe strategies (bite, gouge, scratch, and pull hair). During one fierce fight with life, which was about money and patience, I first excused it away as insignificant and unimportant, but later I started to sulk, then drank booze and yelled obscenities. When that did not bring victory, I grabbed a 12-gauge shotgun, racked in a round, and discharged buckshot into the nearest sumac tree. And even with a record of zero wins and all losses, I stubbornly kept fighting life with an intensity undiminished.

Once I fulfilled my enlistment, I moved to Detroit and enrolled in business courses at Wayne State University. I believed I was prepared, motivated, and more focused; that I would succeed. With zeal, I organized and managed closely my daily schedule and time, determined to attend all classes and complete all work assignments before their due dates. I worked part time to pay for living expenses not covered by the GI bill and student loans.

During the first half of each semester, I performed very well. I stayed current on my reading assignments and completed all homework on time. I typically scored very high on midterm exams. During the latter half, I had trouble maintaining such efforts. I enjoyed formal education and learning but not fulltime, not day after day, and not all subjects. Consequently, I became increasingly preoccupied with distractions outside the classrooms, study sessions, and libraries. The top distractions, often sought out simultaneously, were parties, alcohol consumption, and pretty girls. But during the final weeks of each semester, I would refocus my efforts on my studies. After three years, I completed a bachelor's degree in economics, with a minor in psychology. That was the first time I felt like I had accomplished something significant in the world out there.

Two weeks after graduation, I secured employment at a manufacturing company in Cadillac, Michigan. I worked in the quality management department, crunching numbers and generating reports for the executive team. When I received my first paycheck, I believed that, finally, I was on my way to a better life. I felt happy and certain. My confidence grew. *Success would come for sure*, I thought. *But I need to find a good woman, then get married, have children, and build a good family environment, while at the same time advancing economically through my career... That—all of that would bring paradise.* I believed that with all my heart, as much as I believed in anything else. So, I worked hard, did well, and received raises and promotions for my good work. I spent most of my leisure time dating, engaging in social activities, learning to play guitar, and reading.

After a few years, however, I became bored with my work and lifestyle. I was told by a trusted colleague that I had outgrown the company, that I should look for employment elsewhere. I also dated several women, most relationships lasting less than three months. The relationships seemed to follow a similar cycle: intense physical attraction and excitement, then commitment and routine, followed by disagreement, conflict, and decay.

I continued to have occasional fights with life. Some battles were fierce, some involved new grievances. Sometimes I would yell aloud at God. "All I want is to live a good and happy life... I want to marry, have children and be happy! *You* gave me that longing. Why, then, do You make it so difficult and painful to achieve?"

One day, my life changed hard and fast. It was on a Friday, around one in the morning. I had just left Baker's, a popular biker bar in downtown Frankfort. I had been drinking heavily—Coors Silver Bullet beer and shots of Jose Cuervo Gold tequila; "silver and gold" I often called the combo. I was pulled over by the police, questioned, and given a sobriety test. I failed. When the police searched my vehicle, they found a small amount of cocaine, a vice I enjoyed two to three times a month. I was taken to jail and booked on charges of driving under the influence and possession of cocaine. I was eventually convicted and spent time in jail.

This was another critical point in my life. Once cruising through life, at times carelessly, then suddenly rushed onto the hard rocks. Now I came face to face with reality and truth—I was nothing more than a frail human compared to Nature and God. Everything I worked for was gone in a flash—job, livelihood, possessions, credibility, trust. I became ashamed, doubtful, and hesitant. I began to distrust, and even dislike, who I was. I had to start over again, do something different; something that would ensure that I never experienced jail again. "To fear God is the beginning of wisdom," I often whispered to myself during the aftermath. *How could I make such poor decisions?* I thought. *What drives me? How do I accept the things I cannot change? I am not invincible.*

After several weeks of reflection, I came to believe that to live better in the world out there I needed to go inward. I needed to examine my beliefs, actions, and emotional functioning. After my jail term, I sought help from a clinical psychologist. I attended sessions one to two times a week regularly. I also began to read books on psychological theory, personality, and cognitive development. I wanted to know what drove me, what motivated me, and how to make changes. I was on a quest, first driven by fear but one that eventually became a hunger for knowledge. Within a year, I had read most of the classic and historical works by Freud, James, Watson, and Pavlov. Two years after that, I reviewed many contemporary textbooks in clinical psychology and psychiatry.

During my quest, I thought about the profession of psychology—what would I have to do to become a clinical psychologist? I researched the various universities, formal education requirements, career opportunities, pay ranges, and clinical specialties. The more I researched, the more I believed it was possible for me to make a career change. And so, at the age of thirty, I took a very significant turn in my life and enrolled in a graduate program in clinical psychology.

At that time, I focused primarily on the distance outcome of my decision. I relished the idea of being an educated professional, an expert. I fantasized about the financial returns, the status, the respect. I especially liked the idea of pursuing a career in a subject matter I thoroughly enjoyed. But I would soon discover that the effort and costs were tremendous, that graduate school required more from me than I had ever given to anything else before. This long and intense experience would include challenges and setbacks, including grieving the death of my father.

***

Despite the many trials and harsh experiences, my abilities, sustained focus, and grit helped me to prevail academically and professionally. At the age of forty, I had achieved a PhD in Clinical Psychology. I was known in graduate school as highly intelligent and very ambitious, although some thought I was over the top and grandiose.

I now had a two-year-old son. I knew my son's mother long before we courted. She was from a northern suburb of metro Detroit and lived across the street from my relatives. She had a bond with them, attended the same schools, and shared many of the same friends. When my family visited these relatives, she was often around and shared in activities and social interactions. When we became adults, we pursued our own ways and lost contact with each other. Fifteen years later, I saw her at a wedding event. We talked about things we did when we were younger and about what we had done or achieved since the last time we saw each other. I was stunned by her beauty. She was no longer a girl; she was woman, matured, with all potential natural beauty fully realized. The day after this event, thoughts of her dominated my mind. I asked to see her again, to spend time getting to know more of her. She said yes. So, we began dating. After nine months, we moved in together. One year later, we had a child, a beautiful baby boy.

While we were courting, I relocated, and secured employment at Wayne State University. I was hired as a clinical psychologist and research associate, and managed administrative functions for some of the research clinics. This was a good move for my career. My clinical knowledge and experience expanded exponentially. I was mentored by prominent clinicians and researchers. I continued my education by attending workshops and conferences and reading the latest research articles and textbooks on the technical aspects of psychology. In addition, I gained knowledge and experience in the business and service delivery aspects of mental health care.

A typical work week: I arrived early to work. I looked at my caseload for the day. I had five returning clients and two new ones. Returning clients received approximately forty-five to fifty minutes of psychotherapy, and then I spent five to ten minutes documenting this session. New clients received an initial assessment, typically lasting sixty to seventy-five minutes, that consisted of identifying the primary concern or problem, gathering background information, and assessing their current mental state. The information gathered from a new client was used to make a diagnosis and an initial treatment plan. Occasionally, a new client's concerns or problems were highly complicated, and a diagnosis was difficult to determine. In such cases, a provisional diagnosis was made, and a follow-up session was scheduled to gather more diagnostic information including via psychological testing.

I remember a clinical case from back in those days which I will describe here. (I changed the names and circumstances so the person could not possibly be identified.) I called the client, Mr. Thompson, into my office.

"Hello, I'm Dr. Smith. Mr. Thompson, have a seat here please."

"Thank you," Thompson said as he sat down. Thompson was holding documents he had completed while in the waiting room.

I asked for the documents. I looked briefly at the first page of the background questionnaire, which listed the reason why he was seeking treatment, and asked, "You indicate that you are here for treatment because your family doctor said you were experiencing stomach pain that does not appear to be due to a physical health problem, that maybe there is a psychological cause. Did I state that correctly?"

"Yes, that's what my doctor told me. I told my doctor that I was not crazy… it's got to be something that was not in the labs and tests. I don't know."

I said, "If you don't mind, I'm going to review these documents briefly."

"Sure. Go ahead."

I reviewed the referral letter, background questionnaire, and other forms and documents: *Thompson, a 34-year-old male, married, no children, complains of intermittent stomach pain… did not appear to have a biological basis, or at least not a primary one.* There was nothing else in the background questionnaire or other documents that seemed clinically significant, except one very profound incident that occurred two years ago: the death of his son. There were no details.

After review, I began, in a very empathetic tone, with, "What was your son's name?"

"Charlie," Thompson replied quietly.

"How old was he when he died?" I delivered cautiously.

Thompson replied with no apparent emotion, "Charlie was six months old."

"How did he die?"

Again, with neutral emotion, he replied, "He was injured in an accident."

"How has your wife handled this loss?"

"Well, it was very difficult, as you could imagine. Charlie was our first and only child. When my wife couldn't function or when she fell apart, I did what I could to support her. When I could not function or fell apart, my wife was there to support me. But there were times when we both fell apart. When that happened, her family, my family, and our friends were there to support and help us. They were truly great. The first few months were very difficult, as you could imagine. My wife couldn't go to work. She works as a bank teller. I took a week off from work... It was difficult mostly because my wife was having a very difficult time. I am a mechanic, and I own my own shop. I had to work. But gradually we were able to go on. And still, now and then, we have very emotional periods... as you could imagine." Thompson's response was delivered factually with some mild hints of emotion.

"Yes, I can imagine that was very difficult," I replied with empathy. I sensed there was more but shifted to questions about stomach pain. I would come back to this in a follow-up session.

Through assessment and questions, I ascertained the following: Thompson was experiencing sharp pains in his stomach, mid region, for about an hour each day, over the past twelve to fifteen months. Interestingly, Thompson's pain occurred at the same time each day, around ten in the morning. Thompson could not identify anything that might have triggered or caused the stomach pain, and had tried various over-the-counter medications and some prescribed medications but experienced only partial relief. Thompson had no previous history of stomach pain or problems, no history of any chronic health or emotional problems. The death of Thompson's son seemed to be the only clinically significant incident.

Toward the end of the session, I gave Thompson a provisional diagnosis of psychosomatic disorder and discussed an initial treatment plan. The plan included some additional assessment, psychological testing, and psychotherapy one to two days weekly. Our next session was set for the coming Friday.

For the remainder of that day, I had deep, ruminating thoughts about Thompson's case. This was not unusual for me. There were cases that interest me more than others, and this was one of them.

That night I had a vivid dream. I dreamt of the mythical tale of Prometheus Unbound. In this myth, Zeus punishes the Titan Prometheus for giving humans the gift of fire. The punishment is a terrifying, painful, and ongoing torture. While being chained to a large rock, an eagle flies down, landing on Prometheus, then tears and rips into his stomach and eats his liver. Prometheus feels all the grueling pain of a mortal. At night, Prometheus' liver rejuvenates; his stomach heals. The next day, the eagle flies down again, and tears into him and eats his liver. This punishment is repeated every day for a generation, until Heracles rescues him by breaking the chains. Prometheus is then unbound. When the chains hit the ground, I woke up.

I laid in bed thinking about the dream. *Is Thompson the chained Prometheus? Had he sinned against the gods? What were his sins? Am I Heracles? Am I a savior of sins? Do I have that power as a psychologist? Or am I the eagle?* I knew well the different theories about dreams, classic and modern. I was insightful and perceptive, skills I developed from professional training and deep personal reflections. Based in science and my own direct clinical experiences, I knew psychosomatic symptoms were often associated with extreme stress and trauma.

That Friday in session, I began asking Thompson questions about the death of his son. After the third question, Thompson suddenly interjected with, "I dropped my son on the floor... he slipped right out of my hand. The fall broke his neck. I killed him." Thompson paused, took a deep breath, then continued, "My son was taken to the hospital... he died four hours later." Another pause, then Thompson cried out, "Oh my sweet, sweet Charlie boy!" He broke down into a deep, roaring cry, his body heaving and convulsing as he became flooded with very painful emotions.

I thought as I observed this man, *The body holds on to everything—severe traumas, losses, and stressors seem to live on in the body for years, even decades.*

Thompson eventually recovered, then went on to explain that the hospital called the police and other agencies to investigate his son's death. A forensic pediatric physician from the hospital was brought in to evaluate and determine whether Thompson's explanation of how the injury occurred matched the physical evidence. Some personnel from the Department of Health and Human Services were skeptical of Thompson's explanation. He could hear them talking to each other outside of the emergency room. He was also questioned by the police for nearly two hours. The investigation process went on for nearly two months. He was asked to come into the police station twice for additional questioning. One the officers made a flippant comment, "If your son's death was not an accident, then it's murder." Human Services called for "follow-up questions," mainly to ascertain the reliability and truthfulness of his explanation and testimony. Thompson received little, if any, empathy from those conducting the investigations.

I thought: *How does someone grieve the loss of another while facing decades in prison? Does the fear of facing prison interfere with the normal bereavement process?*

Absolutely. But more than that, this client blamed himself for his son's death. How does a person grieve under those conditions?

Then I looked straight into Thompson's eyes and said, "There is nothing in life that can prepare you for such a thing, not even if you had previously experienced the death of a parent or a sibling. The death of a child is horrible... it makes you crazy. It's the worst. And on top of this, you blame yourself for his death, which has complicated your grief and bereavement." Thompson was tearful and breathing hard but seemed very receptive to my words.

I went on, "I believe that you need help working through the loss of your son. And I believe there might be a connection between your stomach pain and the loss of your son." Thompson nodded in agreement. "Do you mind if I ask you more questions about your son?"

"No, I don't mind."

"Where were you when you accidently dropped your son?"

"At home."

"Where at in your home?"

"In the kitchen."

"Was anyone else there?"

"No, just me and Charlie. My wife was at work."

"What time of the day did this happen?"

"About two hours after my wife left for work, so around ten a.m. That is my best estimation. That's what I told the hospital, the police, and Human Services."

The session went on, with me focused on the accident, the death, and how that all settled in Thompson's mind.

During the following session, I introduced the possibility of a connection between his current stomach pain and the loss of his son two years ago, explaining in lay terms the psychological mechanisms involved. This possible connection and the explanation resonated deeply with Thompson.

Two sessions later, Thompson stopped having daily stomachaches. He went on to have very infrequent stomach discomfort, about once per month, for three months, then nothing. I continued to work with Thompson one to two times a week for an additional three months, focusing on complicated bereavement and severe guilt. Thompson's wife joined sessions on occasion.

At this point in my career, I had already evaluated and treated hundreds of cases like Thompson. My employment at the university provided me with excellent ongoing technical training and skills development, decent income, and health insurance. But the big money was in private practice. Most of my colleagues worked part time outside the university. I was encouraged to do the same.

***

I joined a small private clinical practice working ten to fifteen hours per week. I conducted psychological testing and psychotherapy, and provided consultation and expert testimony. Within six months, I was making in private practice seventy-five percent of what I made at the university but working only a quarter of the time. Within two years, my overall income quadrupled, with seventy percent coming from consulting and private practice. My clinical caseload outside the university was expanding exponentially. I was in high demand, not only because of my clinical skills, but I had a rare ability to empathize with and deeply understand human suffering. "To believe that you are deeply understood—that your pain and suffering is understood—is itself significantly therapeutic," I would often say to interns training under me.

Although thriving, I found it hard to set limits on my work and ambitious endeavors. I worked long hours and worked more weekends than not. I took urgent and emergent client calls in the middle of the night. Consequently, I became very overextended and stressed. I began to experience problems in my marriage, mainly arguments about me neglecting my family.

After six years of high intensity work, I left Wayne State University and launched my own private clinical practice. I also parted ways with my son's mother, which was a devastating blow. I blamed myself for excessive overworking and poor stress management. We settled on 50/50 joint custody of our son. Now, as a single parent, I had to make changes in my schedule and priorities to accommodate the healthy development of my son.

I began my private practice by renting two clinical rooms from an owner-doctor of an OB/GYN practice. This arrangement was far from ideal as we shared the same waiting room and the client populations were significantly different. I employed an administrative assistant part time and a full-time clinician. After six months, I moved the practice into my own office suite located one block away on the same street. Through smart marketing and high customer satisfaction, the clinical referrals poured in. I was able to bring on more clinicians and add administrative staff. After one year, I opened a second location twenty-five miles due west from my existing clinic. After the following year, my personal annual income exceeded $600,000, and I had over one million dollars in net assets.

As success grew, I was approached by colleagues and professional acquaintances expressing a desire to have what I had: the money and lifestyle. I encouraged these people to strive for their dreams, that "by doing so, you will learn things about yourself.... and maybe surprise yourself by all that you can do."

Then I would quote Thomas Wolfe: "If a man has a talent and cannot use it, he has failed. If he has a talent and only uses half of it, he has partly failed. If he has a talent and learns to use the whole of it, he has gloriously succeeded, and won a satisfaction and triumph few men will ever know."

CHAPTER THREE: THE CRIMINAL

My pep talks motivated people. They were ready to "go for it." But I also warned them about the costs of success and often emphasized that what I achieved was one of the most difficult endeavors of my life. That it will take long hours… it will take many hours away from other important areas of your life, such as family, personal health, and recreation. Also, you will have challenges, very stressful and worrisome challenges. At times you may experience intense dread and agony.

I'll give you an example of what I mean: Despite planning for a crisis, on three occasions, I did not know how I was going to make payroll of nearly $100,000 only days away. There was a very sudden and significant negative change in cashflow (bills had to be paid, but income was delayed), and there were no reserves. This occurred in 2008 and 2009, after the crash of the housing market, which put the country and most of the world into a recession. Banks called in business loans, closed out credit, and stopped loaning money. The company bank froze our business credit account that had a $75,000 limit. I was alone and desperate.

No one could or did solve these crises for me. Nearly everything was on the line—not just for me but for eighty employees. Those were some of the scariest and most agonizing days of my life. Moreover, I am constantly protecting the business from theft, lawsuits, and other risks.

Believe it or not, some clinicians were siphoning off referrals into their own mini practices, which was in violation of their professional contracts. I let them go. I had to fire a clinician because he had an unethical and inappropriate relationship with a client. He eventually lost his license to practice due to that poor decision. Also, I fielded many of the loudest client complaints that did not get resolved by the immediate frontline staff. And much, much more. I sometimes questioned whether the upside of success is worth it... that maybe I would be happier with much less.

In almost every instance, the person I shared this wisdom with considered the downside very little, and would ask follow-up questions like, "How much money can I make?"

Despite the hectic demands on my life, I made time to date women. I met a very beautiful and dazzling woman who was sixteen years younger than me. We met during a coordination of care for clients we shared. She worked as a clinician treating substance abuse disorders. Less than a year after meeting, the relationship ended, but she was pregnant. Months later, we had a daughter. Chronic arguments and conflicts arose because she refused to separate herself fully from previous intimate relationships.

A year later, I married a third time. This wife, a native German, was a teacher with a master's degree in education. She taught at schools in several different countries. I met her through one of her relatives. I had two children from this marriage, a son and a daughter.

***

Years of rapid growth and stressful success were realized as I, now in my fifties, built my business up to become one of the largest private outpatient practices in the region. At its peak, the practice consisted of four clinical locations, over eighty clinical and administrative staff members, and tens of thousands of clients. This was an unbelievable feat for anyone, and more so for a man who was once a barefooted country boy who bit a dog and lived by the animal code.

I became very wealthy. Could afford almost anything I desired. Bought a large country estate, other properties and investments. Paid cash for new vehicles. Children were spoiled with expensive gifts and toys. Went on expensive travels to desirable destinations in the United States and foreign countries. Had millions in net assets.

But as with anyone brave enough to establish and grow a business, employ many, provide something of value, and risk it all, that person must always be prepared for the worst yet to come. Unfortunately for me, the worst that came was exponentially more devastating than anything I had ever before experienced. The Sword of Damocles came down on my head.

As a private business owner, I was ultimately responsible for the business, including the goals, plans and operations, and assumed all legal and financial risk. These responsibilities caused a constant stress for me, which intensified greatly when operations ran roughly and cash flow was tight. But when the business crashed, my neck was in a noose. Many indeed suffered to various degrees. But I alone would stand before the hangman.

Though I could only know in retrospect, my descent, a complex mixture of factors, began a few years before, in 2013. It began when the federal government required changes in how insurance companies covered mental health and addiction care and reimbursed clinical providers. The change was potentially very positive for my practice in the long term because of broader coverage and better reimbursement rates. But in the immediate and short term, this change caused severe problems in the billing and reimbursement processes. My business was ready for the changes; all administrative and clinical staff had been trained. However, the insurance companies, those that controlled the purse, had not fully implemented the new schedules and systems by the rollout deadline. Consequently, my practice, like many other private practices, went without insurance reimbursements for several months. Many private mental health businesses not subsidized by government funding were financially crippled. Many smaller private businesses closed for good as they could not operate without having steady predictable income.

After months of poor or no revenue, contracted clinical providers began to leave the practice. This exacerbated the situation. Fewer providers meant fewer services being rendered, and consequently, less future income. I suffered through many days and nights trying desperately to find a solution for paying bills. Several more months went by. Massive cuts were made but had to be done strategically and over time. Eventually, all business savings were depleted… and much of my personal assets were liquidated and loaned to the company.

Then my situation got worse. I was hit with several lawsuits by former contract providers and vendors demanding money. I intended to pay everyone I owed. But insurance reimbursements were still slow, taking several months, and in some cases, multiple years or never. I understood the situation and empathized with those I owed but had to defend myself in court. I hired an attorney to fight over twenty lawsuits. The costs were mounting, and the stress became unbearable.

My situation got even worse. I experienced serious problems in my marriage during these times. We had frequent arguments about money. I often complained about my wife not working and spending too much. "Why do you have the kids in daycare five days a week for six to eight hours a day? We need to reduce our living costs. You must find work… I need help with paying the bills." She complained about me not helping around the house and with the kids. When we both drank alcohol, which had increased significantly, we engaged in vicious verbal abuse back and forth. We eventually separated and she left the state with the children.

My stress was beyond my limits, far more than ever before. I was desperate and scared. I began to consume alcohol daily. I suffered from chronic insomnia. At some point, I experienced a deep despair. I felt a sensation of slowly falling, down and down, into a bottomless black hole. The further down, the darker it became, the harder to breathe. I had trouble catching my breath. My overall mental and physical health disintegrated.

Unfortunately, as I was responsible for everything, I did not have the luxury of taking a break or letting myself fall apart. My grit kicked in, as it had been done many times before, and I kept going forward.

By random chance, during review of financial and billing records, I noticed there were significant errors. There were services being billed for treatment that had not been rendered. I researched this issue and found there were recurring appointments set on an automatic schedule, and those appointments were billed automatically by error. I noticed the errors occurred over several months. I wondered why clients had not called in to complain. Clients would occasionally call if they had a dispute, which is not uncommon for any medical practice. There are ongoing billing issues that go back and forth between the provider and the insurance company, sometimes with the provider owing money back and sometimes the insurance company making additional payments. This was all very common in a healthcare delivery system. But I noticed that few clients were complaining and I had received no complaints from the insurance company. I then thought that maybe, because my business generated tens of thousands of units of service monthly, most of these billing errors basically went unnoticed.

Later that day, I received more bad news from my attorney. Several additional lawsuits had been filed against me. I felt dizzy. I sat down at the kitchen table, put my elbows on the table, and hands over my face. I wanted to disappear. Then thoughts came to the top of my mind. These thoughts formed a plan, a desperate plan: I would create *more* billing errors, and if anyone complained, I would reimburse the money to the insurance company. But if I did not receive a complaint, I would not correct the error and keep the money.

This is criminal, I thought. *But maybe I could pay down some bills and then pay everything back.* I did not contemplate long. I executed my plan that day. I did not allow myself to ponder long the consequences of my decision, intentionally distracting myself, sometimes with pain, when such thoughts came to mind.

Within a few months, I was able to resolve some immediate and extreme financial problems. I began to breathe better. But my mind was unsettled. I hated the decision I made and hated myself. My thoughts became obsessive and twisted. *I can't let my life fall apart... if it falls apart, I will die.* I convinced myself that I had no other choice. I began to employ desperate and unhealthy ways to cope, such as drinking alcohol, blaming, projecting. After several months, I deteriorated into a husk. I could not look at myself in the mirror anymore, but I also did not stop these criminal acts.

On the day of the summer solstice, I received a call from my attorney, Mike Cronkright, regarding a federal indictment for healthcare fraud and money laundering. The indictment included eighteen counts and alleged that I had defrauded nearly five million dollars. Mike informed me that I had to turn myself in to the Eastern District of Michigan US Attorney's Office Building in Detroit. There I would be booked and stand before a federal magistrate. I was fully exposed, way out in the open for the world to see. And I yearned, desperately so, to hide in darkness on the day of longest light.

CHAPTER FOUR: IN THE SEVENTH CIRCLE

It was a Thursday afternoon when I received a call from Mike regarding a multi-count federal indictment for healthcare fraud and money laundering. I was at my summer house entertaining a small group of family and friends on the front deck. The sky was clear, and the temperature was warm and comfortable. Many other people in the community were out and about—walking the streets, landscaping their yards, enjoying conversation with others.

I took the call, then walked into the house for privacy. "Hello, Mike."

Mike delivered the bad news. "The indictment was unsealed earlier today. I will send you an electronic copy immediately. This is a very serious matter. You will need an attorney who has expertise in healthcare fraud and is familiar with the federal legal system. I do not have the expertise you need in this area of law, so I will send you referrals. Also, I spoke briefly with the federal prosecutor assigned to your case. You must turn yourself in next Thursday—that is when your arrest is formally processed. Later that day, you will go through an arraignment, where you will be brought before a magistrate for an initial hearing on your case. The judge will explain your rights and the charges against you and decide if you will be held in prison or released until the trial. Now, it is highly likely you will be released that day on a bond because your alleged crimes are not violent, you don't have a history of violence, and you are not a flight risk."

I was extremely focused on my attorney's words. I did not move. My breathing paused for an extended period, then a short breath, then paused again. The only stimuli penetrating my conscious awareness were the words being spoken to me. I was not aware of any other sounds. I was not aware of what was in front of me—not the warmth of the sun, not the noise from the wind or conversations around me, nor the smell and taste of the summer air. The physical world became dark and distant.

I responded, "Thank you. I'll call you back after I review the indictment." I ended the call abruptly. I had no memory of what I said or how the call ended or certain whether I said anything at all until several months later.

Suddenly, like a clap of thunder, my body became flooded by severe panic and terror. My heart pounded hard, breathing became rapid and shallow. I felt nauseous and dizzy and began to sweat heavily. Throughout, I was profoundly confused and felt insane. I would have no relief for the next five minutes.

Slowly, I began to move, and regain, partially, the ability to attend and comprehend. My breathing remained rapid and shallow, but less so. My panic lessened to a high anxiety. More minutes passed, but my condition improved only slightly. I began to shake from an overdose of my own internal chemistry. I took in a deep breath and let it out slowly. I briefly looked at myself in a mirror. I looked better than what I felt. I then walked back out onto the front deck, but over to the side to avoid eye contact and conversation.

Something in the distance caught my attention. Across the street, there was a car parked way out on the edge of a large vacant lot I owned. Nearby, there were two women: one appeared to be talking while holding a microphone, the other was holding a video camera. Looking back at the car, I noticed a logo on the side.

"Holy shit!" I cried out. It was a local TV news company and they were looking for me. *My indictment... they must have received notice of my indictment,* I thought. I was amazed by how quickly they showed up at my property, just minutes after talking to my attorney. *They must have gotten the news earlier today.*

I quickly checked my phone for new text messages and emails. I had several. There was an email from my attorney with the indictment attached. I closed the email quickly without reviewing the indictment and opened a text message from a close friend.

You are on the news. They say you committed fraud. That there are millions of dollars involved. What's going on?

I quickly focused back to the car and two women. My thoughts began to race and my anxiety shot back up again. But I would not have another panic episode right now. I could fall apart later, but not now. I would not allow it. There were very important matters I needed to address. Then, I turned to my family and friends, and sternly said, "I need everyone to go inside the house now... this is very important. I will explain once everyone is inside."

Once inside, I told them, in simple terms, that I was indicted for fraud, that I lived a lie. I told them I fell on very hard times, felt deeply depressed, and overwhelmed. I told them my life spiraled out of control, and I could not take care family obligations or meet the demands of my lifestyle. I went on for about twenty minutes. No one said a word.

Then, suddenly, I felt powerful waves of panic crashing upon the whole of my being, until the waves turned into a constant downpour, all with no waning. All my mental strength and defenses could not block or reduce the raw emotion. I suddenly dropped to one knee and held my heart. I was lightheaded and dizzy, nauseous, shaking, and experienced intermittent loss of consciousness. After few minutes, I got up and left the room without saying anything.

I did not sleep that night, or the next night. My mind was constantly ruminating. The world would now know the truth. "It's a Scarlet Letter," I said to myself. I was convinced that wherever I was, to all others, the dark colors of lies and theft would be revealed by distorted patterns of my gestures, looks, and overall demeanor. "They will see it… they will see it clearly, as if it were branded permanently on my skin."

***

The following Thursday, I attended the arraignment at the US Attorney's Office Building in Detroit. The courtroom was packed with lawyers, law enforcement, legal staff, defendants, and family members. Some of the defendants and family members were standing, as there were not enough seats to accommodate all. I slowly panned over the crowd. I noticed that most defendants and their families looked like the ordinary rank and file of society.

On the right side of the courtroom, near the front, I saw a row of defendants who were chained around the wrists and ankles and closely guarded by US Marshals. They were markedly different than everyone else. I observed that most of them were male, scarred and deformed, heavily tattooed, wild-eyed, and unkempt. They reminded me of the wild animals I often encountered, and occasionally fought, in my youth. I also noticed that some defendants, when measured by outward appearance and gestures only, could not be distinguished from the attorneys. I surmised they were like me, a white-collar criminal. I had thoughts… *the eyes are the best marker of specificity ... their eyes were tainted with shame and despair, just like mine.*

I noticed a short, pale man wearing glasses, with an intelligent look, moving through the crowd, apparently looking for someone. He locked eyes with me but walked slowly past. Then he turned back, and asked, "Are you Paul Smith?"

"Yes, who are you?" I replied.

"I'm Felix Bauer, the US prosecutor assigned to your case."

"Oh. Yes."

"Do you have an attorney?" Bauer asked.

"No. Not currently. I may have one by next week. I'm trying to raise the money," I replied.

Without saying anything, Bauer walked away, heading toward the front area of the courtroom. I walked through a gate that separated lawyers and court staff from defendants, families, and others. I stopped at a table crowded with professional people, leaned downward toward a very striking, slender Black woman. They appeared to be engaged in conversation and reviewing some documents. Bauer then looked in my direction and nodded. The woman looked in my direction and locked eyes. She got up and walked towards me. As she approached, I could see the signs of seasoned experience in her face and eyes.

"My name is Alicia Thomas. I am an attorney with the public defender's office. I was told that you do not have an attorney at this time, correct?"

"Yes."

"And that you are indigent, correct?"

"Yes."

"I'm willing to serve as your attorney for now. That will allow you to get through the arraignment. After the arraignment, if you like, someone from the public defender's office, possibly me, will work with you on your case. If you don't have an attorney for this arraignment, the judge will have you come back again. The arraignment is primarily a formality about your rights and the charges against you."

I, sensing sincerity, responded, "Yes, I would like you to represent me. I want to get this over with. Do you know my case?"

"The basics, yes. Mr. Bauer briefly reviewed your case with me."

"What will happen today… during the arraignment?" I asked.

Thomas reviewed the process with me. My anxiety began to lessen. She handed me forms to complete and sign.

My case was called. Thomas directed me to a podium next to her, and there I stood before the judge. Thomas informed the judge that she was my attorney. The judge covered several procedures and legal formalities, asked many questions, explained my rights and the charges against me. Towards the end, the judge released me on bond and placed me on pretrial services. The process lasted fifteen minutes.

Immediately following the arraignment, I was instructed to meet with Pretrial Services before leaving the building. I was informed that the pretrial staff would maintain regular contact with me, monitor treatment and health issues, conduct random urinalysis, and make monthly house visits.

***

On my way home, my mind became dominated by thoughts and images of my children. I had been agonizing over their well-being: *Am I harming my children? Do I need to save them from me? What have I become? My children… what's best for them? What do they need?* Tears strained down my face. I shook my head back and forth, then howled out a deep cry. "I'm sorry!" I yelled out. "I'm sorry, I'm sorry,"

I repeated. "They are innocent and shouldn't have to suffer for what I've done."

Over several minutes, my emotional state lessened slightly. I raised my head up to the sky and said, "I fucked up my life. I harmed many people. How do I go forward? I don't have an answer." I thought about the seriousness of my crimes, the harm I caused to society, my employees, the profession, and my family. I thought about how my life changed profoundly and permanently.

I ruminated over the numerous hardcore issues, problems, and concerns that required my immediate attention. I had to meet with my attorneys to set up plans to dissolve my multi-location practice, including transferring all clients to other providers, which would likely take several months of intense focus and effort and the cooperation with existing admin employees who knew their days were numbered. I had to address the many employee and clinical contract provider issues: last and back pay, helping them find other employment, or assisting them in receiving unemployment benefits. The banks would likely shut down business services and may also freeze accounts. I had to get the money out now and transfer it into some other account other so I could pay my debts.

I anticipated several potential lawsuits coming my way, most from major vendors regarding outstanding balances or contractual financial obligations—office property leases, clinical contractors, phone and communications systems, office cleaning services and trash, land and building maintenance and repair, and many more. I also needed to prepare for potential client lawsuits.

In addition to everything else, I had to take care of my family. I had to maintain income for housing, food, and other essentials. Moreover, I had to care for myself and manage my personal affairs, and much more. I was overwhelmed and began feeling sick and desperate. *I put myself in a situation that I can't overcome*, I thought.

Then suddenly, an idea lit brightly in my mind. I experienced a fleeting calm, and then a certainty, as I pondered the idea. *There is a solution. I have experienced severe despair and hopelessness before. I have, on occasion, wished that I would fall asleep and never wake up. I've had fleeting thoughts of how I would end my life, maybe gunshot to the head, maybe carbon monoxide, maybe hanging. But this is different. I have never experienced a clear intent. But now I do. Yes. It is an answer... it is a solution.* I was deeply fascinated with this idea. No other previous decision in my life was more important.

I would wait to determine the "how" and the "when" until after I got my affairs in order. I thought about my children, how I would set things up for them. That would become my immediate and supreme concern. During my drive, I had developed the outline of a plan. Once home, I wrote it down.

All my remaining assets, if any, shall be placed in a trust for the children. My attorney, Leif Anderson, shall serve as executor of my estate and trustee of this trust until my oldest son's eighteenth birthday. Upon his eighteenth birthday, my oldest son will replace Leif as executor and trustee. Leif shall remain involved advising my oldest son as needed and shall be compensated fairly.

Once these affairs were set, I was intent on ending my agony. It was not difficult for me to think about "the plan" or "the act." I did not imagine if or how I would feel, think, or react, because intellectually I knew I would be dead. I imagined how my suicide would affect the children and family. I concluded that it would be difficult for them at first, especially for the children, but over time, they would adjust and carry on. I had studied suicide for years and worked with this kind of loss in my clinical practice. I weighed the possible outcome of doing the act and not doing the act. There would be some residual effects, for some, but overall, they would do just fine. The trust fund would be set up to help the children and to communicate my love for them… though I did recognize the bottom-line contradiction—*if I love my children, then live for them*. But heavy alcohol use and an overwhelming desperation impaired my ability for rational thinking.

I thought about how painful the method might be. Would I feel a gunshot to the head micro moments before I died? Are there painless methods, maybe overdose or carbon dioxide poison from vehicle emissions (maybe that will not work because of the ever-higher EPA standards)? I would have to do some research. What about jumping off a cliff or bridge, running in front of a semi-truck, driving a vehicle off a cliff? Should I take medication just prior to the act to reduce anxiety and fear, and maybe stifle my impulse toward self-preservation? Would I not do it in that moment? Would some instinct prevent me?

"Stop!" I shouted. Then talking to myself, "You know what to do."

I would not leave a suicide note. I would leave this book instead.

Two weeks after the arraignment, I retained an attorney from the Chapman Law Group to work on my federal case. The attorney was refined and tough, highly intelligent, and very experienced. During our initial meeting, the attorney told me that the period time from indictment to sentencing would likely take several months, and possibly two or more years if the case went to trial.

I replied, "I don't want to go to trial. I am guilty and I want to get this over with. Is there any way to shorten the time?"

The attorney did not directly answer the question but instead said, "I understand this is extremely painful for you. We can talk about a plea deal later. But first, we must go through the discovery material and other evidence to know how to proceed. That will take some time, as there are several thousands of pages to review. Who knows, we may discover that some or most of the government's evidence is exaggerated or incorrect or possibly misinterpreted. So, what I recommend is that you hold off on a plea deal until after we have thoroughly examined the evidence."

"Yes, I agree." I knew she was correct and I was being impatient. I came to understand the entire process may take several months, possibly years.

Months dragged by. Court dates and processes were extended, then extended again for various reasons. Eventually, seven months post-indictment, my attorney and I met with the US prosecutor and the insurance company representatives to discuss a plea deal. After additional months of back and forth over the total amount of intended fraud, both sides agreed to an amount of $3.1 million intended fraud and $2.9 million in restitution. After factoring other relevant variables, my federal sentencing guideline score recommended fifty-one to sixty-three months in prison. I was informed by my attorney that the judge did not have to follow the recommendations; he could give a "downward departure" (less than recommended). After researching this matter, I discovered that downward departures were very common. Based on national DOJ data from 2019, on average, federal judges gave sentences that were nine months less than the recommended guideline range. The largest downward departures tended to be for non-habitual, non-violent defendants.

The agony of not knowing my fate became unbearable. But why? For several months, I had planned to end my life. That would end all agony and other pain permanently. So why worry? I was not afraid to die. I had been dead for nearly a year.

But time and my children began to change my resolve. I could not and did not want to reconcile with my wife, so I moved into a smaller house in the suburbs of Macomb County. The house was at the end of a cul de sac, surrounded by deeply wooded land. I spent more time with my children—exploring the woods nearby, teaching them, comforting them, verifying their precious value. I saw the joy in my children's faces and realized again the supreme importance of parenting to their development. I began to have doubts about what I would do.

***

And time marched on. I had settled into a tight routine. I spent ninety percent of my waking hours sitting in a faded brown leather chair positioned in my living room so I could watch TV or look through a sliding glass door into the backyard and woods beyond. When not watching TV or a video on my phone, I observed the behaviors of a particular black squirrel roaming the backyard and nearby woods. Daily, starting around noon, I consumed large amounts of alcohol. I tried not to drink before noon or while my children were around. But when they left, I started drinking. By the end of each night, I was slurring, pathetic and severely impaired.

Weeks and months passed. Still, each day was like the next: sit in brown leather chair, drink alcohol, watch TV, observe a squirrel. I dreaded leaving my house and routine. When with the children, I remained at or around the home. I went to medical appointments and to pick up food, but only when urgent. I often asked family or a friend to drop off alcohol and food supplies. When I did leave the home and was around others, I was very guarded, aloof, and impatient. If required to interact with others for an extended period, I began to experience high anxiety, motor tension, and hypervigilance.

At sixteen months post-indictment, I was still unsure when I would be sentenced but was told possibly the upcoming January. My sentencing date was rescheduled multiple times due to unforeseen reasons. By then, most of my financial assets were seized and I had little money left to live on. I was incapable of holding any kind of employment. My mental and physical health had deteriorated significantly. I had given up on any consistent self-care and grooming; I showered only when required to be in a formal setting or situation. I experienced deficits in attention and memory, and other cognitive functions. My mood was severely depressed. I had difficulty relating to people in social situations, often feeling high anxiety, struggling with what to say and how to react and behave. My ability to respond to the needs of my children was diminished. I had reached a point where the fear of facing prison became much less painful than the agony of maintaining my present stagnant situation. I no longer cared about the length of my sentence, whether thirty-six months or seventy-two months. I did not care about much, about living or dying. I just wanted to get on with it. When speaking about my health condition with a medical professional, I insisted, "The only thing I looked forward to… the only thing that gives me a break from this absolute hell… is watching a damn squirrel."

I did not know why observing Scrap the Squirrel interested me, but it did. So, I observed. It became an intellectual interest and exercise, the only thing stronger than alcohol to give me a respite from the insanity of his situation.

Several times a day, Scrap traveled the same route. Scrap climbed the old walnut tree in the backyard, crawled out on a branch above the house, and jumped down onto the roof above the garage. I could hear the *thump* when she landed. Scrap then gained access to my attic space via a hole through a vinyl ventilation cover. I discovered this hole when I searched the garage attic one day. I also discovered a massive pile of walnuts about six feet in diameter and six inches deep, enough rations for a family of squirrels for multiple years. After a closer look, however, I noticed some of the walnuts appeared newer than others; many had teeth marks and were empty, parts of shells were scattered throughout the mound and beyond. It appeared this pile was added to for several consecutive years. Next to the attic wall, Scrap had built a nest. From the nest, Scrap would make her way back through the vent, climbing back out up on the roof, jump down onto a bush, then onto the ground. Once on the ground, Scrap went around the west side of the house to the walnut tree or an area nearby. This was her full route.

Most of Scrap's life was spent on or very close to the walnut tree or inside the house, going up and down, back and forth, over and over on this route. She had traveled the same route so many times that she no longer had to think about what to do. She no longer had to think about the amount of force she needed to put on her back right leg (or back left leg or front legs) to make a certain left turn at the northwest corner of the house, or how much thrust from her hind legs was needed to jump out far enough onto the roof above the garage. Her movements became automatic. This route appeared to be used for gathering food and providing safety. When she needed food, she took off on her route where plenty was available. If she was chased by a predator, the route gave her an edge as she knew well all the movements needed. This repetitious behavior seemed to be a gift from evolution via natural selection and was reinforced and modeled by direct experience. Unlike humans, Scrap did not possess high order consciousness, and therefore was never inspired by abstract ideas, such as a grandiose lifestyle. Scrap would never risk her life or deny her basic needs for an idea. But I did.

Over time, I discovered the outer geographical boundary of Scrap's life domain, which was about a 150-foot radius from the old walnut tree. Scrap was rarely at or near the far boundary, mainly because she gathered nearly all the food she needed from the walnut tree. I knew that squirrels can travel miles to look for food, but not so for Scrap. When she was far out, she never stayed long. There was no need or desire to go further. What lay beyond the boundary was excess, unimportant, and therefore unknown.

But one cloudy afternoon, Scrap was scrounging way out on the edge of her life domain. Then, quite unexpectedly, a large yellow dog came up barking loudly and startled her. Cut off, Scrap ran straight out beyond her boundary and stopped. Then, she ran off at a different angle, deeper away from her domain. The dog followed in pursuit. Scrap jumped to a bush, then onto the trunk of an adjacent tree, climbing up about six feet. Her behaviors appeared erratic, uncertain, hesitant, and inefficient as she weighed choices. Scrap positioned herself on the opposite side of the tree trunk. The dog ran to the other side, then Scrap moved again to the opposite side. Around they both went for a while until Scrap decided to climb higher, way up into the tree, and chattered. She moved to a crotch, and then a few inches away, then back to the crotch, then to another crotch. Her movements were quick, short, and jumpy. The dog barked for a while, then moved away and began sniffing the ground nearby. Scrap soon climbed back down the tree, circled the trunk, and got close to the ground. Again, the dog ran back toward Scrap, barking. And again, Scrap tried to remain on the opposite side of the tree trunk instead of simply climbing straight up the tree, which she eventually did. A few minutes later, the dog left for good.

Scrap climbed down and scurried towards her familiar domain. She kept running until she got to the walnut tree. She ran up to a limb and settled into a crotch. Her behavior suddenly changed. Her movements became smooth, effortless. Within minutes, Scrap was back on her familiar route, where decisions did not have to be weighed.

Why did Scrap behave so strangely? Her movements were not quick, accurate, and smooth as they were when she is within her life domain. What would happen if Scrap were pushed miles out and away into a completely different wood? Did she have enough models and inherent qualities to survive? Or would natural selection be the executioner of an unfortunate and unfit?

Beyond her domain were trees, brush, and landscapes she not directly experienced. She had no memorial images or events, no cognitive models for the beyond. She did have experiences and images similar enough from her present domain to be valuable when needed. But she had never sought for more than what she needed. All she needed in terms of food, shelter, and climate were within her existing life domain. Combined with her gifts from natural selection, she was surviving and prevailing. She would project into the future through her offspring. To seek more would be excess and luxury, both abstract ideas, which would require something she did not possess—a higher order consciousness.

Deep thoughts came to me. I was depressed and dispirited. I began thinking about my youth, back in the wilderness, and a simpler life. I believed that at the very core of life is a force which has existed since the beginning of time, and that the force is a command: to endure and prevail, no matter what. I had long believed in this idea and many other simple principles of evolution, but over time, I became educated and arrogant, on a quest for something more complex. Scrap shined with that life force. I had no doubt Scrap would survive and project through her offspring into the future. I, however, viewed myself as a disgrace in comparison. A pale, sickly drunk who gave up. I had some work to do. I knew this, but at the same time, I had lost my willingness, strength, and grit. I needed a new route to live by, one that provided me and my family the basics and safety.

I thought, *The questions I ask myself about Scrap's behavior are ones I need to ask about myself. I pushed myself to the beyond, in search of excess and luxury and other over-the-top, grandiose things not needed. I don't believe exploring the beyond and expanding my life domain is wrong or bad... it seems to be a universal innate drive for humans. But I need to ask myself... what motivates me to do so? Am I looking for fame, excessive possessions? Am I looking for validation, anything that confirms I'm good, worthy, special? Unfortunately, all I found were big yellow dogs. Maybe that's what I've been looking for... big yellow dogs.* It could be argued that, in fact, Scrap was chased by a yellow dog specifically because the dog viewed her as valuable, for whatever reason. That's validation, right? Yeah, a kind of fucked-up validation... that Scrap never needed. All that Scrap and I need to live and prevail is, and has been, a much simpler and more manageable life domain. So, now I am standing deep in the beyond. I chose to enter the beyond eagerly in search of excess and luxury. I was far beyond what was comfortable, healthy, and safe. Now I am heading to prison, several steps further into the beyond. I have no memorial images, direct experience, or models for prison and prison life.

Over the several months, I was beaten down by the consequences of my crimes and situation, and because there was simply too much truth to handle. Whether ready or not, I was scheduled for sentencing. The only way to move on, whether for self's sake or not, was to move through. The willingness to move forward by one's own volition was unnatural for the situation, so time had to push me through. For how else does a person proceed to a guillotine?

On January 7, 2020, I was sentenced to fifty-one months in prison. I was also ordered to pay nearly three million dollars in restitution and fines. I was given two months before I had to self-surrender at the federal prison camp in Duluth, Minnesota. On March 2, 2020, twenty months after the indictment, I began my prison experience.

CHAPTER FIVE: THE RIDE

I began to wake up, though not fully. Dull internal pains gripped me. Nausea swirled in my gut. I shook uncontrollably, then dizziness hit me—disoriented, sickly. When I opened my eyes, blurred flashes and surreal shadows danced across my vision. I blinked hard, again and again, trying to straighten my mind, sharpen my senses. I was in alcohol withdrawal. Severe.

Where the hell am I?

A vehicle. I was in the passenger seat of a vehicle. I could feel it moving. The low hum of car tires mixed with the faint conversation on a radio, though I couldn't make out the words. And then—like lightning splitting through the haze—one thought struck me with absolute clarity: *I am heading to prison. I am to self-surrender today.*

My body reacted immediately, a full-body wince. Every symptom intensified, all at once. Federal prison—Duluth, Minnesota. That's where I was going. My friend, Tommy Lowe, was driving me, a full nine-hour drive. Tommy was then and still is the best kind of friend.

The misery climbed higher for a few brutal minutes before it plateaued. I shook my head slowly in disgust and whispered, "You are a pathetic, broken man, Paul Smith."

More minutes passed. My thoughts circled the drain of my situation. Despair sat heavy in my chest. Then suddenly, I dissociated. My mind numbed out, seeking refuge. I became strangely fascinated by my imminent situation and the cold logistics of my new reality. My brain, desperate for control, started constructing mental lectures. Anything to stay anchored. But focus was hard. My thoughts jumped like jazz—tangents, obsessions, random riffs—punctuated by rare bursts of clarity.

I needed to accept the things I couldn't control. But how? I'd never done well when my liberty was stripped away. I would need to toughen up. Harden. Or I'd fail—badly—in prison. I clenched my teeth. Tightened my upper body. Forced my mind to focus.

Only an especially hard individual from a dangerous or deprived background—say, a rough inner city or poor rural environment—could survive prison without suffering serious distress or trauma. Civilization and savagery are not equal partners in hardship. A savage is more prepared.

Could I define those concepts? I tried. A civilized individual—like the one I believed I had become—was educated, indoctrinated into society, gainfully employed, socially adept, emotionally regulated. Civilized people follow norms. We temper our emotions. We strive to be lawful and acceptable. But even the civilized fail. We falter. Our self-control slips. *And what happens when that person—someone who has built a life around civility—commits a crime and is sent to place that does not follow civil codes of conduct? Can he stay civilized? I don't think so.* Solzhenitsyn asked, "If we live in a state of constant fear, can we remain human?" I believe not. But what is "human"? If being human includes being civilized, then constant fear erodes that humanity.

And when disregard, disrespect, and violence—real or threatened—becomes the environment, instinct kicks in. Self-preservation. The fork held properly in your left hand, your academic degrees, your perfect spelling—they're all useless. The uncivilized—callous, hardened, hypervigilant—know how to survive. They're already living the lifestyle. Poverty, addiction, mental illness, violence, death—those aren't exceptions. They're norms. To the civilized, it's trauma. To the savage, it's just another Tuesday.

The closer we got to Duluth, the more my panic broke through the intellectualizing. I was a felon. Separated from my kids. Nearly broke. Depressed. Detoxing. Heading to prison. I needed to survive. But how?

I thought about prison. The dangers, the unknowns. Violence. Rape. Sadism. Would I find safety? Would I find anything resembling peace? I had to become a hardened savage. I had to be willing—without hesitation—to defend myself. Even with violence. I worked myself up into a mild frenzy. The uncertainty clawed at me. I had read the books, talked to the ex-cons—some full of advice, others full of bravado. Most treated prison like a rite of passage, a badge of twisted honor. I tried to prepare. I tried to become savage.

Eventually, exhaustion overtook everything. I fell back asleep.

I dreamt of a leopard, a lion, and a she-wolf.

CHAPTER SIX: THE DESCENT

March 2, 2020, Tommy dropped me off at the Duluth Federal Prison Camp. The place was officially designated minimum security—low custody, no violence in the last fifteen years, no sex offenses, and under ten years left to serve. I met the criteria.

Inside the Receiving Department, I stripped off my civilian clothes and handed over what personal property I had. I was searched, screened for suicide risk, and issued prison gear. The Camp itself had once been a US Air Force base. It had the bones of a town—administration buildings, a cafeteria, berthing units built like military barracks, and separate buildings for recreation, religious services, gym facilities, a library, and even a defunct bowling alley. According to bop.gov, it was almost a vocational haven, offering certificates in electrical, plumbing, welding, and other trades. I read about all that before I came. I thought maybe I'd learn a skill. I had hope.

But that illusion would crack soon.

After moving through Receiving, I was sent to meet several prison staff for the initial parts of the Assessment and Orientation process—A&O, they called it. Most of it was focused on health assessments and a few broad prison policies. I was told I'd be scheduled to complete the rest of A&O later, but that never happened.

I sat for two interviews—one with a nurse practitioner, the other with a physician. They asked questions to gather my medical history, assess my current health, and determine any diagnoses or necessary medications. It was clinical and impersonal, like being processed on an assembly line.

Afterward, I was placed alone in a room with a table and two chairs. I sat quietly, waiting, not knowing what was next. A few minutes passed. Then the door opened.

A man around my age walked in and sat down across from me. We locked eyes.

"I'm Dr. Swanson, chief psychologist," he said.

We stared at each other for a moment—mutual surprise blooming into recognition.

"I know you," I said.

"Oh my God," Swanson replied, eyes wide with disbelief.

"Wow… it's been like twenty years," I said, my voice a mix of shock and embarrassment. We'd gone to the same university, been friends. He'd even kissed my sister once when she came to visit me at school.

We talked briefly, mostly about my current mental status. He was professional, but the history between us was obvious. At the end of the conversation, he said, "I have to inform the warden about our past connection. There may be a conflict."

"Okay." I nodded. "Good seeing you. I just wish it were under different circumstances."

He left the room. Ten days later, I was informed I'd be transferred to Morgantown, West Virginia. Apparently, the warden had decided our history was, in fact, a conflict of interest.

After my health service meetings, I was sent to the main CO's office to receive my unit, cell, and bed assignment—what they casually referred to as my new "house."

"Well, you're assigned to the shithole unit," the lead CO informed me flatly.

I nodded.

"I'll take you to the shithole soon but first, go down the next hallway until you see an ugly fucker. Ask him for your ID card."

"Okay," I said, keeping a straight face, though mildly amused.

I followed his directions and walked down the hall. A CO stopped me and asked what I was doing. I told him exactly what I was told.

He processed my ID card, then asked what unit I'd been assigned to.

"The shithole unit," I answered.

"Oh. You're in Building 208. Here's your ID. Now go back to the dumb bastard who sent you to me," he ordered.

"Okay," I replied, still not smiling but finding the whole exchange surreal.

When I finally walked into Building 208—my house—everything in me tensed. The place was loud and chaotic, packed with inmates. I followed the escorting CO through the building, scanning the strange and unfamiliar surroundings. The sounds, the smells, the stares—it was overwhelming. My body snapped into a fight-or-flight state, but there was no fight to be had, no way to flee. I had to take it. Endure it. Try to adapt.

That first night, after the final stand-up count at nine-thirty p.m., I climbed into my top bunk. I barely slept. My mind churned with thoughts of what I'd already experienced—and what I had yet to face.

Early on, I learned that prison operates by three sets of rules. First, the official, written Bureau of Prisons' rules. Second, the verbal instructions COs give—sometimes aligning with the written ones, sometimes not. And third, the inmate code. That last one? It's the most important. It's unwritten but strictly enforced. Usually learned the hard way—through trial and error—or, if you're lucky, from a seasoned "celly" willing to teach you how things work.

I was lucky. My cellmate, Rodney, had twelve years of prison time behind him. I had one day. Rodney was a skinny, wiry guy. A meth dealer—second offense. He'd already served ninety-six of a 144-month sentence. With good time, he'd be out soon. Before this, he did fifty-one months for his first offense. Street tough, smart as hell, even though he'd only made it through the ninth grade. I pegged his IQ around 120. His body was covered in tattoos—except his face. A dog had bitten off his left index finger during a house party gone wrong. My favorite tattoo of his was a zombie riding a motorcycle.

He also had a pretty severe case of OCD.

On my second day, Rodney pulled me aside. "Hey, man," he said, "there's a rule you're breaking... someone a few cells down told me about it."

I was confused. "What'd I do?"

"You've been looking into other inmates' cells as you walk by. That's a serious problem. You broke one of the Ten Commandments—the fourth one: don't look in someone's house."

"I wasn't doing it on purpose," I explained. "Sometimes someone moves fast, or there's a sudden noise. I glance without thinking. Most of the time, I don't even realize I'm doing it."

Rodney nodded. He got it. "I know... I do know. But it doesn't matter. One day, someone's gonna think you're snooping, and it'll turn into something."

"I hear you," I said, grateful for the warning.

Rodney gave more advice. "I look at the floor when I walk through the hall or outside. My guess? You're not from the city. City people never look around or make eye contact. Just watch—see how most inmates stare at the floor or straight ahead. They won't acknowledge anyone unless they're tight with 'em. It's about timing. When to say something. When to keep quiet. You'll get it."

Eventually, I was approved to use the phone and email. The only number I could remember was my attorney's, Leif Anderson. I called him to check in, give him an update, and get contact info for friends and family.

I dialed the number and waited through the BOP recording. "This is a call from a federal inmate. You will not be charged for this call. If you wish to accept, press 5." Leif picked up and pressed 5. The line opened.

"Hey, Leif, this is Paul."

"Paul, how are you doing? Are you okay?"

"It's tough," I admitted. "I feel lost. Nobody tells you anything here. But I got lucky—I've got a decent cellmate. He's been showing me what to do, what not to do."

We talked for a while, catching up. I didn't know BOP calls had a fifteen-minute limit, or that they were interrupted every few minutes by a robotic voice reminding you that you're a federal inmate. Five minutes left. One minute left.

As the one-minute warning hit, I wrapped it up. "We've gotta end the call," I said. "I'll try again when I can."

"Stay strong, Paul," Leif said.

"I will. Thanks for everything."

And then the line went dead.

***

Later that afternoon, I wandered into the upper TV room. One other guy was already there, sitting at a table. He was white, looked to be in his mid- to late thirties—maybe 5'10", around 220 pounds. Solid build. Muscular. Clearly someone who worked out regularly.

A few minutes passed in silence. Then I decided to break it. "The Camp here's not so bad, is it?" I asked.

He barely looked up. "This place is a fucking shithole. There's a lot of bullshit going on," he said flatly. Then added, "Name's Sam."

I didn't offer mine.

Sam continued, "I've been in high-security, medium, and low prisons for over ten years. This one? The worst. Total shithole."

"Really?" I asked, surprised. "Why?" Then, before he could answer, I followed up, "So… are higher-security prisons actually better?"

"Yeah. And it's about the people," he replied. "White people here are pussies. No pride. They don't stick together. You go to medium or high—you've got people watching your back."

Maybe it was a little impulsive, maybe I just needed to connect in some way, but I decided to tell Sam about what happened to me on my first day. I told him how I walked into the cafeteria alone, sat at a table next to the wall, and started eating. A few minutes later, a white inmate approached me and explained—quietly but firmly—that the table I was sitting at was claimed by Black inmates. In fact, he said, all the tables along that wall were for Black inmates. I looked around and, sure enough, he was right. He pointed to the opposite wall and told me those tables were for Hispanic inmates. The rest of the tables—the center ones—were for white, Asian, and "others." He told me a lot of guys come down from higher-level prisons where that kind of racial segregation is the norm. It's territorial. Aggressive. I admitted to Sam that I felt embarrassed. I must've looked like the new guy I was—lost and clueless.

"Fuck that!" Sam snapped. "If whites stuck together, you wouldn't have that shit. No fucking nigger or spic would talk that way to a white if whites had each other's backs." Then he pulled up his shirt. Tattooed across his chest was a swastika. "They see this, they know I'm serious!"

He told me he was part of the Aryan Brotherhood—AB. A violent and notorious gang. Claimed he'd convinced the BOP he was no longer affiliated.

What I didn't know at that moment—but would later learn—is that anyone with active gang affiliation doesn't make it to minimum security. To be eligible, they must disaffiliate, in writing. Even then, it's not guaranteed. Many who try to break from gangs request to "Drop Out" or be "Sent Up Top," which basically means they go into protective custody or transfer to another facility. But right then, I had no reason to think Sam was lying. Or exaggerating.

I tried to steer the conversation somewhere else. "Must feel good... knowing someone's got your back."

"Damn right!" he said. "There was this inmate who owed me money. I beat his ass in public to show I'm serious. You've gotta strike in the open so people know to fear and respect you."

There was a pause. The room felt heavier.

"Got to go get my medication," I said, needing an excuse to leave.

"Later on, Paul," Sam replied, nodding.

I nodded back and left the room. But as I was walking away, a thought hit me like a jolt: *how the hell did he know my name? I never told him.*

Back in the cell, I sat down at the little metal desk and opened a book I'd checked out from the prison library. Rodney was already there, lying on his bunk. We didn't speak for a while.

Then he said, "I'm proud of you. I noticed you looked down when you walked." He paused. "And... I noticed you were talking to Sam."

I looked up, surprised. "How'd you know?"

"I walked by. Saw you two through the window," he said.

"Sam's... spooky," I said. "He's got a swastika tattooed on his chest." I lowered my voice on the last few words, as if saying them out loud would cause trouble.

Rodney nodded. "Yeah, he's a weird, crazy fucker. Thinks he's living in a movie. That guy runs a poker table in the Rec Building—high stakes. Like five hundred to a thousand a hand." He started chuckling. "There was this dude, Hernandez, who lost money to Sam and couldn't pay. Sam blindsided him, right out in the open. Tried to beat him down."

Rodney laughed harder now. "But Hernandez was with this little guy, Lopez. Lopez picked Sam up and body-slammed him. Little dude—maybe 5'2", 140 pounds. But he kicked Sam's ass. Sam got up and started threatening to kill both of them. All three—Hernandez, Lopez, and Sam—got sent to the SHU." He was laughing fully now, shaking his head.

I was trying to process all of it. "What's the SHU?" I asked.

"The Special Housing Unit," Rodney said. "SHU's just another word for the Hole. They use the SHU to punish inmates who act up, fight, or break the rules."

"How violent does it get around here?" I wasn't sure I wanted to know the answer.

Rodney gave a few examples. "Not frequent. Sometimes. Like, about a month ago, five Black guys beat the hell out of a Mexican guy. Ten minutes—non-stop. The Mexican had been snitching on them. They beat his ass good. The COs didn't punish any of them."

I raised an eyebrow.

"It's a rule," Rodney said flatly. "The Mexican asked for a transfer after that. Said he felt unsafe, that his life was in danger. They moved him out immediately."

"Damn," I said, stunned.

Rodney went on. "Month before that, two Black dudes owed a Mexican guy—Alejandro, he works in the metal shop—some money. They refused to pay. Alejandro walked into their cell with a sharpened metal bar, raised high. They ran. Tripped over each other trying to get down the stairwell. Scared shitless." Then he added, "Blacks are the worst to deal with. They try to cheat too often. Even some that seem nice."

I was still processing the image. "Did Alejandro get his money?" I asked almost mechanically.

"You bet your ass he did," Rodney said with a smirk.

***

On the afternoon of my fifth day inside, I headed back to the upper TV room. It was empty. That never happened. Not in here.

Thank God, I thought. *Alone time. I can watch what I want.*

I grabbed the remote and settled in. Finally—some peace. I had two goals: watch the news and enjoy the company—albeit through the screen—of smart, beautiful women.

I turned the TV on to Fox News. With just one click, I could flip over to CNN, MSNBC, CBS, or ABC. All of them had striking female anchors and reporters. The news kept me connected to the outside world. And when it came delivered by a gorgeous, intelligent woman, it made things feel… lighter. It was a small pleasure, but in here, small pleasures were everything.

It was March 7, 2020. The coronavirus epidemic in China, market meltdowns, talk of systemic racism, and the presidential election dominated the coverage. Trump hadn't declared a national emergency yet. Non-essential government services were still open. But the Dow Jones was down over a thousand points from its high. Bad news.

Still, somehow, the women on Fox made it all feel manageable. I watched, not just for information, but for comfort. Martha, Dana, Harris, Sandra, Gillian, Laura, Trish, Marie, Ainsley, Abby, Shannon, Lisa B., Lisa K., Arthel, Kimberly… and oh my sweet Lord—Dagen.

It's been a while since I enjoyed the company of a beautiful woman, I thought. There's no substitute. None. And it's not just their physical beauty. It's their eloquence. Their intelligence.

I flipped the channel.

Don't worry, CNN, MSNBC, ESPN, ABC, CBS—you have your own set of brilliant, beautiful women too. Kaitlyn C., Christi, Pamela, Briana, Katy, Sage, and Amara. I laughed under my breath. "Damn, Kaitlyn C. and Sandra S. My darlings, you both look fabulous today," I said out loud before glancing over at the door and window to see if anyone heard me. Then, in a quiet whisper to myself—again, checking the room—I added, "Thank you, ladies, for all the hugs and kisses you've given me... even though every single one exists only in my imagination."

Fantasy had to end sometime.

The door opened and in walked Roger—a sixty-year-old Black inmate. He took a seat at the table next to mine. Convicted of meth distribution, second offense, he'd already served sixty-one months of a 120-month sentence. Thanks to the First Step Act, Roger was eligible for early release after completing sixty percent of his time because he met all the necessary criteria: over sixty, no violence in the past fifteen years, no sex crimes, solid prison conduct, and completion of required programming.

Roger had a reputation. He often spoke about race, especially when talking to white inmates. He fancied himself a scholar of the 1619 Project—the controversial piece by Nikole Hannah-Jones, whose father was Black and mother white. Roger hadn't read the project, not a single page of it, but he absorbed every bit of commentary and advocacy from others who had. He believed the US was founded on racism, that the American Revolution was really a fight to preserve slavery. He wasn't interested in hearing criticism. That didn't stop him from preaching about it.

Then came his analogy.

"Let's say we havin' a running contest between a Black and a white, and they're runnin' a total of 1,600 meters," he began. "Startin' gun goes off—bang—and the white takes off, but the Black? He don't start until the white passes four hundred meters. That's a four-hundred-meter head start. Now... is that fair?"

"No, it's not fair," I said. "And no, the Black person probably can't catch up. I get your point."

Roger leaned in. "It don't matter how much you give Black people—assistance, reparations—we ain't never gonna catch up."

I nodded, but responded, "Well, I think ending slavery was a good start... civil rights laws made a big difference. And there's been billions in taxpayer money spent on Black communities—for housing, education, employment. Plus, the president recently made permanent a $225 million commitment to historically Black colleges. There are programs out there meant to help. I don't think a Black person today starts four hundred meters behind. And in my view, reparations have been paid."

Roger's eyebrows lifted. "What do you mean *reparations was paid*?"

"I don't say it lightly," I told him. "But to me, there's nothing more degrading, more despicable, than enslaving another human being. And based on everything I've read, there were plenty of white people—even before the Civil War, even before the Revolution—who believed slavery was immoral and wrong. Many of them were willing to risk their lives to end it. During the Civil War, around 750,000 soldiers died—about 450,000 Confederates, 300,000 Union. Most of those Union soldiers were white. They gave their lives to end slavery. Their blood, their sacrifice—that was the payment."

Roger thought about it. "You're right about whites dying to end slavery," he admitted. "But 450,000 others died tryin' to keep it. And we still never been treated right after that."

"You're right," I said. "Black people were not treated well." The conversation stayed respectful, mutual. But even so, I felt uneasy when it ended—embarrassed, almost. I knew better. I'd been told before: prison is not the place to have those conversations.

Back at my cell, Rodney gave me a look. Then came the warning. "I saw you talkin' to Roger," he said with urgency. "He's a racist fucker. Hates white people. He'll be nice at first, but I've seen him go off on white guys over dumb political shit. Equal rights, race stuff. He's full of hate and bullshit. Watch yourself. Race talk can set off violence in here. Stay away from it."

"You're right," I said. "He wasn't rude, and I wasn't either. It felt civil, but yeah, he seemed laser focused on race. I think this place brings out the worst in people. Maybe he's not so bad outside. Still, it was foolish of me to go there."

Just then, the callout for mealtime came. Rodney took off fast.

I threw on a jacket, gloves, and wrapped a scarf around my neck, then walked out the door and down the stairs. The cafeteria was about three hundred yards from our unit. A crowd of inmates was already making its way there, all careful to stay within the marked walking path. Step outside the boundaries and you could get written up—maybe worse.

At the cafeteria entrance, the line had already curled into a zigzag outside the building and into the foyer. Hundreds of inmates, all hungry. When I got there, I joined the line and took off my hat—no hats allowed indoors. If your shirt was untucked, a CO would snap at you, no hesitation.

Then came Terrell. A large, pudgy, gay Black inmate, Terrell hustled past the line. He worked kitchen duty—cook and food server—and was late. Suddenly, from somewhere behind me, a loud voice rang out. "Terrell, you are a disgrace to homos everywhere! How can you advance homo rights in prison when you won't even ask for pink clothes?"

The line erupted with laughter.

I turned and saw who it was—Anthony. A nutty, troubled inmate from the next unit over. Funny as hell though.

"How would you know about gay rights?" Terrell shot back instantly.

Terrell was in his fifties, doing time for embezzlement and money laundering. Just a month away from finishing his sentence. He'd soon be headed to a halfway house, then probation. He never hid the fact he was gay—probably the right move. Better to own it than pretend otherwise. Some gay inmates still tried to hide it, fearing violence. But that kind of violence had become rare.

Terrell was smart, thoughtful, and likeable. That got him respect.

Inside, the cafeteria ran like a well-worn assembly line: plastic spoon, tray, then food and drink. Sit, eat, return your tray, leave. Fifteen minutes tops. If you lingered, a CO would bark orders. And if you tried to take food with you, expect trouble. Officially, BOP policy forbids it.

Inmates mostly sat by race. Some mixed it up, depending on the dynamics, but race divisions were the norm. I sat with a small group of so-called "white-collar" criminals— two securities fraud guys, one money launderer, one wire fraud. They'd taken me in after that white inmate—same one who told me I was sitting at the Black table on day one—introduced me.

It was an educated group: a PhD, two MBAs, and two BAs, including myself. One of them had been featured on the show *American Greed*—he stole hundreds of millions.

Among white-collar inmates, most were older, late thirties to eighties. And over ninety-five percent were white males.

After turning in my empty tray, I walked toward the exit but stopped when I noticed a laminated meal plan posted beside the door. It listed every meal—breakfast, lunch, and dinner—for the month of March 2020. I'd later learn this plan wasn't unique to Duluth. It was part of a Bureau of

Prisons (BOP) systemwide menu, carefully controlled and standardized across all federal prison facilities. That meant every federal inmate across the country was eating the same thing on the same day.

Later that evening, I was napping back in the unit—something that had already become a routine—when Anthony stormed into my cell unannounced and shouted, "Hey, you got my payment?"

I sat up instantly, like I'd been startled awake by a fire alarm. The day before, I'd agreed to buy a pair of leather boots from Anthony. The BOP-issued ones had been tearing up my feet with blisters.

"Hey! Anthony! Why are you in our room?" Rodney yelled from down the hallway, storming toward the cell.

"I'm getting payment for my shoes," he replied.

"I didn't ask what you were doing. I asked why you're in the room. My celly is sleeping and you should not be in there," Rodney snapped, laying down the prisoner code.

"Well, he's up now," Anthony said, not missing a beat.

Anthony was thirty-seven, white, and had a history of severe traumatic brain injury. He got bashed over the head and body in a brutal bar fight, left unconscious for hours. Since then, impulse control, mood swings, and memory lapses plagued him. Mix in drugs or alcohol, and he was like a lit fuse. He'd already done five months of a ten-year sentence for conspiracy to distribute meth—another mandatory minimum casualty.

Around eleven p.m. that night, I was in the cell alone, restless. I wasn't looking for anything, just fidgeting when I noticed a bit of dirt on the floor. Rodney—OCD to the core—had already swept and mopped four times that day. I figured it might ease his nerves if I did it one more time.

I went to the cleaning room to grab a mop, bucket, and broom. I opened the door, flipped on the light—and immediately regretted it. Right there, in the harsh fluorescents, was a white inmate kneeling in front of a

Black inmate. The Black guy was already mid-orgasm, his body jerking as the last of it streamed onto the floor. I froze, stunned, not even sure what I was seeing. The Black inmate, breathing heavily, didn't seem to care I was standing there. But the white inmate snapped, "Get the fuck outta here!"

I got out. Fast.

I'd seen a lot of wild things in life, but that moment—a full-on gay, interracial, prison sex scene playing out right in front of me—was a first. The next day, I saw both of them. Neither made eye contact. No nod, no sign of recognition. Not that I expected it. *Maybe they didn't recognize me*, I thought. *Good.*

I had zero interest in reliving it.

***

At three a.m. on my tenth day in prison, I was jolted awake by a female CO flashing her light in my face.

"Time to get ready for transfer," she said in a soft voice so she wouldn't disturb Rodney.

My heart started pounding—not from the transfer, but because she was stunning. Easily one of the most beautiful women I'd ever seen, let alone in prison. Early thirties, brunette, long legs, fair skin, slender frame. A vision. I nodded that I understood, and she left.

No one warns you about transfers. It's policy. For security reasons, inmates aren't told when or where they're going. Some guys catch hints. I didn't. Not until the day before. Still, I pieced together what my itinerary might be from things I'd heard. First, a stop in Sandstone, Minnesota, to pick up others. Then Stillwater, then down to Terre Haute, Indiana, for a holdover. After that, the infamous Con Air would take me to Oklahoma City. Another stopover. Then a flight to Atlanta, followed by a long bus ride north, swapping inmates along the way, before finally landing in Morgantown, West Virginia.

That was the plan—or rather, the best guess. It could change at any time.

I climbed down from my top bunk, got dressed, grabbed my mesh bag, and headed out into the dark cold. The wind cut through me like a blade. It was black as hell outside.

At the administrative building, I knocked on the Discharge door. Another female CO opened it, and again—stunning. My eyes widened. Heart skipped again. Tall, gorgeous. *What is going on here?* I thought. *Thank you, God, for these gifts.* I tried not to be obvious, but it had been so long since I'd been around a beautiful woman. Prison, up until that point, was basically void of any contact with women. I never noticed that kind of loss before.

While processing through Discharge, I thought about the two women. I enjoyed being around all women, the way they look, the feminine voice, their smell, the interaction, loving them. I experienced a sudden ache, then the attached thought, *Something happens to a man who has been denied, voluntarily or by force, access to women. He suffers... when deprived of experiencing and reveling in the intimacy of, deprived of caring for and loving an adored woman. Women motivate and give purpose.* I felt a loss.

I was the only inmate to be transferred from Duluth that morning. The bus had metal bars on the windows and very uncomfortable seating. There was a protective mesh cage to separate the front and the very back of the bus from the middle section where the inmates were placed. In the back caged section, one CO sat with a shotgun, keeping an eye on the convicted. Up front, one CO drove and another CO sat with a shotgun. The COs rotated positions during the long drive. I noticed that both COs with shotguns occasionally dozed off. But why not? They knew I was no problem and long understood what rules could be ignored.

The bus was now on the road. The sky was dark. The headlights revealed a light snow and a strong wind. *The winter lasts long in Northern Minnesota*, I thought. To the onlooker, my immediate situation would appear miserable and stressful. But it was not. For the first time since my surrender, I felt relieved and relaxed. The marshals did not chain me, which is rare during a transit. The chains are always uncomfortable. Also, the first stop was six hours away, which meant I would have uninterrupted alone time with no obligations or duties.

I inhaled deeply, then exhaled slowly. I let my mind go, no effort to direct attention or censor the emotion related to thoughts. She entered my mind, that tall and slender ideal, evoked by illuminating beauty and the prolonged deprivation of a basic need. I could not resist her image, nor did I want to. The last time I shared a romantic embrace with a beautiful woman was years ago. Passion… what was once a painful loss, eventually faded and numbed, but now became an intense eruption.

I entered a deep state of fantasy, imagining we were together in a private place, wondering what it would be like to embrace her. I closed my eyes, relaxed further, and imagined her in a soft white t-shirt and panties, embracing that tall, slender body, inhaling her exotic scent, kissing her lips and then down her neck and around her shoulders. She was dazzling, fantastic, perfect. With all my might, I imagined gently caressing her soft skin and firm body with the palm of my hand, straight down, slowly, and back up in circular motions, and her responding with a delicate quiver and a soft moan. My body started to shake as yearning became an imperative to feel all of her; yes, to enter her. And she was with me, at all levels. She needed me in her as hunger became more than desire.

I imagined her removing her t-shirt and as I pulled down her panties with her laying on the bed, naked, long dark hair fanned out on both sides of her shoulders. Each thrust into her was met artistically with a slight upward arching motion she made with her lower back and pelvis. We created a kind of energy only found in live flesh, the building up and more, until finally our bodies released it all in waves so powerful and so extended, we temporarily lost all pain, all doubt, all sense of time and space. A few moments passed. We woke up, lying in each other's arms. She would not let go of me, not yet. I saw nothing but her... the world disappeared... the pain of prison, of the world, was gone, if just for a moment. She would be my religion for that day.

Now emerging from fantasy, my eyes welled up with tears... that was my only release... there was nothing else I could do.

CHAPTER SEVEN: THE SHU

After an overnight in Sandstone, Minnesota, and a quick stop in Stillwater to swap inmates, the prison bus finally rolled into Terre Haute, Indiana. The place was massive—the Terre Haute Federal Corrections Complex. Built in 1940, it housed everything from a minimum-security camp to a high-security penitentiary with a death row unit. The Complex could hold around three thousand inmates, mostly medium and high security.

As we drove from the main gate toward the FCI, I sat by the window, taking it all in. On the left side, I spotted the high-security USP and the minimum-security federal prison camp (FPC). The bus continued until we reached the medium-security FCI entrance. The guy sitting next to me acted like a tour guide. He'd been here before. Hispanic, mid-forties, in for a probation violation. Smart, judging by his vocabulary, but he came off kind of shady, maybe a little too full of himself.

I noticed a strange black building that didn't match the rest of the architecture. It stood off to the left side of the main FCI.

"What is that building over there, the black one?" I asked.

"That's where death row inmates go to die," he said, then added, "Death row inmates are housed in the penitentiary. There's a separate max-security area just for them."

That got me curious. "So, what's the difference between all these BOP prisons—minimum FPCs, low and medium FCIs, high USPs, and then death row?"

He explained, "Security levels are based on two things: One, the inmate—what kind of crimes he committed, if he's violent, and how dangerous he's assessed to be. Two, the facility itself—how restricted movement is, and how many staff they've got per inmate. Did you see the Camp?"

"Yeah," I said. "It was the second set of buildings on the left when we drove in. There was a sign."

He nodded. "Right. Camps usually don't have fences at all. The housing's open—dorm style—with four to eight, sometimes sixteen inmates in one space. Nothing's locked. An inmate could literally walk right out. They've only got a couple COs walking around for a few hundred guys. But those dudes aren't dangerous. A lot of them go straight to Camp when they start doing time. Some work their way down from medium or low. It's rare to drop from high to Camp, but it can happen. Break the rules, though, and you get bumped up."

"I was designated minimum security," I told him. "I was at a Camp in Duluth, Minnesota. But that one had a fence."

"Sometimes they do," he replied. "But it's not to keep you in. It's to keep people out. Smugglers—people trying to sneak in booze, drugs, tobacco. Still, most Camps don't bother with fences."

"Got it."

He kept going. "Lows and mediums are both FCIs—Federal Correctional Institutions—but there are differences. Low security guys are usually non-violent or at least haven't been violent in ten or fifteen years. And if you've got over ten years, they won't send you to a Camp... probably start at a low if you're not violent. Lows are dormitory-style, more open interaction. They've got double fences and more COs around."

I pointed out the window at the medium FCI fences. "So, this place has the double fences like a low?"

"Yeah, but mediums also have electronic detection systems, sometimes even high-voltage fences. They treat guys here like escape risks—potentially dangerous. You get a lot of repeat offenders, people with violent crimes—robbery, drug dealing with a gun, attempted assault, molesters. Oh, and a fucking child molester is called a 'chomo' in here. At mediums, you're in cell-style housing—usually two or four bunks. Doors lock at night. Most guys are doing ten to twenty years, give or take. There are more COs, and it's what they call 'constant and direct supervision.'"

I nodded. "I was told I'd be in the SHU here, just as a holdover, before I transfer to Morgantown, West Virginia."

"Same here," he said. "Then I'm off to Leavenworth. It's temporary. We won't be in general population... but the SHU? Man, that place is a motherfucker. You're locked in like an animal. But just for a bit."

I wasn't too concerned. I figured I'd be in the SHU for a couple of weeks at most. Still, I had one more question. "What about the penitentiary?"

"That's the real deal. High-security prisons are called USPs—United States Penitentiaries. Or the Pen, the Joint, Behind the Wall, or the Big House. They've got serious walls, reinforced fences. Housing is cells, locked at night. Staff-to-inmate ratio is high. There are cameras everywhere. It's full of the most dangerous guys—violent gang members, career criminals, murderers, drug dealers with weapons charges, rapists. A lot of them are doing fifteen to life. That USP here? It's also got a death row unit. Those guys are on lockdown twenty-three to twenty-four hours a day. They've got nothing. No hope. Some live that way for fifteen or twenty years before the government executes them."

Before I could respond, the bus pulled to a stop. COs started unloading us, shackled inmates, one by one. I thanked the guy for the information, and we were marched off toward Receiving and Discharge.

They took us to a large holding cell. Ankles and waists unchained, but wrists still cuffed. I noticed three inmates with a different shackle setup—more restrictive. Later, I learned those were for inmates deemed an imminent risk of harm. In the cell, inmates started talking, some loudly, some like they were old friends. I stayed quiet, realizing quickly that this wasn't Duluth anymore. I was in a mix now—medium- and high-security inmates. People with violent histories. Guys who'd spent years in the system.

Hours passed. No staff said a word to us. Finally, the cell door creaked open.

A CO stepped in and began calling names. One by one, inmates were led down a hallway into a room with four open stalls. Prison clothes and shoes were stacked on shelves. A giant bin of dirty clothes sat in the corner. Two COs ran the process—checking names, numbers, handing out uniforms.

I sized them up. One was short, maybe 5'4", bearded, slender with a round gut. He had a high-pitched, gravelly voice and a weird smirk. He reminded me of a mad, evil gnome. The other was tall—6'4", glasses, medium build, monotone voice. He seemed like the one in charge. "What's your full name and number?" the tall CO asked.

"Paul Smith number 7757321."

"You look like a double X. Shoe size?"

"Size 10. But I'm not a double X. Maybe just an X."

"You'll want a double X," he said, handing me an orange jumpsuit, boxers, socks, and slipper-style shoes. "Go to a stall, strip, toss your clothes in the bin."

I followed instructions. Stripped down, stood there naked, facing forward.

The CO ordered, "Run your fingers through your hair. Open your mouth. Lift your tongue. Arms out. Spread fingers. Show your palms. Lift your nuts. Turn around. Lift your right foot, now the left. Squat. Spread your ass cheeks and cough."

I did everything he asked.

"Get dressed," he said.

Then the shorter CO barked, "Come over here."

He cuffed me behind the back and led me to an adjacent room. I sat down.

I understood the search. It was necessary. Inmates smuggle things in. You can't trust anyone in here. But still, standing there naked, exposed, and inspected like an animal—like a pig during a livestock sale. And the damn scrotum and rectum thing! "Lift your nuts and spread your ass cheeks." Damn! Maybe the cough is supposed to cause the rectum to wink. Apparently, the act of coughing pushes out and exposes anything hidden up inside—drugs, pills, even a small phone. Hell, maybe next time I'll just shit on the floor and let them sort it out.

After the Receiving process, I was led down to the Special Housing Unit—the SHU, pronounced *shoe*—to be held in transit. Based on what I'd learned in Duluth and overheard on the bus ride, I figured I'd be here maybe two weeks, give or take, before heading to the Oklahoma City Transfer Center via Con Air. From there, maybe Atlanta or Harrisburg or somewhere else entirely before finally landing at the Federal Prison Camp in Morgantown. So far, the path seemed to be unfolding just like the BOP manual said it would—predictable, in that bureaucratic, fucked-up kind of way.

We stopped in front of cell B-31. The short CO patted me down, then ran a handheld metal detector around my body and ankles. He clicked his radio. The door unlocked with a heavy clunk and slid open with a grinding metallic screech, rolling left on its track.

"Inmate, walk to the back wall. Don't turn around," he ordered.

I shuffled inside and did as I was told. Behind me, the door slammed shut with a thunderous echo, locking me in. Then came the clank of a metal slot opening behind me—about four inches by twelve inches. The CO's voice filtered through. "Put your hands through the opening."

It wasn't easy. My wrists were cuffed behind my back. I had to bend at the knees, press my spine against the door, and angle my hands just right to fit through the slot. My wrists wouldn't line up. The metal cut into my skin. After a few failed tries, the CO broke protocol—reaching through to yank my wrists into place, leaving himself exposed in the process (for safety reasons, a CO never reaches into a cell).

"Are you all right?" he asked with a rare hint of humanity.

"No—but keep going until you get this damn thing off," I grunted.

Finally, the cuffs came free. The slot slammed shut and I was alone.

I turned around and took it all in. Roughly ninety square feet of concrete and metal, maybe thirty-five square feet of actual usable space. Upper and lower bunks. A small stainless-steel toilet-and-sink combo. A filthy, bacteria-riddled shower stall in the corner. The walls were off-white, cracked, chipped, covered in graffiti, crude poetry, Bible verses, gang tags, and cryptic symbols. The floor was layered with grime—food, feces, God knows what. The air reeked of mildew, mold, and old shit. The shower was the worst. Mold climbed the walls and clung to the curtain in black and green streaks. I felt like I needed a hazmat suit just to breathe.

The mattress on the bottom bunk was three inches of plastic-wrapped foam. About eighteen inches had been hacked off and stuffed into the top bunk to act as a pillow. I swapped them. Pillows weren't allowed, but I needed something.

I walked to the narrow window—about five inches wide and maybe three feet tall—embedded into the far wall. Through the dirty pane, I could see barbed wire fencing, a patch of dirt, and little else. No sky, no freedom. Just containment.

The next day—March 13, 2020—I received an Inmate Bulletin. It was a one-pager, handed to everyone. President Trump had just declared a national emergency due to COVID-19. Effective immediately, all inmate movement was suspended across the Bureau. No visits. No transfers. No lawyers. No exceptions. The prison world stopped spinning.

That's when I knew—I wasn't going anywhere anytime soon. Con Air? Grounded. Morgantown? On hold. No Duluth, no Oklahoma, no nothing. I was stuck.

I wasn't afraid of the virus—not yet anyway. But based on my relatively brief experience, I did not trust government bureaucracy. Somehow, they'd fuck this up.

I'd spent months mentally preparing for Duluth. I studied the place, visualized the routines, made peace with what was ahead. I was going to enroll in RDAP—the Residential Drug Abuse Program. I qualified for it: years of heavy drinking, an actual diagnosis of severe alcoholism, and a clear connection between my addiction and my crime. It was my ticket to twelve months off my sentence. That, plus Good Time Credit, gave me a plan, an estimated release date, and a path forward.

Then this transfer to Morgantown came out of nowhere. I had no internet access, no books, no way to research anything. But I got resourceful. I started gathering info, word of mouth mostly. Morgantown had an RDAP program. It had training, apprenticeships, education. Not bad, all things considered. I would find a way to adjust.

Then came Covid. Now I was sitting in the SHU with nothing. No info. No plan. No timeline. Just this box.

I had no idea what was next, and apparently, nor did the BOP. This feeling of unpredictability, not knowing my future, neither immediate nor remote, was becoming a strong theme of the prison experience.

I started asking questions. "Hey, CO—any updates on the virus? How long are these lockdowns supposed to last?" I asked as my lunch tray came through the slot.

The CO ignored me. Flat out ignored me.

Thirty minutes later, when they came back for the tray, I asked again.

"CO! CO… anything new about this corona situation?"

Nothing. Not a glance. He took the tray and walked on.

Maybe there were no answers. Maybe there were and they just weren't talking. Either way, the uncertainty gnawed at me. The anxiety built in slow waves—like the tide rolling in under the floor of your mind.

I'd only been locked up for ten days, but I was already losing my grip on the basics. No orientation. No handbook. No communication. The SHU was max confinement with no guidance. I didn't know how to make requests, who to ask, what forms to use. I heard staff throwing around acronyms and lingo—COPOUT, BP8, Standing Mainline—but I didn't know what any of it meant.

I understood the basics: COs wore uniforms, ran the units. Health Services did medical. There were admins handling HR and logistics. The warden sat at the top. But the in-between was a blur. Chaplains, assistant wardens, lieutenants, captains—no one told me who was who, or how to reach them.

I was lost. Completely and utterly lost.

One afternoon, I ran out of toilet paper.

"CO!" I yelled as one passed. No response.

"CO, I need toilet paper!" I said louder. Still nothing.

"God damn it! I can't wipe my ass properly. Who the fuck do I ask for toilet paper? I can't make a fucking written request—I don't have any goddamn paper or pencil. Do you want me to shit in a sock and send it out with an empty food tray?"

That got the attention of other inmates. The whole tier exploded—banging, laughing, shouting.

Eventually, when the noise died down, a voice from the next cell over called out, "Keep askin'… they get you some shit paper soon. Or I'll throw a line and gets you some." I didn't respond. Just thought to myself, *How the hell is he going to 'throw a line' and gets me some?*

Still, I kept observing. Listening. Watching movement through the crack under my door. I tried to identify which COs were walking by, what times they came through, who talked and who didn't. I tuned in to the conversations between inmates and staff. I picked up some prison slang— OG, punk, baby momma, range boss, lock in a sock, sweet in the ass, roll up on someone, poke, stick.

At first, I only understood a third of what they said. But that third mattered. It was a start. It was the beginning of learning how to survive in a world built on strange codes.

I made mental notes about the words and language I heard during observation and interactions. I learned that "OG" meant an older, wiser inmate—sometimes referred to as "Original Gangster." "Leaving a body" or "he's got bodies" meant the inmate had killed before. "Lock in a sock" or "I'm gonna lock in sock his ass" meant creating and using a flail-like weapon. It was simple and brutal: take a metal combination lock—authorized for purchase through commissary—drop it into a sock (the longer the better), grip the open end, and swing. The lock end does the damage.

Then there was the word "bitch." Before prison, I thought it referred only to a subordinate inmate used for homosexual gratification. In prison, I learned it was most often used as a pejorative—like calling someone an asshole, but more forbidden, more provocative. "Bitch" sat on a tier above "motherfucker" but below racial slurs like "nigger," "cracker," and "wetback." When one inmate called another a "bitch" with intent, violence was sure to follow.

Within a couple of days, I started to orient myself. The frustration and anger started to dull—slightly. I learned the SHU was built for maximum restriction and deprivation. Solitary confinement was its core design. All inmates, no matter why they were there, were treated the same: locked in a cell twenty-three and a half hours a day, with a supposed thirty-minute recreation window. Most inmates never saw those thirty minutes.

Counts were random or every thirty minutes. The randomness wasn't just for show—it was strategic. It confused us, kept us from syncing up for planned misbehavior.

Most cells were double occupancy. They called it "double-celled solitary confinement." When two inmates were housed together, they had to share the same security level—minimum with minimum, low with low, and so on. Apparently, COs weren't allowed to mix different levels. I felt lucky to have a cell to myself. The space was tight, and the last thing I wanted was to be locked in with someone I didn't know.

COs barely talked to us. Communication was limited to meds, meals, clothes exchange, or the rare miscellaneous request. Inmate-to-inmate communication was limited too, mostly due to the architecture of the SHU. COs never used names. It was always "Hey" or "Take this," or a sharp rap on the door with a baton.

"Throw a line" or "send a line"—I heard that one early, during the funny outburst from the guy in the next cell. It meant exactly what it sounded like. We made strings from whatever we could—threads from blankets, strips torn from sheets or towels. The line had to be longer than the distance to the next cell. A weight—usually a bar of soap—was tied to one end, thin enough to slide under the cell door. You'd angle it out toward the cell you wanted and the other inmate would do the same. The lines would cross, and he'd snag yours by slowly pulling his own back in. Once your line was in his cell, you could start passing messages or items back and forth.

In the SHU, you were either under Administrative Detention or Disciplinary Segregation. Administrative meant holdover, transfer, protective custody, or under investigation. Disciplinary was for inmates who violated BOP regulations. The two guys to my right were holdovers like me—one was from Detroit, a connection to Michigan. The guys on my left were under protective custody, supposedly because their lives were in danger. Two cells over, a guy was doing thirty days in disciplinary segregation for getting caught with a phone. Some inmates had been stuck in the SHU for three months, six months, or longer.

On day six, I overheard a confrontation down the hall. I watched from the little cell window. A shackled Black inmate was being brought in and was about to be placed with a white inmate. They were both medium security, and there were no other open cells. Usually, COs ask if an inmate is okay with a celly from another race—but they didn't this time.

The white inmate shouted, "He ain't coming in here! Fuck that!"

The lead CO warned, "If you cause any problems, you'll rot in there for a long time. You want that?"

"Fuck that!" the white guy yelled back. "If he comes in here, there'll be fucking problems."

Then the Black inmate chimed in, "Fuck you, cracker bastard! I'll kick your mothafuckin' ass!" It went back and forth like that until the COs led the Black inmate away.

It could've easily gone the other way. A Black inmate refusing a white cellmate. Or Hispanic. Didn't matter.

In my view, the situation was resolved without violence. No incident report. No write-up. Just experience and wisdom guiding the moment. In prison, the rules were different.

This wasn't the place for civilized morality or progressive policies. Racism might not even have been the reason for the white inmate's refusal—maybe it was fear, maybe safety. Just two days earlier, a Hispanic inmate stomped a Black inmate to death in the penitentiary. It was a gang hit—hate with intent to kill.

In prison, hate had to be tolerated—at least to a degree. Otherwise, more inmates would die.

The progressive ideologies around racism and hate have failed in society. If they're forced into prison culture, chaos and riots will follow.

The race policies weren't written or spoken aloud, but they existed. White inmates bunked with white inmates. Hispanics with Hispanics. Blacks with Blacks. Only if both parties agreed and security classifications matched would they mix. And even then, only if same-race pairings weren't available. That's how it worked in most medium- and high-security federal prisons—where violence was likely and gang affiliations mattered.

Later that day, I sat cross-legged on the floor and meditated. I did a sensory review—a full assessment of my new world, sense by sense.

Sound: Everything was the same, every day, just reshuffled. The drip of water from the sink and shower repeated endlessly. Muffled voices passed like tides through the hallway. Then, out of nowhere, the loud bang of fists on a wall, someone screaming obscenities into the void. At night, a guy somewhere down the range would rap for hours, slapping rhythm on his door, projecting his talent to an involuntary audience. Then another inmate would lose it—"Shut the fuck up!"—because it was one in the morning. But the worst sound, the one that crawled under my skin, was the metal-on-metal creak of the electronically controlled gate. It opened and closed twice an hour, like clockwork, right near my cell.

Sight: My vision was limited to the cell. The same walls, the same faces of COs during count, meal delivery, or medication. Through the narrow window, I saw barbed wire fencing thirty yards away and a patch of grass. Sometimes a bird flew by. Sometimes a CO circled the perimeter in a security vehicle. If I laid on the floor and peered through the half-inch gap under the door, I could see a short distance down the hallway. On the walls were messages—names, poems, Bible verses, gang symbols. I scratched my own into the paint beneath the window: *To fear the Lord is the beginning of wisdom.*

Smell: The smells were the most honest. Food came three times a day, each with a different—but fleeting— scent. The rest of the time, it was just the sour, pungent odor of the cell and my own body.

Taste: Bland. The meals were predictable and dull. No commissary. The water had a metallic, oily taste. I used the flavor packets—grape, orange, cherry—to mask it.

Feeling: Touch was the rarest and harshest sense. The temperature stayed cold—62 to 67 degrees. I wrapped myself in a sheet during the day, slept in all my clothes at night, tucked under a thin blanket. The fabric was coarse. My pillow was a rolled-up towel. The shower temperature was insane—cold, then scalding, then for a few seconds, just right. But it never lasted. I had to dance in and out, dodging the extremes. And the tension—I felt it in my gut, my jaw, my neck—every damn day.

***

After eight days, I felt the anxiety start to devour me. It wasn't just psychological anymore—it was physical. There was a constant tension in my jaw from grinding my teeth and a pressure that settled deep in my stomach. I ruminated endlessly: what had happened, what was happening now, what might happen next. I couldn't stop the spiral. At times, the anxiety peaked into full-blown panic—heart pounding, sweating, dizziness, and that terrifying thought: *I'm about to lose it.*

All I did was worry, eat, sleep, and use the toilet—circling through those activities inside a rectangle smaller than a parking space. The uncertainty only made things worse. I had no idea how long I'd be stuck in the SHU. Eight days? Eight weeks? Eight months?

I started pacing. Four steps back and forth, over and over again.

The next morning, desperate for something to do, I asked the CO, "How do I request books, paper and pencil, a phone call, and recreation time?"

He answered flatly, "The afternoon CO should be able to take care of those requests... so ask him, or you can put in a COPOUT."

"I haven't had access to anything," I said, trying to emphasize my urgency. "And I haven't been out of my cell."

He barely reacted.

"What's a COPOUT? And how do I submit one?"

"A COPOUT is a request on a piece of paper. Write your request, fold it, slide it through the crack between the door and the wall. A CO will pick it up and someone will respond... eventually."

"But I don't have a piece of paper or anything to write with."

He shrugged. "I don't have time right now and I don't have paper and pencil to give you. Ask the CO on duty this afternoon." Then he turned and walked away.

Later, I tried again. "May I ask a question, please?" I said to a CO walking past my cell.

He stopped at the door, stared through the window, but said nothing.

"May I ask a question?" I repeated.

"I'm staring at you, aren't I?" he replied, clearly annoyed.

"How do I request items—books, paper and pencil, the use of a phone, and rec time?"

"I'll see what I can do about paper and pencil," he said. "That's usually done on the weekends. Every Thursday, the CO on duty pulls out a book cart... though I don't think anyone's done that in weeks. For the phone, there's one CO—Godfrey—who maintains the list. You get one fifteen-minute call per month. Rec Cage? You have to ask the morning CO."

"Thank you," I said, finally getting a somewhat straight answer.

The next morning after chow, I asked, "Please put me on the rec time list."

"Rec time has already been scheduled for the day," the CO responded.

"But I was told to make a request with the morning CO," I said, frustrated.

"You need to make the request at five a.m. That CO will make the list."

"But I have no watch or alarm. I can't track the time—there's no clock, no routine. I estimate by meals and daylight. That's all I've got. What am I supposed to do?"

The CO shrugged. "A CO will tell you the time if he's generous," he said and walked away.

"If he's generous? What does that even mean?" I called after him. No response. I seethed.

It wasn't just the indifference—it was the implication. We weren't seen as humans deserving of answers or clarity. The disregard, the rudeness, the smugness—it was in their training. But worse than how they acted was why they acted that way. They truly saw us as unworthy.

The next morning, I woke while it was still dark and stood at the cell door. I waited until I heard footsteps.

"CO, what time is it?" I called out.

"Three a.m."

I had two more hours. I was exhausted, but I didn't dare lay back down. If I did, I knew I'd fall asleep and miss rec time again.

At five a.m., I heard something—barely audible. I pressed my ear to the gap between the door and the frame. A CO was softly calling out, "Rec time," as he walked the range. I caught him and asked to be added to the list. Finally.

I went back to sleep.

At seven a.m., I woke for breakfast, ate, then crashed again. Around nine-thirty, I was up for the day. I stretched on the floor, waiting for rec time. An hour passed.

"Are we doing rec time today?" I asked a CO.

"Rec is over," he said.

"What? It never even started!"

"Started and ended. I walked by your cell and you were sleeping."

"Why didn't you wake me up?!"

"I don't wake inmates up," he said, smirking.

I lost it. Rage surged through me. I wanted to tear his arm off, beat him with it, then eat it.

But instead, I snapped verbally. "This is intentional! God damn it! You bastards designed this. You make us request rec at five a.m., knowing we don't have a way to tell time. Then, whenever you feel like it—maybe morning, maybe afternoon—you come by quietly and say we missed it? It's all to avoid work! Because taking one inmate to rec is a whole process—chains, escorts, door coordination. Multiply that by ninety inmates and it's a pain in your ass. So you don't bother! You're fucking lazy bastards!

"I'm not even in here for disciplinary reasons! I'm a holdover. I'm in transit, damn it! But it doesn't matter— you treat everyone the same. Whether someone's here for shanking a guy or waiting for transfer, same punishment. Same dehumanizing bullshit. This is a jail within a prison—it's the lowest level of existence. It's harmful. It's inhumane."

The CO just smiled. "Welcome to prison," he said and walked off.

Those words echoed through my head the rest of the day. I felt sick. Like my mind was breaking from itself.

And yet... I wasn't punished for the outburst. That surprised me.

Later, I reflected. Was I exaggerating? Was I paranoid? Was the system really set up to deny rec time... or was I just cracking under stress? I didn't land on a conclusion at first.

But then, it became obvious. The pattern was too clear. The staff was trying to reduce their workload by cheating inmates out of rec.

This place wasn't just inhumane. The people (staff) made it worse.

How could someone treat another person being this way?

The answer came, painful and sharp: You treat someone like that when you no longer see them as human.

By day twelve, I could no longer ignore a growing pain, a mixture of yearning, desire, loss, and suffocation. The onset occurred sometime after indictment, then increased significantly after I surrendered to prison. But now, since my time in the SHU, the pain was full blown. The strength pierced through my chronic depression and anxiety to become most prominent in my conscious mind. I knew what caused it; it was a reaction to a total loss of the sensations and stimuli—obvious and subtle—of a free life: watching the news, listening to jazz music, enjoying conversations with colleagues and friends, feeling the soft hair of my children, enjoying the warmth of sunshine on my face, the scent of a flower, and the taste of pizza. The pain worsened as more freedoms were taken away, reaching the highest severity while in this maximum isolation, confinement, and deprivation. That kind of pain was the worst I had ever known. At no other time before then was it more severe. I knew it would get worse. And that very thought pushed me closer to a point of insanity than I had ever been.

At about fifteen days, my level of anxiety peaked. I began to experience brief but frequent periods of panic. During waking hours, I paced the cell (about four steps), back and forth obsessively, looking out the small window on the wall, then the small window on the cell door, then back again. I was checking for something that would give me an experience other than what I experienced repeatedly each hour and day. Through fantasy, my hope began to morph into belief that a change meant the BOP was ready to transfer me. I knew I was behaving compulsively and knew my thinking was irrational, but I did not resist because my disordered state granted me some small relief, however briefly.

A couple days later, that energy gave way to a deeper depression. Hopelessness. I felt like I was fading.

By twenty-five days, I felt detached from my body, sense of self, and disconnected from the world. I experienced a numbing of physical sensation, and a decrease in range and strength of emotion. When I passed by the mirror, I saw an expressionless, dead face. When I spoke, which occurred only when I was required to, I used few words, slowly, softly, with poor articulation and pronunciation.

For hours, I stared in a direction for no reason, not focused on anything. Time became an illusion, as the days had no cyclical rhythm; one never began, the next never ended. Counts, meals, and random communication with COs became rude interruptions to a preferred somnolence state. I wolfed down meals, the only action done quickly and with zeal, in a desperate attempt to experience something, anything strong and different. My mind was undisciplined, thoughts ruminated and wandered at the same time, then suddenly nothing but loose, themeless associations.

After twenty-seven days, I was experiencing a moderate degree of indecisiveness and indifference. I had difficulty making choices, so I made no choice. I laid in the bunk and stared at the walls and ceiling, getting up only for food trays and using the toilet. I had not showered in the past seven days. My sleep-wake cycle became flipped, awake all night, asleep during the day, then flipped again. But day and night did not matter anymore. When I was awake, I did nothing. I did nothing because there was nothing of value, no stimuli, internal (an idea, image) or external (the sun shining), available or strong enough to prompt a decision.

It was on the twenty-ninth day when I first became aware of experiencing transient perceptual distortions and illusions. At first, I perceived sights and sounds that would normally evoke immediate and strong curiosity, but in my current state, that level of curiosity was lacking.

For an example of such illusions/distortions: I saw insects crawling on the ceiling, legs moving, the bending of the long thin body back and forth, surveying the area during travel. Then suddenly, the insect disappeared for a second and reappeared at the very spot it began. I heard my name being called from somewhere outside the cell down the range walkway. I heard a keychain clinking, as often occurs when a CO is walking or in motion.

But there was no external sensational link to these perceptions, or there was a gross misperception. They were distortions of a disordered mind.

That afternoon, laying in the bunk, I opened my eyes slowly, moving my head on a roll of dirty laundry. An overcast day darkened my cell in shades of gloomy gray. The rank scent of urine and sweat lingered. My lungs labored to draw in the thick, pungent stale air. I felt a dull ache throughout my body, a stiffening, which came from weeks of no movement. I became nauseous, as from a hangover. I felt a transition—the becoming something else, something less than. Not only was I disconnected from others by space due to incarceration but had become separated by species or kind. This chasm caused a loneliness beyond anything I previously contemplated or experienced. I was unsure about myself, except I was certain I was no longer healthy.

Suddenly, I became flooded by vivid ruminating thoughts of my terrorizing situation, the utter disregard and disrespect, the total lack of any kindness or decency, and the torturous conditions of maximum isolation. I felt a strong mood heat my body.

Then, I howled, "How dare you! How dare you fucking bastards treat another human being this way. How dare you, fuckers?!" But there was no one there to give a damn.

Day thirty-two—the banging on the door woke me. The slot opened.

"Come here," a CO said.

I got up. Through the window, I saw another inmate—cuffed, held by another CO.

"Turn around," the CO said. I complied. He cuffed my wrists. "Stand back." The door opened.

In walked Ted Gunderson. My new cellmate.

Ted was a fifty-nine-year-old white guy, minimum security, transferred down from Sandstone. A big man—275 pounds, 6'2", tattooed all over: naked ladies, death, skulls, panthers, clowns. His head was shaved, goatee thick. He looked at me, nodded, and smiled.

"We're gonna do just fine," he said. "Where you headed?"

"Morgantown, West Virginia."

"Well good," he said. "I'm going to McDowell, near the North Carolina border where my family lives. We're gonna be just fine."

Ted threw his bag on the top bunk and began unpacking.

At first, I hated the idea of a cellmate. The courtesies, the annoyances, the lack of privacy. But surprisingly, Ted made it bearable. He was easy to live with—funny, knowledgeable, "been around," as they say. I learned a lot from him.

He was a hillbilly—more Iowa than Deep South. Used to do mason work, had a thing for eating sheep testicles. When he described how he'd cook and eat them, I fought back my gag reflex.

After a few days, I finally asked, "What are you in for?"

"Drug charges. Conspiracy. Got 240 months for manufacturing meth. My second time."

"240 months..." I paused, stunned. "How many years is that?"

"Twenty."

I went silent. My head spun. I'd never met someone doing twenty years. I felt a wave of sadness wash over me. "Have you seen violence?" I asked.

"Yeah. Some."

"What causes it?"

"Food's number one. Race is a close second. Then personal property."

We talked more.

"Most guys won't fight," he said. "They don't want to lose their classification or good time. But if you have to fight—if it's unavoidable—swing first. Don't hesitate."

I nodded. "My biggest problem is my anger. I've been losing it lately."

"Keep to yourself," he advised. "Focus on you. Make a routine. Do your time."

He moved on to other topics, "Stamps are the main form of money. I recommend you don't get a prison tattoo... they melt down chess pieces and use the soot as ink... Not good. Infections can get real bad."

Instead of moving to other matters, I brought back the issue of violence, "What kind of violence have you seen?"

"I saw one inmate stabbed another inmate in the neck with a pencil. The inmate grabbed his neck and blood was gushing out between his fingers."

I was stunned. "Why? Was it a race thing?"

"No, they were both white," he answered.

"What security level?"

"Medium security,"

Ted continued, "A Black inmate hit a white inmate in the head with a meal tray, right in front of me. The CO was fucking around, told this white dude to sit at a table where only Blacks sit. The white dude didn't know better. There was no more to it. After being hit, the white dude just left. What that white dude did was a disrespect. Saw several Mexicans beat up one of their own with a broomstick for not sticking up for himself. That was gang related. When I was at a prison that had separate low- and medium-security facilities—I was in the low—heard about several Mexicans, beat up three Black guys to death with baseball bats, but I don't know if that's true."

I asked, "How did they get bats?"

"They got them from Recreation."

"Was it in the low-security facility?"

"No, a medium," Ted replied quickly. Then he added, "I did see some Arab throw a shoe at some white guy. I heard that's some cultural thing."

I added, "There are no rules in fighting. There are no rounds, no refs, none of that. If your life is in danger, there is one goal—survive."

"Amen," Ted agreed. "Years from now, you can tell everyone I helped you survive prison."

I smiled and chuckled.

On day thirty-five, a CO rapped on the cell door, and said, "Get your personal property together. You have both been redesignated to the Terre Haute Prison Camp due to the COVID-19 pandemic."

About fifteen minutes later, Ted and I left. As we were escorted from the SHU to the Camp, I thought about what Nietzsche wrote.

"What doesn't kill me, makes me stronger."

CHAPTER EIGHT:
PANDEMONIUM 1

In early April 2020, despite the spread of COVID-19 and the implementation of protective measures, the entire Complex was operating fully, except the rate of incoming and outgoing inmates had decreased moderately. There was no indication from the warden or staff that Covid was a serious concern. Boldly, the warden boasted zero cases at the Terre Haute FC Complex, which, at that time, was based solely on voluntary self-report of symptoms from staff and inmates. By late April, regular temperature screening (a temperature detection device placed on the forehead) was implemented during facility-to-facility inmate movement within the Complex, such as movement from the SHU to the Camp. Regular screening of staff, vendor, and visitors who entered and exited the Terre Haute Complex frequently had not yet begun. According to the Inmate Bulletin, information gathered from staff conversation, and from inmates using contraband, the BOP systemwide positive Covid rates and related deaths were increasing significantly, creating an urgent and serious situation. As a result, inmates were being released to home confinement under recent federal legislation, passed on March 27, 2020, titled the CARES Act.

After leaving the SHU, Ted, five other inmates, and I were escorted to Receiving and Discharge to finalize the redesignation process. Once there, cuffs were taken off, then we all endured the standard strip search. The same two COs, the short one and the taller one, were directing the process. This time, the four stripping stalls were used by four inmates simultaneously. The shorter CO began the cadence, which was slightly different from before. "Run your fingers through your hair. Pull your right ear forward, now the left ear. Lift your arms and spread your fingers. Now lift your sack. Turn around, lift your right foot, now your left foot. Spread your ass and cough. Here are your clothes. Get dressed."

One inmate, however, did not keep up with the strip search procedures. I spoke to this inmate at length in the holding cell and suspected neurological problems, primarily frontal lobe. This provisional diagnosis was based on several years of experience in conducting literally hundreds of neuropsychological assessments. While in the holding cell prior to the search, I noticed on six occasions the inmate would be in the middle of describing something about his past, often prison related, then interrupt himself with some trivial matter such as noticing and commenting briefly on the length of his thumbnails, then try to go back to the previous train of thought but forget what he was talking about. On three of those occasions, he eventually remembered what he was talking but started back at the beginning. Among the signs I observed, deficits in working memory, distractibility, and awareness were most pronounced. Therefore, it did not surprise me the inmate could not keep up with the pace of commands and easily confused right from left.

The CO pointed at the inmate and barked, "You, do it over," then started yelling out the commands. But the inmate did worse. The CO walked up next to the inmate, and shouted, "Spread your fingers! Now lift your sack. I said lift your fucking dick and balls. Lift them, goddamn it! Turn around! Lift your right foot. I said your right, damn it. Now your left foot. Hurry up! Spread your fucking ass cheeks."

When done, the inmate stated, "I see you don't follow the California procedures."

"Shut up and get the fuck out of here!" the CO growled.

I chuckled. I knew sometimes the order of body parts examined in the strip search varied slightly from prison to prison and even CO to CO. This inmate's statement about "California procedures" was clearly an attempt to excuse or explain his performance.

Ted and I were taken out the medium-security FCI main doors and told to wait for a ride. I was moderately confused about the situation and commented, "We have no chains on, we're outside, and no COs are watching or guarding us... this is strange."

Ted replied, "We're minimum-security inmates going to a minimum-security Camp, which is nothing like maximum. Things will be way different."

A few minutes later, a Camp van stopped for pick up. The driver, who was also an inmate, asked, "You guys going to the Camp?"

Ted replied, "Yes, we are."

We entered the van and traveled toward the prison Camp. I asked Ted, "What is the difference between a Satellite Prison Camp and a Federal Prison Camp?"

"There is no difference. 'Satellite' means the Camp is part of a larger prison complex, like it has one or more higher security prisons—like Terra Haute has a medium FCI and high USP. When a Camp is a standalone prison facility, like at Duluth where you were at, it's referred to as a Federal Prison Camp, FPC. But there is no difference. They have the same security, same policies, same everything."

The Terre Haute Satellite Prison Camp (SCP) was built in the early 1960s. The main facility included administrative offices, housing, food service, and a recreation area. There were outbuildings for various programs, functions, and operations, including education and training, general facilities, and ground maintenance, shop and garage work, food depot storage, and UNICOR. The physical structures looked rough, neglected and poorly maintained. The interior of the housing units, where the inmates resided and spent most of their time, was extremely filthy and in poor condition. The bathrooms were the worst: grime-stained doors and walls, rusted pipes, areas layered with mold and mildew, nonfunctioning fixtures. The main facility of the Camp was infested with rodents and cockroaches, with heaviest concentrations found in food service areas and housing units.

I was assigned to Unit S08, Cell 4, Bed 160. Unit S08 was another shithole, worse than Duluth but better than the SHU. Unit S08 was on the top floor of the housing building farthest to the east, where the morning sunrise shoots rays of light through the hallway windows. The floor plan of the unit was simple: 120 feet long, thirty feet wide, all cells and the bathroom were lined up along the west side about twenty feet deep, and a long hallway stretching from one end of the range to the other, about ten feet wide on the east side. Cell 4 was next to the bathroom, about midway down the unit range. From the hallway windows, inmates had views of the high-security USP facilities and the Complex's main entrance.

The prison counselor, Mr. Clark, took me and Ted to Unit S08 and our respective cells and bunks. Ted was in Cell 6, two down from me. Neither cell had yet been given any personal care items or a change of clothes. The counselor told us to stop by his office later that afternoon for temporary clothing items, combs, shampoo, soap, and shower slippers.

Immediately after the counselor left the unit, there was a sudden change in inmate behavior. It was like a movie director yelling, "Cut!" and suddenly all the inmates stopped acting. The inmates were instantly louder, and, within a few minutes, several openly used cell phones and two began smoking tobacco at the backend of the range. I was shocked by such bold behavior.

"My name is Paul Smith," I introduced myself to my new cellmates, all white: Richard, Mathew, John, Bradley, and James. The counselor intentionally placed me with white inmates for safety reasons, which was a fairly common practice in the BOP, and also occurred at Duluth. John politely, and as casually as possible, informed me that inmates don't normally disclose their full names nor ask another for his during introductions. I nodded, acknowledging I understood, and stated, "I didn't know."

Mathew was quite friendly and explained some basics about the cell, including common courtesies, the location of cleaning items, and general routine and expectations. "The system does not treat prisoners in transit well. So, here's a bar of soap and washrag to get you started if you want to clean up," Matthew offered, handing me the bar. "I also have some shampoo, and we can locate a towel if you want to take a shower. And later, we'll get you coffee and some food to hold you over until commissary."

"Thank you, very nice of you," I replied sincerely. I then started pounding the soap on the corner of a concrete windowsill, trying to break it. I wanted to give a piece to Ted. But the bar didn't break.

A Hispanic inmate suddenly came out of an adjacent cell, approached me, and offered a sharpened thin piece of metal, custom made. "Try this," he said. The metal was in the shape of a flat rectangle, approximately three inches wide by five inches long, one-sixteenth of an inch thick, and sharpened on one edge.

"Wow! Thanks for the offer. But I got it." I then slammed the soap harder into the concrete corner and this time it broke. I was surprised by the inmate's offer of what seemed like serious contraband, and more so by his casual and open manner. The inmate exhibited no concern, as if offering the use of a pen or a deck of cards. I wondered why the inmate had such an item. *Was it for protection? Or intimidation?* Later, I discovered the Hispanic inmate used it to chop food, likely considered by staff as mild to moderate contraband but not serious, nothing that would send him to the SHU.

About an hour later, Mathew approached me about purchasing a cell phone, considered major contraband. "There are ways of communicating with your family on a regular basis. I have something you can use a couple of times." He showed me a cell phone, then continued, "But you should think about getting one for yourself. There is one available for $150... I can help set you up."

"Thank you, I mean it, but I am damn afraid of getting caught, losing some good time, and being sent to that fucking hellhole, the SHU. It's not worth the risk," I replied.

Mathew seemed slightly offended, as if he had just been called a fool. "It's not what you think; most people in the building have a cell phone. There is a lookout system where someone is always watching for COs, and there are places to hide the phone. Where COs never find it."

"Well, right now I'm too nervous about having a phone."

He replied, "You will want a phone eventually, when you see it's not a big deal."

My thoughts began to swirl as I tried to make sense of the prison environment, the code, and selfish philosophy. I had very limited knowledge about what "regular" general population prison was like. I had been down seven weeks, but five and a half weeks were spent in the SHU, which is nothing like regular prison. I knew there was a lot I did not know. I vowed to avoid impulsive decisions, infractions, and any problems, and I did not want to be known. These were very serious vows. I planned to remind myself frequently during meditation and prayer. It seemed simple: don't break the rules and lay low. But I would find that it was very difficult.

It was nighttime, and toward the end of my first day in the Terre Haute Camp. I made a phone call to my children, which was the first time since surrendering to prison. I wasn't able to call them before because the BOP did not set up my phone code until the day before I left Duluth. I was anxious and excited. I was uncertain how they would respond to me, given the situation, and I desperately wanted to hear their voices and to tell each I loved them as much as I knew how.

The call went very well. I explained to my oldest child how the email system worked, and that I would contact him frequently through this mode of communication. My oldest daughter understood I was in prison and was naturally curious about my situation. She asked me questions like, "What do you wear? What do you do? Can you go outside?" The call lifted my spirits significantly. Afterwards, exhausted, I walked back up to Unit S08 and decided to end my day. I was unable to speak with my two youngest children because their mother disallowed phone calls and emails. She would only accept regular mail.

I changed my clothes and climbed up into my bunk. Unfortunately, I was assigned to a top bunk right next to the cell entryway, which happened to be the worst bunk. I was bothered by frequent traffic flowing in and out of the cell and had zero privacy. But worse, I was placed directly above cellmate Richard, who, while asleep, snored very loudly on the inhale of breath, whistled often during exhale, and flatulated frequently. He weighed 345 pounds, which was likely the main cause of his sleep disturbance.

That night, Richard's snoring and flatulating were worse than anything I had witnessed in my lifetime. The onset of the loud noises and rank smell began around 11:45 p.m. Initially, the cellmates seemed to tolerate the harsh sensory stimuli emanating from this large inmate. I was a coward and did nothing. After an hour, however, the cellmates and some inmates in the adjacent cell were losing sleep and began to voice their frustration. I felt trapped, as bellows of the foul stench moved upward from its source, resulting in a smell more powerful than a Russian bear slap.

Bradley was the first to act. He tapped Richard on his shoulder to wake him, then told him to roll onto his side. As Richard attempted to roll, which was very difficult for a large man on a very narrow bunk, Bradley assisted him to succeed. But the rank smell alone was violent enough to disturb sleep. Then, John turned on six fans, already pointed in the right direction, as if he had dealt with this situation before, and began to pull in rapid succession the trigger of a spray bottle containing an industrial strength fragrance called Cherry Blossom. The speed in which he pulled the trigger was impressive as the spray appeared to be a near-constant flow, like the bullets spraying out of a machine gun. John oversaw cleaning the bathrooms, so he had access to special cleaning supplies. These countermeasures seemed to work. The inmates went back to sleep.

Unfortunately, they did not last through the night. At 4:36 a.m., I, having suffered enough of noise, harsh smells, and an overdose of cherry blossom fragrance, got out of bed, went into the hallway and tried to sleep on a plastic chair. I had no idea how I would survive prison without going crazy.

Four days later, I felt compelled to do something, as each subsequent night was the same as before. I was determined to assert myself, to lay down the law and the harsh consequences for noncompliance or violation. I imagined and rehearsed the scenario in my mind, over and over. I knew the words I would use, the tone and loudness of voice, and the assertive gestures for emphasis. But when the moment came to lay it all down "with some stank," I instead begged for mercy.

"Every night it smells like someone shit a cherry tree. Can we do better than this? I think we can. Anyone else think so?" This started a conversation among the cellmates, focused with the intent to resolve the situation. But the next day, and all days after, there was no evidence of a sincere plan or effort to change.

Over the following weeks, I became acquainted with my cellmates. There was respect, courtesy, and relative calm mostly. On occasion, tensions would rise because of some political outrage or mild disagreement.

Mathew "Flamethrower" Richardson, a forty-three-year-old German-English white man, had served twenty-one months of a ninety-six-month sentence for four counts of mail fraud. He refused a plea bargain and instead took his case to trial. He was accused by the prosecutor of setting fire to his house, then receiving an insurance payout check for the total damage through the mail from the insurance company. He was never charged with arson or insurance fraud.

I reviewed, upon Flamethrower's request, the trial transcripts and other documents confirming he was indeed not charged with arson or insurance fraud, but the prosecutor accused him of both as facts. I was intrigued. Typically, on those occasions when an inmate professes his innocence, I exhibited all the signs of thoughtful listening but my mind often went elsewhere, and I did what I could to cut the conversation short. I had never met a prison inmate who was not guilty.

However, Flamethrower's case was different. It appeared the US prosecutor was able to use "backdoor prosecution" loopholes to add arson and insurance fraud as enhancements to the sentencing guideline calculations. Those two enhancements basically added four years to his sentence. Flamethrower was charged and found guilty "beyond a reasonable doubt" for mail fraud. Then, during the sentencing phase, he was given enhancements for arson and insurance fraud, where the burden of proof to establish facts in trial and sentencing is "preponderance of the evidence."

I asked Flamethrower, "But I don't understand. What if you drove to the insurance company and picked up the check instead of receiving the check through mail? Would they—"

Flamethrower interjected, "That's correct! My attorney asked the prosecutor that very question and added would he have a case if the US mail service wasn't used? The prosecutor said no."

Flamethrower was now in the appeal process, hoping to hear something soon from his appeals attorney.

He was highly intelligent, having completed all but three courses of a master's degree in avionics. He achieved his commercial pilot's license and been employed as a pilot for a major airline company. He owned his own construction business for several years. Also, he was a professional UFC fighter for a short period in his early thirties. He bared no tattoos. He had six children from three different women and was currently on his third marriage. I sympathized. Apparently, his wife was very supportive, from what I gathered, and he was in frequent cell phone contact with her. I viewed Flamethrower as friendly and reasonable; he was the first inmate at Terra Haute Camp to introduce himself and make a friendly gesture.

John "Machine Gun" Kelly was a forty-nine-year-old white man of Irish-Italian descent. Machine Gun had served twelve months of an eighty-four-month sentence for delivery of cocaine and illegal possession of firearms. He had prior convictions but a good attorney dealt with his current case. The attorney was able to avoid any "violent charge" enhancements.

Machine Gun got his name partly from owning hundreds of guns (pistols, rifles, some fully automatic, some with bump stocks or silencers) and other interesting weaponry, including flamethrowers, high-powered CO_2 pellet guns, blow darts, and explosives, which he talked about frequently with inmates he knew well. His guns were not for hunting rabbit and such, but rather for enforcing his will, defending himself, and for showing off. His nickname was often expanded to Machine Gun Kelly, because he looked and behaved like George Kelly Barnes, the OG during the prohibition era of the 1920s, who preferred the fully automatic Thompson gun (Tommy gun) to perform his craft.

While in conversation, I overheard him talk about collecting money on the streets of Chicago back when he was in his twenties. "One guy didn't pay, he owed, a lot," Machine Gun said.

"What'd you do?" asked an inmate.

"What do you mean, what did I do? I put a gun in his mouth and told him to pay, and he paid."

Machine Gun told me a story about a drug rehab he once completed. He was down in South America to some untold place in a house owned by persons who possessed several kilos of cocaine. The owners of the cocaine knew Machine Gun had a drug problem, so they helped him out. One of the South American's laid out the intervention plan as follows.

"You can enjoy the girls, you can smoke the weed and drink the booze," he then pointed to the cocaine, "but if you touch any of the cocaine over there? Then," he pointed to a deep hole, "we will bury you in the ground." Machine Gun claimed that was the greatest twelve-step program he ever attended.

Machine Gun was obsessive compulsive about showering, cleaning his small area of the cell, and organizing and tidying his possessions. Sometimes he showered four times in one day, wiped the floor under his bunk three to four times a day, and reorganized the possessions in his locker for hours. He often complained to his cellmates about not cleaning and tidying up their respective areas. However, I enjoyed my conversations with him.

Machine Gun had multiple tattoos, most done while in prison. I noticed he had no tattoos on his face, neck, arms, or hands—any areas not covered by clothes. His tattoos were typically of skeletons in some kind of action. He used a cell phone on a disciplined schedule to reduce risk, smoked tobacco daily, and occasionally drank alcohol that was smuggled into the prison, typically huge quality. During the first nine months of his current prison stint, he completed his GED. The BOP punishes inmates without a GED by granting less good time credit than those who have a GED or higher.

Bradley "Gay Boy" Lutz was a thirty-eight-year-old gay white man, who had served twenty-four months of a thirty-six-month sentence for delivery of methamphetamine. His crimes were clearly driven by his severe addictions. After serving two-thirds of his time, he was being released early under the CARES Act. He was expecting an out date any week. Gay Boy showed me a picture of himself, dressed in drag, the day he surrendered to prison. I noticed how thin he was in the picture and guessed it was likely from ongoing meth use.

Gay Boy did not hide that he was gay, nor could he hide if he tried. He exhibited, with flair, many traditionally feminine gestures, and his voice was signature homosexual. Some inmates teased him for being gay; lightheartedly, for prison. "Bradley, I heard you tested positive for a virus called G-A-Y-19."

Gay Boy was on his cell phone obsessively every day. He smoked tobacco, hand rolled. He was arrogant, unrealistic, and had a bad habit of playing the devil's advocate way too often while in social situations, which sometimes caused outbursts and harsh words. I was surprised he had not been beat down. He disclosed he'd had several discrete sexual encounters while in prison but never gave names. He completed some college.

Richard "Big Baby" Ford III, a large forty-eight-year-old English-Polish white man, had served four months of a 134-month sentence for possession of multiple illegal firearms in the furtherance of a crime and delivery of cannabis. He was assigned a court-appointed attorney from the public defender's office and plea bargained his case. After some initial interaction, I found it was hard to believe Big Baby was able to contribute adequately to his own defense. I read his court transcripts and sentencing documents, then talked to him about his educational background.

"Did you complete high school?" I asked.

"Yes, but at a school for disabled," he replied.

"What disability did you have?"

"I didn't read or write too good and had that ADD," he replied. Then he added, "My mom said I didn't talk 'til I was two. I had problems in school, startin' out in kindergarten. I was put in a different school 'cause I needed help. I stayed in that school 'til I graduated. When I got out of school, I was helped in getting work. I took some kind of test to see what would be best for me."

I felt angry and sad about Big Baby's situation, as I knew he wasn't able to adequately comprehend the complexities of his own case nor the legal process enough to make good and meaningful decisions or contribute to his own defense.

Big Baby was 345 pounds, 5 feet 7 inches tall, and had multiple chronic medical problems due to diet and severe obesity. He snored and shat himself at night, a combination that caused sleep disturbances to nearby inmates. As frustrating as it was, no one used any measures to resolve this noxious problem because all knew he could not control what happened while asleep. However, he did eat very large meals just prior to sleeping, a very bad habit, which some inmates insisted was the cause of his flatulence and demanded he cease that habit immediately. On several occasions I saw him during late evening hours, spoon in hand, digging deeply into a large bowl of food, which was held very close to his mouth. I thought he looked like an ox with a large grain sack strapped around his mouth. Big Baby did not cease, but instead became worse, as food seemed all he had to counter the horror of an eleven-year sentence. I came to understand this, and ceased efforts to change the situation, vowing I would not interfere with another inmate's methods to cope with life in prison.

Big Baby had a tattoo on his chest and one on each calf. I never observed him using a cell phone, or being in possession of any other significant contraband. He was good natured and friendly.

James Walker was a seventy-three-year-old, white man called The Liberal. He was imprisoned for securities fraud involving over ten million dollars, had served forty-eight months of a seventy-two-month sentence. He took his case to trial and lost, which added about twenty months more of prison time than if he had plea bargained. He was seeking an appeal. Fortunately, due to the First Step Act and CARES Act, which were approved during Trump's presidency, he was only weeks away from being released to home confinement and probation.

The Liberal had an MBA from an Ivy League school, and spent most of his working years in the financial and investment industries. It was rumored he had previous convictions for fraud, but he never talked about any prior legal history. I never confirmed whether the rumor was true. The Liberal was very witty and humorous. But he was also an obnoxious liberal, who, at times, was very difficult to live with. The cellmates, consisting of a hardcore progressive, a moderate democrat, a libertarian, and two MAGA conservatives, barred him, under punishment of severe slapping, from saying the president's name, or making any direct or indirect references about the president. If there was such a thing as Trump Derangement Syndrome, he had a very severe case.

Liberal shared the Flamethrower's phone almost daily. I did not observe him use any other contraband.

In late April 2020, I received a callout notice via the TRULINCS email from the Camp Counselor, Mr. Clark, indicating I was assigned to work in General Maintenance 1 (GM1), to begin the following morning. During open hours, I went to the Camp counselor's office to ask Clark what GM1 entailed. After entering the office, I remained standing and tried to be concise; I learned most administrative staff tolerate only very brief inquiries and discussions, if at all.

"Mr. Clark, I was assigned to GM1, and I have no idea what that involves. I was hoping to get into a skills training program or apprenticeship, like welding, plumbing, electrical, or construction. Prior to entering prison, I read on the BOP website most prisons have training and apprenticeships available, and even some offer certifications through the Department of Education. Are any skills training or apprenticeships available here at the Camp?"

While listening to me, Mr. Clark initially had a look of confusion, which turned into a slight smirk. I was not sure how to interpret Clark's expressions, but sensed I possibly said or did something wrong. Maybe I should have said less.

Clark replied, "You must do work while you're in prison, and you often do not have a choice about where and what that will be. Mr. Riley, the staff supervisor over at GM1, needs inmates, which is why I assigned you to work there. With this coronavirus situation, a lot of inmates have been sent to home confinement and very few are coming into the prison. The inmate numbers are way down. Right now, all staff supervisors are desperate for inmate labor. So, if you want to work somewhere else, you need to see Mr. Riley first and ask if he is willing to transfer you to another job. Then, you need to go the staff supervisor of the job you seek and ask if he or she is willing to accept you. I don't know of any kind of training or certification going on right now, but that will be dealt with by the Education Director. The prison stopped most activities involving groups of inmates. In fact, starting tomorrow, that will include food services. Inmates will no longer gather in the cafeteria to eat. Instead, inmates will pick up a tray, one unit at a time, and go back to their unit to eat. Things are changing around here."

"All right, I will speak with the Education Director about training and apprenticeship opportunities. What about the 2018 First Step Act? It's my understanding inmates would receive 'evidence based' programming based on a needs assessment. What is that about?"

Clark responded, "That's down the road. That's not happening now, and probably not for several years, if it happens at all."

"Thank you," I said, then left the room.

I was very disappointed. Programming was my key to early release. I felt a sick anxiety, like I was trapped and could barely breathe, but there was nothing I could do. I was told I qualified for the Residential Drug Abuse Program (RDAP), a nine-to-twelve-month intensive treatment program. Upon successful completion, my time in prison would be reduced by up to twelve months. I also understood the First Step Act would allow inmates to earn additional time off by participating in "qualified programming and activities." The BOP was about to implement this part of the Act. However, the pandemic was causing delays and disruptions.

While heading toward the building exit on his way to Mr. Riley's office, I heard a loud, harsh, and startling command, "Tuck in your shirt, inmate!"

I turned around quickly and stopped.

It was Mr. Parker, one of the case managers. My startled look quickly turned to white-hot anger. I hated being talked to in such a disrespectful and completely unnecessary manner. Parker repeated, "I said tuck in your shirt!"

While fixing my shirt, I said in a moderately loud voice and with a glaring stare, "I heard you the first time."

Parker walked past me, then turned into his office. He was about six feet tall, 190 pounds, white, and exhibited signs of an autism spectrum disorder. It was as if he existed in some parallel world, self-absorbed and mostly shut off from the real world. He had no friends at work. His general approach to inmates was odd, awkward, and at times troubling, especially when he made some half-assed attempt to appear wickedly tough. He was not mean or tough in any real sense. Inmates did not fear him but found him highly annoying.

Another inmate, Jerome Pugh, witnessed the brief interaction. "That guy an asshole. Man, he should be no case manager. He ain't no good with people," Jerome stated.

Jerome, nicknamed Black, was housed in a different unit than me, but we talked occasionally as we were headed to an RDAP once our transfers were redesignated. Black was in the SHU at the time I was there, one cell over to the right. He was a forty-nine-year-old Black man from Detroit, Michigan, who had served nearly forty months of a sixty-three-month sentence for delivery of opiate-based medication. Apparently, he moved thousands of doses while living with friends on an Ojibiwe reservation in Minnesota. He served prior time on three felony drug charges and many misdemeanors. He had nearly thirty arrests and fifteen convictions, many petty crimes such as operating a vehicle without a license or with no plates or insurance. Half of his arrests and convictions were due to probation violations. Black had a moderately tragic childhood: neglectful parents, lived in multiple foster homes, sent to juvenile detention twice. Academically, he completed the ninth grade, struggled in most basic areas, but had great penmanship. Remarkably, Black had never worked a "real" W2 or 1099 job or filed a tax return. Yet this man survived, created income (albeit illegal), owned multiple houses, and had a family. Black got his nickname because, as most inmates pointed out, he was

"Black as a mothafucker." I believed Black's celly said it best, "That motherfucker is so Black he's blue."

"Jerome, the first time I met with Parker was for my initial team meeting. That meeting lasted about two and a half minutes. He said three things to me: get a job while you're here, stay out of trouble, and don't bother me. After that, he entered some things on a computer and had me sign a document. After I signed, he asked if I had any questions, and I told him no. That was it."

Jerome said, "Yeah, he is not helpful at all. They say his father is high up in the BOP, and somehow that gives him an excuse to be an asshole."

"So, what the hell is a case manager? What do they do? And how is that different from a counselor?" I asked.

Jerome answered, "Case manager, he do team meeting, and progress reports every six months. He also do classification, security level status, if you got any changes. When you get released to halfway house or probation, he do that. Team meeting is what you do when you meet him the first time, when you got here. The counselor gives you a bunk assignment, job, and supposed to be part of the team, whatever the fuck that means."

I ranted, "Yes, I'm shocked by the vast difference between what is presented and described on the BOP website and the reality of this shithole. It's a huge lie based on laziness, incompetence, and irresponsibility. The BOP mentions unit meetings and team meetings, which are attended by a team of staff who help an inmate set a plan to succeed in prison. I have found no evidence of meetings, no unit or team. And get this; the Terre Haute A&O Handbook describes the counselor as someone who provides counseling and guidance to help an inmate's adjustment to prison, and plays a leading role in programs relating to an inmate's activities, including work and training. That is the biggest piece of horseshit I have come across in prison so far. The BOP uses titles like 'case manager' and 'counselor,' which traditionally, and even in the broadest sense, mean to help or assist others achieve a goal or an outcome. That's just BOP BS."

Black and I ended the conversation. I headed towards the woodshop to speak with Mr. Riley. On my way, I crossed paths with Flamethrower. I knew Flamethrower worked for GM1, so asked him about the work and Mr. Riley.

Flamethrower replied, "GM1 is okay. It's basically light construction, repairs, some modifications. Also, there are certain set of plaques we make out of wood, for staff retirements and annual awards of the USP, the FCI, and here at the Camp. We also have staff requests for unique projects, like the assistant warden wants us to make a wooden BOP transfer bus about thirty inches long with all the details and designed in a way so the top of the bus can be lifted, and inside are pegs that'll hold all staff chits. I will show you that; I'm working on it. Let's see, there're the tools and equipment needed—saws, planer, joiner, sanders, pneumatic tools, drills, painting equipment, and many other things. You'll see it all. Let's go. I'll go with you and introduce you to Riley."

"Great, thanks."

As we walked, he continued, "He's cool and mellow, never a hard ass. He wants inmates to show up and the work to be completed. A full-time workday is roughly nine to eleven a.m., then one to three-thirty p.m. You'll get paid about $19 a month, which is standard starting pay. I make $45 a month because I'm level 2, and lead inmate; level 1 makes $120. The lead inmate is basically like a foreman or direct supervisor."

Flamethrower directed me around the south side of the Education building, to the back door of the GM1 shop. Flamethrower introduced me, "Mr. Riley, this is Inmate Smith. He has been assigned to work in GM1." After the introduction, he left.

Mr. Riley responded, "Ah yes, I received a notice this morning that you were assigned to work in GM1." Riley did not shake my hand, which would have been appropriate etiquette in the outside world. But no matter the situation, prison staff does not shake the hand of an inmate, or refer to an inmate as *mister*, or use an inmate's first name. Such a behavior communicated equality and mutual respect. I knew well inmates were not equal to prison staff or anyone else.

Riley continued, "Things have been kind of strange lately. This Covid thing has shut down a lot of work that needs to be done. We got fewer inmates and have all the recent six-foot social distancing and no gathering or groups, even though I'm still expected to finish the work. So, what kind of experience do you have in woodworking and construction?"

"Some experience. I worked on construction crews when I was younger. I've done some roofing, painting, tear down," I answered.

Riley showed me around the woodshop, explaining work expectations, safety issues, the various tools, and procedures for checking a tool in and out of the tool crib. Afterward, he stated, "Do your work and don't use a cell phone or smoke tobacco in or around the shop. Other than that, there should be no problems and you'll learn some things. You'll start tomorrow after you sign some paperwork."

"Thank you," I said.

I was sincere about redefining myself and preparing for a new life and lifestyle. I lost my professional license for at least five years and there was no guarantee I would ever get it back. I wanted to develop valuable skills that would help to secure employment upon released from prison and, later, help to create streams of income. Unfortunately, I discovered the BOP website listed many types of available trainings and certifications, but none were offered at the time, and few had ever been offered, even before Covid. I heard buzz about the First Step Act of 2018; inmates would be eligible for "evidenced based" programs according to their personal needs. But I was skeptical: How does the government define "evidence based" programming? How are my needs assessed? And by who? Will these programs be required or voluntary? I liked the rehabilitative aspirations of the First Step Act (FSA). But I was simply asking to receive training in some kind of professional trade. The "evidenced based programming" as defined by the FSA seemed more like therapeutic interventions than certified training programs designed for professional skill development. I thought maybe FSA programming would also include traditionally certified programs.

***

On Tuesday May 6, 2020, after being released from the afternoon count, I went to the TV room to catch up on the news. Nearly all news coverage was of the pandemic. On that day, the total Covid-related deaths in the United States topped 70,000, and the rate of daily deaths reached between two and three thousand. The experts estimated passing 100,000 deaths before June. Likewise, several countries throughout the world were experiencing massive outbreaks and increased rates of death. Many countries, including the US, implemented travel bans. Some countries were imposing mandates, punishable by jail or fines, restricting movement and prohibiting social gatherings. There were no effective treatments identified or vaccines, though the president was working with pharmaceutical companies, the FDA, and other government agencies, and research scientists to develop something. It seemed that human life was headed to a worldwide prison: isolation, confinement, restriction, loss of freedoms. Pandemonium was everywhere.

The pandemic was an enduring prominent news topic in the United States. The upcoming presidential election was a close second. The pandemic was also the dominant topic in the BOP. Two months after President Trump declared a state of emergency, Covid hit the BOP system hard, despite the so-called protective measures. The BOP's measures—restricting inmate movement, social distancing, hand washing, disinfecting surfaces, and later, mask wearing—did not stop the spread or harmful effects of the virus in the prison system. The rates of positive cases and related deaths skyrocketed. It seemed Covid was everywhere. But no. Amazingly, the Terre Haute Complex was spared. According to the warden, as of May 6, 2020, the FCC had no positive cases and no deaths.

I, and most inmates, knew this was a whopping lie. We knew, because we saw it firsthand—the BOP at Terre Haute created an illusion of successful protection. The administrative staff and COs, with exception of the Health Services staff, were the least compliant with protective measures. Placards and notices were placed on walls with instructions to wear a mask, socially distance, disinfect surfaces, and wash hands frequently. Tape was placed on the floor in rooms, hallways, and ranges every six feet to mark social distancing, but were never used or enforced. Most staff never wore masks, and few followed other protections. The staff was most likely to spread Covid in the Complex because they left and returned regularly. Testing did not occur. Staff and inmates were temperature screened infrequently and inconsistently. Visitors and vendors to the Complex were asked if they had any symptoms. Many COVID-positive inmates never disclosed having symptoms to staff because they did not want to quarantine in the SHU for two to three weeks. I knew with certainty I would not disclose if I were positive. And there were many positive cases at the Terre Haute prison.

Back at the cell, Gay Boy, Flamethrower, and I discussed this lie and how it would likely affect inmates. I stated angerly, "I fear, and I mean this sincerely, all of us here are going to suffer for this warden's BS. At some point, the spread of Covid, and maybe some deaths, at Terre Haute prison will exceed the warden's efforts to cover up. Then, he will be outed as a fake and liar."

Flamethrower added, "There's no doubt the warden lies to the public and the inmates, and he's possibly lying to the regional and central authorities of the BOP. We see and hear directly what's happening; he's trying to make himself look good and not look bad. We have no idea what information he sends to higher authority. I think he believes Covid is going to be gone in a couple of months, or at least he did believe it. Many experts are now reporting they believe Covid is going to be with us for a while, maybe over a year."

Gay Boy said, "Ya know, in late January through maybe mid-February, this entire Camp went through a severe case of flu; that's what Health Services called it. I was very sick, and like everybody got it. I mean, it went through this place within four weeks. If someone looked through the medical records of the inmates here during that time, they would see coronavirus-type symptoms."

"I was here then. I was sick, very sick. Health Services gave a No Work Pass and some Aspire, nothing else. I laid in the bunk, coughing, sweating, then chills, for four days. It was hell. I mean, I don't remember being *that* sick from the flu," added Flamethrower.

I asked Flamethrower and Gay Boy, "When you were both sick, did either of you experience any difficulty with smell or taste?"

"I could barely taste anything. But I wasn't hungry," answered Flamethrower.

Gay Boy stated, "I couldn't taste much either."

"I ask this because it's been reported that a common symptom of this virus is temporary loss of smell and/or taste" I added.

"But it doesn't matter; even if what happened here in January and February was the flu and not Covid. The fact is we know staff are not currently testing, not screening, and people are coming in and out of this Complex without masks, without being screened thoroughly. The warden can't possibly know how many positive cases there are in this shithole," Gay Boy stated.

I concluded, "There is a lot of noise in the news about Covid, a lot of arguments, and confusion. It seems like an ideal time for what journalists and politicians call 'disinformation.' The BOP and other experts know the prison system was and is inherently vulnerable to the spread of disease. This is common knowledge. However, the BOP was caught way off guard, which was solidly confirmed by the increasing rates of new positive cases and related deaths. Also, the BOP knew the protective measures could never be implemented fully, consistently, and adequately because doing so would critically compromise the basic functioning of the prison system. Think about that. If the Camp administrator were to implement and enforce the protective measures strictly, then who would perform the work, like food service or laundry service or any other service that are provided by inmates? It's impossible, and the BOP knows it."

I observed directly the inherent vulnerabilities of Camp and the Complex to the spread of highly contagious viruses. The complex and operational systems were designed for masses living in close proximity. Inmates stood in groups for food trays, pills, count time. Inmates were stacked on top of each other in the housing units. On Unit S08, there were eight bunks per cell and seven cells total. There were eight separate housing units at the Camp, with a total capacity for around three hundred inmates. At the time, there were approximately two hundred and fifty inmates.

I observed at least seventy percent of admin staff and COs refused to wear masks and other protective gear, and very few followed other protective measures. I noticed staff never wore protective gloves when touching an inmate's property during room searches or patting down an inmate. I was not given a mask when I was released from the SHU and still had not been given one.

Unit S07, directly below my unit, was used to quarantining inmates transferring in and out of the facility, with increasing numbers being released to home confinement under the CARES Act. The staff went in and out of the quarantine unit without wearing masks multiple times a day. Also, the housing units had areas in the floors so decayed, an inmate could see and talk with other inmates on the adjacent unit and pass objects back and forth.

Until the spread of Covid became rampant, the inmate and staff movements throughout the Complex were as usual, regardless of what the BOP website indicated. Even at its worst peak, movement occurred. COs rotated duties from Camp to USP, from FCI to Camp, and so on. Initially, the spread of COVID was worse in the USP and the FCI, which caused lockdowns. Staff took shifts of Camp inmates, including me, by threat of punishment, out of lockdown to work in food service and other service areas at the USP and the FCI. The inmates who refused to work stated they had fears of contracting Covid in facilities with very high exposure rates. All were sent to rot in the SHU for three weeks.

COVID-19 did indeed spread rapidly in the BOP system. The ratio of positive cases and related deaths in the BOP were five times and three times higher, respectively, than in the general national population.

A scare overcame me. I believed the pandemic was getting out of hand and my life was in danger. I started sharing this concern with other inmates. Many had the same concern. Not an hour would go by without me discussing, one way or another, Covid and the risk of harm. I became obsessed with watching news on major news channels. I started having difficulties with sleep, constant tension, and worry. There was talk about natural immunity, but a potential for the mutation of other strands. The entire country was in lockdown, yet the virus continued to spread, causing fear and harm. I was frustrated with the BOP and the warden for not being forthright and open about the spread of the virus within the FCC. The only communication I and the other inmates received was from Attorney General Barr, which was passed down the ranks.

On May 18, 2020, a prison union official told the news media a case of COVID-19 had been reported at the Terre Haute FCC. This was the official first case at the prison.

Within a week, the complex warden sent a Bulletin to all inmates via TRULINCS email. This basically consisted of two memoranda from AG Barr, dated March 23 and April 6, 2020. The memoranda communicated a directive that the BOP maximize use of home confinement and the factors for determining eligibility. In his March 26, 2020, Memorandum, AG Barr directed the BOP to "utilize home confinement, where appropriate, to protect the health and safety of BOP personnel and the people in our custody." To this end, AG Barr issued the following directives to the BOP with respect to the use of home confinement.

In assessing which inmate should be granted home confinement pursuant to this Memorandum, you are to consider the totality of circumstances for each individual inmate, the statutory requirements for home confinement, and the following non-exhaustive list of discretionary factors:

The age and vulnerability of the inmate to COVID-19, in accordance with the Centers for Disease Control and Prevention (CDC) guidelines;

The security level of the facility currently holding the inmate, with priority given to inmates residing in low and minimum security facilities;

The inmates' conduct in prison, with inmates who have engaged in violent or gang-related activity in prison or who have incurred a BOP violation within the last year not receiving priority treatment under this Memorandum;

The inmate's score under PATTERN, with inmates who have anything above a minimum score not receiving priority treatment under this Memorandum;

Whether the inmate has a demonstrated and verifiable re-entry plan that will prevent recidivism and maximize public safety, including verification that the conditions under which the inmate would be confined upon release would present a lower risk of contracting COVID-19 had the inmate would face in his or her BOP facility;

The inmate's crime of conviction, and assessment of the danger posed by the inmate to the community. Some offenses, such as sex offenses, will render an inmate ineligible for home detention. Other serious offenses should weigh more heavily against consideration for home detention.

In his April 6, 2020, Memorandum, AG Barr directed the BOP to "move with dispatch in using home confinement, where appropriate, to move vulnerable inmates out of [BOP] institutions." AG Barr also indicated that he was exercising his authority under the CARES Act "to expand the cohort of inmates who can be considered for home release upon [his] finding that emergency conditions are materially affecting the functioning of the Bureau of Prisons." AG Barr directed that under the CARES Act, the BOP was to expand its review of inmates to "all at-risk inmates—not only those who were previously eligible for transfer." The BOP interpreted AG Barr's directive as removing the requirement that an inmate have served at least fifty percent of his sentence to be eligible for home confinement.

About two months later, the BOP essentially reversed the decision and reimplemented their fifty percent sentence completion requirement for eligibility of home confinement, though there was nothing in the memoranda supporting their decision.

In early May, an administrative official bulletin sent by the Complex warden stated all inmates were being reviewed for eligibility of home confinement under the CARES Act. But if an inmate wanted, he could contact the case manager directly to discuss whether their case met the criteria.

That same day, I emailed the CARES Act criteria and my supporting information, showing I clearly met eligibility criteria, to the warden. The following day, the warden replied, instructing me to see the Camp administrator. I sent an email straight away to the Camp administrator regarding the warden's instruction for me to see him, and that I would stop by later that day. An hour later, I knocked on the administrator's door and walked in.

The Camp administrator shook his head dramatically and said rudely and loudly, "No. I am not talking to anyone today. Come back on Monday." I left the office, wondering who the hell gave that man permission to speak to me that way.

The Camp administrator was a 6 foot 2 inch tall, 175-pound white man who had worked for the BOP for eighteen years. He worked as a correction officer in the USP, prior to his current position. I was shocked by how wrong this person was for the duties of an administrator of any type. He was often moody, inconsistent, and socially awkward. Many seasoned inmates claimed he did not have the right temperament to work in a prison, that he incited anxiety and confusion. I believed he lacked social finesse and confidence, and posed a security risk, as many inmates expressed a desire to harm him.

I received an email response from the Camp administrator, stating, "The BOP takes the safety of inmates and staff very seriously," that all inmates have been reviewed for eligibility home confinement, and he hoped his email answered all questions. This email response was the same one given to all other inmates inquiring about home confinement eligibility.

That same day, I replied, thanking him for his email, but stated he had not answered my specific question. The administrator replied promptly, instructing me to see the case manager for questions concerning home confinement eligibility under the CARES Act. I followed up with the case manager but received no clear response, mainly some rambling about having enough time to be eligible for release to home confinement.

The following day, I reached out to Leif, my attorney, via email to explain the COVID-19 outbreak at the prison. I informed Leif the prison had been being overtaken by the virus, and despite efforts, the BOP could not stop the spread or ensure safety of staff and inmates. I also informed Leif of the recent memoranda by Attorney General Barr, and I wanted to be considered for a compassionate release.

I understood a compassionate release or release to home confinement under the CARES Act would decrease my risk of harm. But I also understood that if granted either, I would be leaving that shithole. I was not confused about my motives. I believed my life was in danger and refused to do nothing about it. I also believed my current situation was cruel and harmful, and I would do risky or dangerous things, maybe a round of Russian roulette, to get the fuck out of that hell.

On a follow up phone call, I informed Leif, "I have medical vulnerabilities—history of pneumonia and I am twenty pounds overweight—both are listed by the CDC, and that puts me at an increased risk of harm and death. Many inmates are filing motion for compassionate release, and some succeed. I would like you to put together a motion for compassionate release."

"Paul, let me investigate this and I will get back with you soon. Send me an email listing any information or questions you believe are relevant," Leif replied.

"Okay, I will. I had pneumonia when I entered prison. There should be documentation by the doctor at the Henry

Ford Urgent Care of the diagnostic assessment, including x-ray, and treatment. Also, there should be documentation of pneumonia in my prison Health Services record. Through power of attorney, you request a copy of my medical record at Ford. Also, maybe reach out to my family doctor, Rossi... ask if he is willing to give an opinion on the potential risks of harm Covid might have to someone with a recent case of pneumonia. I will send all this in an email."

Leif ended the call with his usual last words, "Stay hard."

The following day, he sent me an email.

I obtained some good initial information. To file a Motion for Compassionate Release to the Court, you must first demonstrate you have exhausted all BOP remedies. That means: You must begin with the warden. You send a request for Compassionate Release to the warden. If the warden does not respond after thirty days, then you can motion the court directly and need not seek an appeal. If the warden denies your request within thirty days, then you file an appeal to the regional authority. And you follow the same process when appealing to the higher regional authority and if needed, to the higher central authority. Once you have exhausted all these remedies within the BOP system, you can motion the Court. I will write a request for compassionate release and send it to you by mail. When you get the request, submit properly to the warden using BOP forms.

FYI, as you know, the BOP has been releasing inmates to home confinement under the CARES Act. This process might get you out earlier, but we will move forward on a Motion for Compassionate Release.

Twelve days later, I received the request for compassionate release in the mail. I attached the request to the official BOP forms and sent them to the warden.

On June 14, 2020, about two months after release from the SHU as a holdover, Ted was called down to the case manager's office. Mr. Parker was assigned to his case. Many other inmates and I heard the callout over announcement system, thought it unusual for a Sunday, and asked Ted for the reason.

I teased, "You are going home, brother! You are going home."

"Don't know. I'm gonna find out," Ted said as he walked toward the range exit.

About fifteen minutes later, Ted returned. He was animated. I asked him what happened.

"Well, I walked down to the case manager office. He told me to have a seat; he had good news. He said I'm eligible for release to home confinement under the CARES Act. Then he paused. I was shocked. At first, I did not say anything. Then he had me sign a document and gave me some forms to complete. The forms are about my place of residence during home confinement and the name and contact information of the person who will be picking me up. I said, 'Wow! I... wasn't... Wow!' I stuttered. I was not expecting that. I have to complete these forms and turn them in right away."

This news came out of nowhere and changed everything for Ted. He was not expecting anything regarding his release for another five to six years—his release date was 2027. But now, after eleven years in the hell called prison, he was finally going home.

Suddenly, Ted had to focus on all aspects of his life outside of prison: Where he would live? How would he gain access to initial money? He needed a vehicle; what kind? Where would he work? What kind of work? What would be his restrictions while on home confinement? No longer did he have years to think about all these things. His mind raced and whirled with ideas.

"You got to be kidding me! Ted, you ol' coon dog. Look at you, you're going home, brother," I said excitedly, extending my hand for a shake, then brought him in closer for a hug.

"Yes. Wow. Got to call my sister and some other family members and start setting things up. Man, I was not expecting this!" he said. His face expressed a smile, then shifted to a contemplative look, then back to a smile. "I am not out yet. I will celebrate once I am in a vehicle heading home."

Other inmates surrounded Ted, asking questions or making comments. He knew this was not a time to go on and on about what happened. He had to prepare himself for release and the rest of his life.

I could tell Ted needed space, that he was overwhelmed. "Ted, I will check back in with you later… Again, I am glad for you."

Two hours had passed; Ted went to drop off the completed form to Case Manager Parker.

After about ten minutes, Ted came back to the range with a tense look on his face.

Something went wrong. "Ted, how did it go?" I asked.

"I went down to Parker's office and had a seat. Immediately I sensed something had happened," he explained. "His voice and actions seemed different. He paused for about a minute. Just looked at his computer screen and acted like he was reading something, but I don't think he was. It just gave him extra time to think about what he was going to say to me. I was feeling something negative. I looked at his face and eyes because I trying to find out what happened. Then told me, in a dull way, 'You are not going to like this, but you have a criminal history of violence, which means you not eligible for early release.' I told him I don't have any violence in my past. He said I had a simple assault from 1989. Thirty fucking years ago. I told him I don't ever recall having any kind of violence charge. He said I did."

I imaged Ted experiencing all the strong feelings of devastating disappointment, then the onset of an intense anger. To the onlooker, there would be no evidence of this. He probably appeared unfazed.

Ted added, "I looked him straight in the face and said, 'Well... that's that. It is what it is.' I then asked him if we have anything else to talk about? He said no."

Ted was questioned by fellow inmates. He told them he was not being released to home confinement. "The cocksucker told me I had a simple assault on my record. I told him I didn't... I knew nothing about it," Ted said with a slight smirk and a gaze that communicated utter contempt. He gave a detailed account of his interaction with Parker, repeated it multiple times, as other inmates approached and listened.

I overheard him tell the story multiple times to others. There was a time just after dinner when things quieted down. I then approached, "So, Ted, what the fuck happened? Parker said you have a simple assault from thirty years ago. You said you did not. I suggest you have somebody research this alleged simple assault... find out whether it's on your criminal record. If it is, it should be on your Pre-Sentence Report (PSR)."

"I don't have any mention of simple assault in my PSR. I could have my sister look into it, maybe talk to an attorney. Yes, that's what I'm gonna do," he replied.

"Also, Ted, it shouldn't matter if you do have a simple assault. AG Barr's memo stated inmates with 'serious offenses' should not be consideration for home confinement. A simple assault is classified as a misdemeanor, and misdemeanors are not considered serious offences. The prison system doesn't know how to define certain criteria for release. This might be another thing you want to share with your sister if she does indeed talk to an attorney. Just something to think about. But what a fucked-up mess... And these kinds of things happen frequently. It's a form of torture, unintentional, but grossly careless."

Ted responded with humor, "I wanted to rip that fucker's leg off, eat it in front of him like I was feasting on the Thursday chicken meal, and then use his toes to pick my teeth."

We laughed.

I observed Ted during and after this severe disappointment. He spent eleven years in prison with seven years to go, then was unexpectedly told he was being released to home confinement. He spent time, although brief, excited about being free and going home. He could breathe. Then suddenly, it's all taken away like a cruel joke. I believed this was beyond wrong because it has serious cruel and torturous effects. I saw several similar incidents— some less severe, some more. Perhaps the most extreme case happened a week prior.

An inmate who was found eligible for home confinement under the CARES Act had completed three weeks of required quarantine, was processed through the receiving and discharge office, then was walking toward his wife, who was waiting in a vehicle ready to take him home. The inmate was only moments away from leaving this shithole, when the Camp administrator yelled out his name and told them to stop. The administrator walked in his direction, waving him back towards the prison facility. When close enough, the administrator told him, just moments ago, Health Services released the latest COVID-19 test results of all inmates who were in quarantine and found three who had tested positive. The inmate asked the administrator if he had tested positive. The administrator told him no but stated it didn't matter because he had been exposed and would have to quarantine for another three weeks. I saw that inmate just after being told to report back to quarantine. He was clenching his hands into fists and had tearful eyes. I imagined he was devastated but only temporarily because in the back of his mind, he knew it was just another three weeks and not another three months or three years. I thought then, *No one would ever believe such a story was true.* But it was.

Ted had let the devastating disappointment go through him. His mind was settled. He felt hurt, but that faded quickly. He went back to the routines and habits that served him well for years and now would help him deal with the rest of the days and years ahead. I believed Ted was hardest motherfucking badass I knew.

After a week, Ted was rarely talking about what had happened. He shared some wisdom with me. "You can't count on anything in here. That is why I can handle the shit in this place. When I am on the road outside the walls, then I can celebrate. I think I surprised Parker. He probably thought I would flip out and start yelling. But I didn't; I stayed calm."

Remarkably, two days later, Ted was called back down to Mr. Parker's office, told his case was reevaluated, and he was set to be released to home confinement in exactly three weeks. Ted had to pack up his things and move down to the quarantine unit that day. Though the BOP set a fourteen-day quarantine standard, Terre Haute extended it to twenty-one days.

After three weeks in quarantine, Ted walked down the hallway toward the front lobby area of the facility. On his way, several inmates, including me, wished him well, said goodbye, and some gave a quick lean-in hug, followed by a slap on the shoulder.

Technically, this behavior spoiled his quarantine status as he was exposed to others not quarantined. But everyone, inmates and staff, knew the protective measures did not work and were not policies that had to be followed.

CHAPTER NINE:
PANDEMONIUM 2

On May 25, 2020, I was shocked by what I saw and heard on the news. George Floyd, a Black man, was arrested by Minneapolis police for attempting to use a counterfeit twenty-dollar bill. During the arrest, Floyd was cuffed, placed on the ground, and eventually held down by four police officers, all male—three white, one Asian—because he did not cooperate. Tragically, Floyd died during the arrest. Many blamed the "white" officers for targeting yet another Black man and using excessive force by kneeling on his back and neck. For nine minutes.

Overnight, Minneapolis ignited with protest and violent riots. In a matter of days, this quickly spread to other major cities in the country. Mayors in some cities told the police to stand down during the violence and destruction. Buildings were set on fire, communities destroyed; there were billions of dollars in destruction and damage. Many people were injured, and some murdered. Groups, supported by big money, like Antifa and Black Lives Matter, were very involved, going far beyond peaceful or lawful protests.

I discovered firsthand the BOP sometimes put inmates in "lockdown" during riots that occurred inside and outside the prison system. During a lockdown, all inmates are confined to their cells or ranges. All inmate movement is prohibited. If an inmate is found outside of his cell or range during a lockdown, which can happen in minimum-security facilities where most doors are not actually locked, that inmate will be sanctioned for being out of bounds.

The riotous destruction continued until the November 2020 presidential election, then quite suddenly stopped, an indication that much of the rioting was, unfortunately, politically motivated. Evidence emerged that financial contributions came from wealthy individuals, corporations, and political action groups.

In my view, that tragic situation, which should have been protested, was hijacked by mobs, ringleaders, and powerful people with selfish and harmful agendas. The lack of adequate law enforcement, prosecution, and accountability, some say due to politics, for the crimes, destruction, and harm occurring in the summer and early fall of 2020 angered many inmates, including me. It was difficult for inmates, who were spending years in prison for a crime, to watch hundreds, possibly thousands of others engaged in criminal behavior, including serious felonies, with little or no consequences.

***

"Another ambulance going to the USP. Lights are on, sirens, and everything. Seems to be moving fast," reported an inmate called Indian Joe to others on the range nearby, including me and my cellmates. He was looking out the hallway windows of Unit S08, where most traffic in and out of the Complex and to and from the USP could be observed. "Could be another death," he added.

Indian Joe was a descendant of the Navajo Nation. He was doing eighteen months for a probation violation. Secondhand reports indicated he had more than two dirty urine drug screens. His previous sentence was 120 months for delivery of cocaine and methamphetamines.

Later that day, a rumor spread claiming the Terre Haute FCC had its first Covid-related death. One day later, during a unit meeting, the Camp administrator confirmed there was an inmate death due to COVID-19 and reported the official Terre Haute FCC count was "3 positive cases and 1 death." The inmates knew this was a poorly contrived, bald-faced lie; there were more cases, and the BOP was trying to deceive the inmates and the public. I also knew about the news of "one death, three positive" the day before it was published in an article by the Associated Press, dated May 26, 2020. I believed the BOP and warden were shamefully deceiving the public intentionally.

Just prior to my transfer from the SHU to the Camp, Health Services staff took my temperature, asked if I had any Covid symptoms, and informed me of the protective measures. I asked the nurse directly about the virus within the Complex, maybe how many cases, and what do they do when somebody is positive. The nurse told me Health Services took charge of setting up the protocols for assessment and treatment for the entire complex. These protocols included quarantine in the SHU for positive Covid inmates, and temperature and symptom screening for all inmate transfers from facility to facility within the Complex and transfers in and out of the Complex, but did not include testing. I asked why there was no testing. I was told there were only four tests for all staff and inmates at that time.

This was later confirmed by a prison union representative, named Smith, during a televised local news interview. During that interview, the representative also stated, "The prison management did not seem to care about the safety of the inmates and prison staff."

The BOP's official statement was "frequent testing occurs, and the safety of inmates and staff are the number one priority." But what the BOP referred to as "testing" was only quick screening, which would not detect positive cases with accuracy and non-symptomatic cases. The screening was not sensitive enough, and Health Services knew this. But that seemed to be fine. As long as the BOP continued current screening practices, the numbers would likely remain low, and low numbers made the warden and staff look good.

On the range, I overheard inmates talking about having frequent telephone and email contact with local and national news reporters and journalists, feeding them information from the inside, including pictures, about the failure of the warden and prison staff to follow the BOP protective measures and other CDC guidelines and recommendations. Local Terre Haute news reporter Heather Good was breaking stories about the prison's first COVID-19 cases and related death two days before they became officially announced by the BOP. I thought her reporting was good, factual.

***

In early July 2020, all inmates at FCC received a Bulletin stating that seven inmates on death row were scheduled for execution. The dates were set for July 13, 16, and 17, August 26 and 28, and September 22 and 24, one execution per day. Most inmates and staff at the FCC knew these executions were a big deal with national, and possibly international, coverage and scrutiny, likely to include attendance by BOP bigwigs, and to involve protests for and against capital punishment.

I read in the news that with these executions, President Trump's administration would end a seventeen-year moratorium, which many critics viewed as part of the president's efforts to burnish a law-and-order reputation ahead of the November election. If carried out, President Trump would set a record for the most inmates executed by a president in a single year. I thought this "record" was not one to be proud of, as it lacks reverence for death. Human death in such a context should not be used to score political points. I was disappointed.

The Camp administrator held meetings at each housing unit, explaining the security procedures required for each execution. Upon entering Unit S08, he called, in his characteristically harsh and rude manner, all inmates into the hallway. "Listen up! Here are orders: Inmates from units S01 through S04 will be placed in the video library service area and the inmates from Units S05 through S08 will be placed in the recreation gym. You'll be in lockdown, which means you are prohibited from leaving these spaces. If you are caught out of bounds, I will give you a shot. You are not to bring any food, games, or any other items except reading material. You are all prohibited from communicating to anyone outside the space, including other inmates, in any form… that is why you are being placed in locations without windows or access to others. Any questions?"

"Can we bring something to drink?" an inmate asked.

"No."

"Can we use the TV rooms?"

"No. No TV. Anyone else?"

"What about pill line?"

"Good question. The Health Services staff will bring your medication to you. Any other questions?"

"How long will we be locked down?"

"I don't know. As long as it takes. I know this is going to be uncomfortable, but it is what it is."

I thought about several potential ways the preparations in security and accommodations would likely cause misery for the general inmate population. The last time the federal government had executed a death row inmate was in March 2003. Many staff were not around back then. There would likely be an overexaggeration of security measures, policy compliance, and orderliness, primarily due to the presence of high-ranking BOP officials. *The situation was reminiscent of the Navy*, I thought.

When an admiral was scheduled to meet with the captain and inspect the ship, I and all the rank-and-file service members had to scramble to create the impression of meeting or exceeding compliance with military standards and a command of orderliness and wartime readiness. This meant the rank and file had to put in several extra hours of work. But the difference, here and now, was the work would be done by inmates, and without compensation, but with all the threats of potential consequences for failure to deliver.

The following day, Mr. Riley, the GM1 supervisor, told me and Flamethrower to build signs with parking instructions for the expected protesters. The idea was to separate the protesters, thereby reducing potential conflict, by sending the pro-death penalty protesters to one location and the anti-death penalty protesters to another location.

After finishing work and walking back to the unit, Flamethrower and I discovered a large tarp had been placed in front of the windows of the quarantine unit.

"What do you think that's about?" I asked.

Flamethrower replied, "I think they're preparing for the executions. That tarp is put up so inmates in quarantine can't see what's going on out on the Complex."

"Good answer," I responded.

Before entering the stairwell to S08, we saw inmates pushing carts full of military-style cots into the recreation gym. "You think those are for us?" I asked.

"Maybe. Maybe it's backup just in case the executions and lockdown are extended into the evening," Flamethrower answered.

Two days later, on July 12, 2020, all inmates were locked down in their cells. The following day at noon, Camp inmates were given a sack meal of bologna, bread, and an apple, and a bottle of water, then ordered to the video library or recreation gym for lockdown. Upon entering the gym, I noticed all the cots were gone. Later, I was told they were for prison staff. The place was extremely hot, exceeding ninety degrees, despite having two fans to push air around.

The rumor among the inmates was the executions would occur around six that evening. Interestingly, the inmates did not fuss or grumble the first several hours for having to sit in a space with temperatures over ninety degrees and nothing but reading material. Many inmates started talking about the execution coming that day and those within later weeks. But eventually there was very little talk. I sensed some kind of group reverence for death. Execution of life was the ultimate punishment—we all understood this. On that day, the inmates did not question whether execution was right or wrong. On some other day, maybe they were loud, open, and stating strongly their opinions whether for or against. But not on that day.

I thought a prisoner code might explain what was happening: it is considered very rude, and in some cases punishable by violence, for an inmate to openly complain about the severity of his prison sentence. Such talk frustrates other inmates who have much longer and harsher sentences. So, in the current situation, when focused only on that day, all that the Camp inmates would and could possibly endure were merely inconveniences and petty torments in comparison. The very few inmates who did complain strongly about their "difficult and unfair" conditions on that day were soulless and incapable of being human.

The hours went slowly on and on, as they do during lockdown. After eight hours, most inmates had finished their meal and water hours ago and were now thirsty. Several approached the CO on duty requesting water. Thirty minutes later, the Camp administrator came through the entry door with a large cooking pot full of water and paper cups, then left without taking any questions. The inmates used one of the cups as a ladle.

By midnight, many inmates were lying down on the hard floor or sitting propped up next to a wall. I placed my shoes together for propping my head on the floor. The temperature was still above eighty. The conditions were barbaric. I was disgusted with the BOP, allowing staff to treat me and other inmates with such careless disregard.

But on that day, I would not complain. I gave due reverence to death.

At 5:37 a.m., the Camp inmates were ordered back to their units. The first death row inmate had been executed.

The seven inmates scheduled for execution were:

Daniel Lewis Lee, scheduled for execution on July 13: Lee, a forty-seven-year-old white man, was sentenced to death for the 1996 killings of gun dealer William Muller, his wife Nancy Muller, and her eight-year-old daughter Sarah Powell, which prosecutors said was part of a plot to steal guns and cash. Lee and an accomplice placed plastic bags over their heads and sealed the bags with duct tape, suffocating them to death. Then, they taped rocks to their bodies and threw them into a swamp.

Wesley Ira Purkey, July 16: Purkey, white male, sixty-eight years old, was sentenced to death in 2003 for raping and killing sixteen-year-old Jennifer Long. Purkey stabbed her repeatedly in the face and neck, killing her, then cut her body into pieces with a chainsaw and placed them into bags. He burned the bags one by one in his fireplace, then took the leftover remains and ashes and dumped them in a septic pond.

Dustin Lee Honken, execution set for July 17: Honken, fifty-two years old, white male, a methamphetamine kingpin and serial killer, murdered witnesses to stop them from testifying against him. Honken, in 1993, kidnapped, fatally shot, and buried Lori Duncan, a single working mother, as well as her two daughters, ten years old and six years old. He killed Greg Nicholson, a government informant who testified against Honken on federal drug trafficking charges. Honken also murdered Terry Degeus, who he thought might also testify against him, by beating him with a bat and shooting him.

Lezmond Charles Mitchell, scheduled for death on August 26: Mitchell, thirty-eight years old, Native American, was sentenced to death for the 2001 slaying of Alyce Slim, a sixty-three-year-old Navajo woman, and her nine-year-old granddaughter, Tiffany Lee. Mitchell and his accomplice stabbed both multiple times; Mitchell slit Lee's throat and bludgeoned Slim with rocks and stabbed her to death. Afterwards, when both were dead, Mitchell and his accomplice dragged their bodies into the nearby woods, decapitated them, and lit their bodies on fire. Their remains were buried in a shallow grave.

Keith Dwayne Nelson, execution set for August 28: Nelson, a forty-five-year-old Black man, was sentenced to death for the 1999 rape and murder of a ten-year-old Kansas girl. Pamela Butler had been rollerblading in front of her home when Nelson abducted her. He raped her before strangling her to death with a wire and burying her body in a forest behind a church.

William Emmett Lacroix, scheduled for September 22: Lacroix, white male, fifty years old, was sentenced to death after raping and murdering thirty-year-old nurse Joann Lee Tiesler in 2001. He broke into Tiesler's home in Gilmer County, Georgia, to further a plan to flee the country after serving ten years in federal and state prisons for crimes including child molestation and statutory rape. When Tiesler returned home, he strangled her with an electrical cord before raping her. He then slashed her throat with a knife and stabbed her in the back five times.

Christopher Andre Vialva, September 24: Vialva, a forty-year-old Black man, was given the death penalty for the 1999 murder of two youth ministers, Todd and Stacie Bagley, in Texas. Vialva and two accomplices kidnapped the couple at gunpoint after Todd agreed to give Vialva and his two accomplices a ride. While later parked on the

Fort Hood military reservation, he shot Todd Bagley in the head, killing him instantly, and shot Stacie Bagley in the face, knocking her unconscious. The car was then set on fire, causing Stacie to die of smoke inhalation. During the kidnapping, the Bagleys urged their abductors to accept Jesus into their hearts and spare their lives.

I thought about the execution. It bothered me, but I wasn't exactly sure why. I believed those who commit violent crimes should be put in prison for public safety, deterrence, correction, and retribution. But the death penalty takes away a person's chance for redemption. A dead man can't right a wrong or make amends. The death penalty was not just an eye for an eye, but an eye for an eye without the possibility of anything afterward.

I believed that if a person commits a violent crime, and in doing so causes severe harm to the victim, then that person should be sentenced to prison at a security level and length of time proportional to the crime. I also believed the person was obligated, and therefore should have a chance, to right the wrong, regardless of the crime or wrongful behavior. All inmates have a chance to redeem themselves if they choose to do so, except the death row inmate. Death cancels the opportunity. A death row inmate may have the capacity for redemption, to go from a premeditated murderer to a person who is authentically remorseful, has openly and fully confessed to the heinous crimes, and worked hard to repay or make right the wrongs committed, however possible, and for as long as it takes. But the inmate's death is worth more than a capacity for redemption, in the collective view of society. I believed differently: the transformations that occur through redemption are among the most powerful and hopeful examples of the human spirit. That has great value.

More than once, I thought about the evil of their crimes, the victims and their families. I imagined the horror and devastation, and what if that happened to one of my children. I could not bear to dwell long because the thoughts and images stirred me to the point of feeling sick. But at the same time, the images and sick feelings ignited powerful emotions within me and a desire to execute the murdering bastards myself. But I understood, in that situation, my capacity for making a free and rational decision would be severely impaired.

I did not have it all figured out. Before committing my crimes and being sent to prison, I had never seriously contemplated the idea of redemption. But now, I thought about it often. I knew redemption was not an inalienable and protected right. No one is guaranteed the opportunity or the achievement. I believed in redemption because I desperately needed it. I knew no other way to go forward in life. For how else can a person go forward when they are nothing more than a rap sheet and a stain?

But how would I redeem myself? Where would I begin?

Later that day, I experienced a harsh episode of emotions. Intertwined in these emotions were all the thoughts that define self-loathing and worthlessness. I had them before. These episodes were typically short lived but severely disabling, nevertheless. But this episode happened to be the worst of all.

My mind ran through painful thoughts and images, failed marriages and relationships, failed work endeavors, loss of trust and integrity, the sad faces of my children, and much more, all bolded and double underlined by a strong thought: *I fucked up my life and have no way to make it right.* With my eyes closed, I whispered to an image in my mind of a younger and hopeful self, "I'm sorry." I shifted my mind to images of my wife and four children, and whispered, "God knows I'm sorry for the pain and suffering I caused." My eyes welled up.

Self-loathing flowed. I viewed myself as a net sum of poor decisions, failures, crimes, and harmful actions. This self-contempt compounded my inner turmoil to the point of despair.

I asked myself repeatedly: *how do I overcome this?*

For most of that day, I remained plagued with thoughts of the catastrophic mistakes I made in my life and of being denied an opportunity for redemption, obsessions of self-contempt, and how I would find a solution.

Toward evening, I was getting tired. I began to read to focus on other things, which worked well. After an hour, I put the book down on a chair next to my bunk, then fell asleep.

That night, I had an elaborate dream. I was in a dark and vast forest. I could not see clearly for more than a few yards. The air was damp, thick and depressed. I was suffering from a deadly self-inflicted wound that caused a lingering smell of rot and despair. I had lists of sins and crimes carved into my body, both front and back. I was searching, desperately so, for a tree with four divinely crafted golden boughs. I was told I must find the tree and take the boughs—if the boughs do not break off, I will be denied what I'm looking for and stay in that hell forever.

There were others in the forest, also with self-inflicted wounds and carvings of sin. Some appeared to be searching for something and others were wandering aimlessly. Then, there were those who were sitting down, doing nothing, not even looking around. All of them were ugly, scarred, and deformed.

I felt tired, pain and sickness, and had a constant hunger and thirst. But despite the suffering, I continued to search onward without rest, up and down hills, across rivers, and through swampy areas. Some of the terrain seemed familiar to me, but most did not.

Then, after what seemed like an eon of dredging through a diseased darkness, I saw the tree with the golden boughs. The surrounding area was lit brightly. I ran to it, then quickly and eagerly tore the four boughs from the tree. It was a sign I was worthy. I held the boughs upward as if an offer to God. The brilliant shine healed my body and mind, helped me navigate through that hell, and lit my way up and out to the upper world.

I woke from my dream. Looking over, lying face down on a chair next to me, I saw the book I was reading—*The Aeneid* by Virgil. I picked it up and read through sections of "Book VI" I read the night before:

…the descent to the underworld is easy. Night and day the gates of shadowy Death stand wide open, but to retrace your steps, to climb back to the upper air—there the struggle, there the labor lies. … Hidden deep in a shady tree there grows a golden bough, its leaves and its hearty, sinewy stem all gold, held secret to Juno of the Dead, Proserpina. The whole grove covers it over, dusky valley enfold it too, closing in around it. No one may pass below the secret places of earth before he plucks the fruit, the golden foliage of the tree. As her beauty's due, Proserpina decreed this bough shall be offered up to her as her own hollowed gift. When the first spray's torn away, another takes its place, gold too, the metal breaks into leaf again, all gold. Lift your eyes and search, and once you find it, duly pluck it off with your hand. Freely, easily, all by itself it comes away, if Fate calls on you. If not, no strength within you can overpower it, no iron blade, however hard, can tear it off.

"They are my golden boughs," I whispered to myself. "They are my way through and out of this hell. They are my way to redemption," I pronounced as I brought the images of my four children to my mind. "They will save my life while I am here and help me find a way out of the hell I created. Without them, I don't see any purpose worthy enough to convince me why I should endure another day in this hell called life."

On that day, I vowed to make changes. My self-interests and desires must now, and must always be, subordinate to the best interests and needs of my children. I would follow a plan to pay my restitution, make amends where I could. I would live a balanced and simple life. I would try to help others going through similar struggles. But the core of my redemption was to devote the remainder of my life to the interests, health, and wellbeing of my children.

***

Thirty days after filing a request for compassionate release, I emailed Leif stating I received no response from the warden and we should now move forward to motion the federal court.

The following day, I received an email from Leif asking me to call that evening if possible. After the supper meal and a quick shower, I called him.

Leif addressed several issues. "Send me your copy of the request you sent to the warden. I will attach it to the motion. I completed most components the Motion for Compassionate Release. I was able to obtain your medical records from the urgent care. Also, I received a letter from Dr. Rossi, your family physician, which states his opinion about your vulnerabilities and risks related to COVID-19. When you obtain a copy of your prison health services record, mail it to me ASAP."

"Great news! Do you need anything else?" I asked.

"Oh yes, I do need you to write up an affidavit detailing your concerns of the prison conditions as related to failure to protect against the virus. That will also be attached to your motion."

We talked about other important matters including finance, my children, and storage of my personal property.

That evening, I completed my affidavit covering many of my observations and concerns about the prison's inherent physical and systematic vulnerabilities to spread of the pandemic. I ended the affidavit with the following statement:

For the past several weeks, my life has been dominated by fear and panic due to COVID-19. Not only am I in a setting inherently vulnerable to the spread of COVID-19 (high concentrations of people in very close proximity to each other) and I am at risk of developing life-threatening complications if I contract COVID-19, but, in addition to, I am unable to take sufficient and necessary action to protect my own life. I was sentenced to prison for committing a crime. That fact is hard enough to deal with. But I was not given a death sentence.

I believed I "laid it on thick," and suspected others would think that, but it was one hundred percent true. I was scared because I was in danger. But prison was a desperate situation in general, so desperate I would have, or at least contemplate having, my pinky finger snipped off in exchange for freedom. In my mind, I did not confuse these two motives.

On July 7, 2020, I received an email from Leif stating he mailed out a complete copy of the Motion for Compassionate Release for my review and would call the Camp case manager to set up a confidential attorney-client call. Ten days later, I received the compassionate release in the mail, which, once again, had been opened by prison staff despite a clear and conspicuous "privilege and confidentiality" notice in the place and format required by the BOP. The entire motion was nearly 139 pages long, which included exhibits. I reviewed all of it carefully over two days.

The attorney-client call was not confidential. The phone call was put on speaker while Case Manager Parker was present in the room. Parker handed me the phone.

"Leif, this is Paul. Hold one moment."

"Okay."

"Mr. Parker, this is supposed to be a confidential communication between attorney and client. Can we have privacy, please?"

"If you want to take the call off speaker, that's fine, but I am not leaving the room."

"Leif, he's not leaving the room, so I'm going to take this call off speaker and we'll do the best we can."

Parker began typing something into his computer, making the appearance he was not focused on the call. I felt an impulse to cuff Parker alongside his head, but I resisted.

"So, Leif, I read the motion. It's outstanding; one of the best pieces of legal work I've seen from an attorney, and you know I have dealt with many attorneys in the past. I really don't have any questions about the motion and think you should submit it immediately. I don't feel comfortable talking about my affidavit in front of prison staff but was hoping it was sufficient."

"Yes, your affidavit included all the relevant points we talked about. There is no need to change any of it. And thank you for your kind words. I'm doing my best to represent your case. I know what's at stake and how important this is to you."

"Thank you. Thank you for giving me your best."

"You bet, Paul."

"So, what are the next steps?"

"Well, the next steps are to submit the motion to the Court, who will then pass a copy on to the prosecutor. The prosecutor will have time to respond to your motion. We will receive a copy of this response, and at that time, we may respond to their response. The judge will review the motion and the responses, and likely set a hearing date. However, sometimes a judge will render their decision without a hearing. But I think we'll have a hearing. At the hearing, you and I will argue your case directly. The hearing will be done over live video."

"Okay. That sounds good. I don't think the prison has video conferencing available." I then asked Parker, "Does the prison here have or allow live video conferencing for legal hearings available to inmates?"

Parker shook his head no.

"Leif, I was informed by the case manager that the prison does not have video conferencing available for legal hearings. Let me check into that a little further at another time."

Parker interjected, "I'm telling you there are no video conferencing for inmates. There is nothing further to check into."

"Okay, Mr. Parker, I'm going to finish my confidential phone call now," I replied sarcastically.

"Paul, take it easy and stay focused. Don't worry about that right now."

We went on to discuss the procedures of a hearing, the main points that should be stressed, and the likely rebuttal by the prosecutor. I understood the hearing was a formality, and the judge would have likely reviewed the motion and rebuttal beforehand and have a provisional decision ready. Leif explained the judge may still ask probing questions, however, as there was the possibility he had not reached a level of comfortable certainty. We also discussed payment and financial matters, and my children, including the trust set up for them.

***

In late July 2020, I received notice that I was being transferred to another prison facility. I asked where I was being transferred but was told inmates are not given dates and places of travel for security reasons. I immediately went to the email system and sent a message to Leif regarding this transfer. I knew, once in quarantine, I was in a twenty-four-hour lockdown and not allowed to use the phone or email. Two hours later, I moved all my property and mattress into Unit S07 quarantine.

Although inmates are not told when and where they transfer, I had an idea. I hoped my destination was still

Morgantown, but I wasn't sure. There was widespread uncertainty throughout the BOP system regarding inmate movement. I was anxious and frustrated because no one knew what the hell was going on and there was absolutely nothing I could do about it. I was trapped and suffocating.

Quarantine was basically a twenty-four-hour maximum-security lockdown, like the SHU. But instead of a small cell, it was in a range, and there were seven to twelve inmates at any one time rotating in and out. There was no use of phone or email. However, several inmates had cell phones—illegal contraband. All inmates were tested within twenty-four hours after being placed in quarantine, not before. Inmates were tested again seven to four days before being released from quarantine. Temperature screenings were taken every morning. The length of quarantine was twenty-one days, seven days longer than recommended by the CDC. I had no idea why an extra seven days were added, despite inquiries. That horrible feeling of wasting life dominated. I had experienced that feeling ever since I surrendered (and on occasion prior) to prison, but it was never more pronounced when in maximum confinement lockdown.

I spent most of my time reading classic works and writing very detailed notes about my prison experience, something I started just after release from the SHU. These activities were a good escape from the day-to-day nothingness of my immediate surroundings and helped to dull the pain of wasting life.

Five days later, Jerome Pugh, Black, was placed in quarantine. He was scheduled to transfer to another prison facility.

"Hey, Black, what's happening? Give me a quintet," I said, surprised. While holding my hand up, Black slapped it. "Where are you headed to? You going home?"

"I'm going to McKean in Pennsylvania. They got a Camp with RDAP." He rarely exhibited emotion or quick action, and talked slowly, as if stuck in a state of perpetual slow motion. But Black was not slow minded. He was clever and keenly aware of what was going on around him.

"I'm going to an RDAP as well, hopefully at Morgantown. I was supposed to be there months ago."

"Yeah, I know. I was in transfer same time as you. But we got put here for a while."

"Man, I'm glad to get out of this shithole."

"Why? This is an easy place to do time. You do anything you want. Most COs don't care about phones or smoking or cooking food in your cell. This is easy."

"Well, you're right about that. It's like the Wild West. Anything goes. I just want to get out of here and into an RDAP. This place is so fucked up—I was worried I would not get out of here in time to benefit fully from RDAP, get the twelve months off my time."

"Hell, I don't know if I'm gonna benefit at all. I don't have much time left."

"All right, man. We'll talk later today."

"Yaaalright," Black replied. The way he pronounced "all right" seemed common among most Black inmates, alternatively pronounced as "isle righ'" and used especially when acknowledging somebody while walking by or when ending a conversation.

On the nineteenth day, the Camp administrator entered the range, aggressively pushing the door open. He was wearing a mask, a face shield over the mask, a full paper gown over his clothes, paper over his shoes, and rubber gloves. I thought he looked ridiculous, like he was prepared to deal with some sort of radiation or nuclear waste. I had not seen any other staff wear such a costume. It was highly impractical but what the CDC recommended. No other staff member, including the Camp administrator on any day after, wore that ensemble of protections. Not even one-quarter the protections. The discrepancy between what was required and what actual adherence was due primarily to an unwillingness by BOP rank-and-file staff to follow fully the protective measures.

"Where is Pugh?" the administrator asked.

Black came out of his cell and answered, "Here."

"You have tested positive for COVID-19. Have you been out of this range? Don't answer because you'll lie to me anyways. You are going to be separated out and placed in the SHU. Leave all your stuff here. Everyone here will be tested today and must redo quarantine for another twenty-one days. You can thank Pugh for that." He then escorted Black out of the quarantine unit.

Other inmates and I set for transfer had our travel itineraries canceled. I was given no information about my transfer status—whether I was classified as a holdover or redesignated.

After an additional three weeks in quarantine, I was sent back to the general population on S08 in my old cell. Bradley and James were released to home confinement, which left Big Baby Richard, Machine Gun John, and Flamethrower Matthew.

At that time, the entire Camp was in general lockdown due to high rates of the virus. Inmates no longer reported to work except for those in food service and laundry. All training and educational programs remained shut down as they had been for the past five months. Chaplain services were closed. The use of phone and email services were being rotated by unit and time by day, where each unit was allowed out of lockdown for two hours twice a week—once during morning hours and once during evening hours. Inmates no longer picked up meal trays in the cafeteria. Instead, cold meals put in paper sacks were prepared in the kitchen and delivered to the ranges. Each morning, two 8-ounce milk cartons per inmate and one serving of cold cereal, often unsweetened bran or corn flakes, and an apple were dropped off. For lunch and dinner, inmates were served either bologna and cheese with bread or peanut butter and jelly with bread, and piece of fruit, and a water bottle. I ate more bologna in one month than I had in all my years before. About once per week, inmates were served hot oatmeal in the morning and shredded chicken on rice or spaghetti for lunch and dinner. The taste and texture were horrible, commensurate to the effort and care put into the preparation.

The temperature outside was above ninety degrees for over two weeks, and five to ten degrees higher inside the units. There was no air conditioning. Inmates could buy fans from the commissary, but it was closed. The temperature at night remained above eighty degrees. I woke up each morning soaked in sweat. I tried to journal the situation and my thoughts, and tried to read, but had difficulty focusing my attention for more than a few minutes. The heat was too unbearable.

The harsh conditions of prison during the COVID-19 pandemic alone were very difficult to handle, but the addition of extended high temperatures seemed to push inmates over the edge. The frequency of inmate-to-inmate fights increased. None were reported to staff, from what I observed. Many inmates started leaving their ranges, an out-of-bounds violation, during times when inmates from another range were authorized out of range. Two inmates from my range, Shorty and JJ, received shots for being out of bounds. They were put in the SHU for thirty days.

The use of cell phones, tobacco, and alcohol significantly increased. The amount of contraband being smuggled into the prison increased very significantly. Three inmates, all Hispanic, unknowingly woke up me at one in the morning as they crawled through the bathroom window with three large bags of merchandise. Among the merchandise were fifteen cell phones, four handle-sized jugs of whiskey, ten fifths of liquor, and eight pounds of tobacco. In all, the contraband was worth about fifteen thousand dollars. These inmates unscrewed a metal panel next to the bathroom showers to access the plumbing and placed the bags of contraband in the available space.

Some inmates began to toss their sack lunches and dinners down the hallway to protest the lack of variety and amount of food. The COs on duty did not seem to care. None of the inmates were punished for the behavior and no changes were made. The bologna and peanut butter remained on the menu.

***

By the end of August 2020, the rate of aggressive altercations increased significantly throughout the Camp. I believed this aggressiveness was mostly due to prolonged confinement and heavy restrictions related to the pandemic but was significantly exacerbated by the rioting and violent behavior occurring in many major US cities and to the shamefully wicked political tactics levied by the media, social media, and politicians during the presidential election season. Mildly surprised, I discovered most inmates were very aware of, interested, and affected by the politics and social issues of the country. I often heard inmates in the TV room and on the ranges talking about specific political issues, the lawless riots during the summer, chronic lying by the media and government, and the details of the upcoming presidential election.

"These motherfuckers are committing crimes, violent crimes, with no fucking consequence," one inmate ranted. He was supported by all in the room.

"This fucking shit is organized by big money. This shit is political, mass evil manipulation of the worst," another inmate added.

Frustration and irritability began to overwhelm me. I started arguing with inmates, then with prison staff. Over a period of ten days, I was involved in a series of altercations.

On a Saturday afternoon while in the TV room, a tall and slender Black inmate, who appeared to be about thirty years old, changed the channel on the TV five other inmates and I were watching.

"Hey, we're watching that! You just changed the channel on the TV without asking if anybody's watching it," I declared loudly.

"This TV is for sports," he asserted.

I rebutted quickly, "Well, it might have been for sports, but for the last three or four months, it's been for news. You've been around long enough to know that!"

"Well, it's for sports," he said, refusing to change the channel back. He then sat down at a nearby table.

I got up and changed the channel back to the news. "Motherfucker. Are you fucking serious? Are you picking a fight intentionally?"

The inmate stood up and reached over to change the channel back to sports, but I chest-bumped him away.

"Man, I'm gonna change the channel. If we got to, we can fight over it," he said, taking a deep breath, closing his eyes, and tightening his facial muscles. "You can take the first punch."

I chuckled instantly. I couldn't help it. His offer was ridiculous and a clear sign of inexperience, but that wasn't the main reason. I laughed because the scene reminded me of the three or four past altercations I had with a certain cousin when we were younger and he offered me the first punch. But, growing impatient, I was determined to put an end to this annoyance.

With volume and force, I said, "You're going to lose this battle, motherfucker. To fear this situation is wisdom. Be wise and walk away."

At this time, two others, who were also watching the news, stood behind me in support, and glared with wild, crazy smiles at the inmate. The inmate walked away.

The following day on the range, I got into a shouting match with another inmate, Stretch—6 feet 8 inches tall, 290 pounds—over food. Stretch somehow acquired a George Foreman grill, a moderately serious piece of contraband. On about a weekly basis, he purchased food smuggled in by other inmates from the cafeteria and food depot, then advertised a menu. That day, he was selling cheeseburgers for two stamps per burger, and other items. $1.08 was the face value of two stamps, but the purchasing power was closer to three dollars. For assisting Stretch in acquiring the raw meat by acting as bag man (or carrier between the food depot and the housing unit), I expected a discount on menu items. But in my view, Stretch reneged, which angered me. So I confronted him strongly. Within seconds, the confrontation turned into a shouting match. We squared off, standing toe to toe; my face was distorted by ferocious anger and a fearless stare. Stretch readied his fist to strike, but showed hesitation and what appeared to be a sign of uncertainty and caution. At that moment, I knew Stretch was not a street fighter, nor someone who once bit a dog, and likely incapable of using his obvious advantages. After a few more "fuck offs" and "motherfuckers," we both walked away.

That following Thursday, I was standing in the range doorway prior to count. I was looking down the hallway towards the Control and CO office. From the other direction, Lieutenant Simms shouted in a harsh, nasty tone, "Get the fuck out of the doorway!"

I was stunned and jolted in surprise, then a second later became flooded with hot anger. *Who gave him permission to speak to me that way?* I thought. I stood paralyzed for moments as internal forces competed for expression. The urge to yell back, which was extremely strong, was successfully checked by a desire to avoid negative consequences.

Then Simms barked out again, "Get out of the doorway and go to your bunk!"

"I am in the range where I am supposed to be," I countered.

"I said get in your bunk."

I looked straight at him, and with a sensation of pleasure that comes from releasing tense pressure, said, "What a fucking asshole." Then I walked to my cell.

Simms followed me, stopped at the cell doorway and said, "I'm gonna deal with you later."

Other inmates on the range expressed varying opinions about the situation. Some, the wise ones, told me I was being foolish, that my actions would bring unwanted attention to the range. Others, the unwise ones, told me that I made Simms my bitch. "You rammed your fist up his ass and made him your puppet!" one shouted.

Two days later, Simms called me down to the control center and explained to me no inmate should ever talk to a prison staff that way, especially not a lieutenant. "You must be new here. You must not be aware of who I am and how far I'll go to cause hell for you and the whole range. Nine months ago, I went down to a particular range with a drill and pliers in hand and tossed everybody's cells, including taking apart all lockers. If I do that to your range, several inmates will be busted for contraband; you and I both know that. Then everybody's going to look at you as the person who caused it. Don't ever talk that way to me again."

"Yes, sir."

"All right, now get out of here," Simms concluded.

The next day, I got in a fight with another inmate, nicknamed Pimp. I was irritated by Pimp, mainly because he was bossy toward others.

Pimp was a thirty-four-year-old Black man convicted of delivering meth and cocaine. He was down thirty months on a seventy-two-month sentence. He had been in prison once before—sixty-one months at a state penitentiary.

Pimp began his current stint at the low-security facility at Sandstone, Minnesota, but was transferred to the Terre Haute Camp about nine months prior. Through the CARES Act, he was eligible for early release to home confinement within six months.

Pimp worked out daily, mainly calisthenics and some weights. He had a muscular upper body, but his legs were thin and weak. He walked with a limp due to an old injury he earned at the penitentiary. Occasionally, he strolled up and down the range hallway, almost always exhibiting a rather tough, hardened look. He looked straight ahead and never appeared excited or hyper animated. When he turned his head to notice something or someone, he did so slowly and artfully, as if acting the tough-guy role. Sometimes, he acted as if he oversaw the range. I was skeptical, however. But I was not sure.

On the unit, Pimp set the schedule for lookout or watch duty, which involved scanning the area for COs or other prison staff. If staff are walking toward the unit, the inmate on watch duty will yell up the stairwell, "Coming this way!" This alert allows inmates time to put away any cell phones or other contraband. Watch duty was usually for one hour per day per inmate, and only for inmates who had a cell phone or other serious contraband. I did not possess either, so I was not obligated or approached for watch duty.

For some unknown reason, I was especially irritable on that day. Maybe it was due to the lack of sleep the night before, or my chemistry was imbalanced. Or maybe it was due to the increasingly harsh conditions of my environment. I wasn't sure.

During the morning of that day, Pimp complained loudly and publicly in front of the entire range at Big Baby for not standing ready for count. "You need be on the wall. I'm getting tired of telling ya!" he barked.

I looked at Big Baby and said, "Who the hell is he to be telling you what to do?"

"He's been after me for a couple of weeks. I just ignore him," Big Baby replied.

"Yeah, hopefully he won't get violent on you."

About five minutes later, Pimp made a mass announcement to the range. "Yo, listen up! Whoever's shitting in the toilet and not flushing, better stop now. And whoever shit in the shower and left it there, you're gonna get fucked up."

Another inmate chimed in, "Yeah, man, that is just fucking weird. Who the fuck shits in the shower and doesn't clean it up?"

I agreed these issues needed to be brought up. The behavior was wrong; there was no defense. But I strongly disliked the way Pimp addressed the range.

I went back into my cell and talked to Big Baby. "You know, I'm getting angry. Pimp yells at you for not being on the wall ready for count. He'll argue if you fuck up count, the COs will come down on us. Maybe it's true. If an inmate fucks up count, there may be trouble... but the trouble will be for that particular inmate, not the whole damn range. He can say he's trying to keep the unit out of trouble. But that's nothing but bullshit. He drinks alcohol, a lot. If the COs catch him drinking alcohol, they'll certainly lockdown the whole unit, like they have in the past. He also smokes cigarettes and uses a cell phone. Pimp is no role model and should worry about himself. Why does he take it upon himself to be boss and sheriff?"

Overhearing the conversation, Machine Gun answered, "Because he wants to be the unit boss."

"What do you mean?"

"Some of these inmates come down from a higher-level prison, mostly a penitentiary, and don't know how to behave at a lower-security prison. They try to run the place, try to intimidate other inmates into doing what they want. But there are no unit bosses at a Camp."

Just prior to the four p.m. count, I was in my cell lying down. I was very tired but trying to wake up. I heard an inmate yell, "Coming this way." This meant the COs had started count and were moving through the ranges. I knew I had a couple of minutes before they arrived, so I sat up on my bunk and drank some water. "On deck!" an inmate yelled down the hallway, which meant the COs were walking up the stairway. I walked out of the cell and stood by the wall.

Pimp shouted at me, "You got to get on the wall, man!"

Then, as if someone pulled the trigger on a double-barrel 10-gauge shotgun, I shouted, "Who the fuck do you think you are?" The entire range was startled and went silent. All inmates faced me with eyes wide. I continued, "You worry about yourself, motherfucker!"

I wanted to fight. I craved it. I did not care if I won or lost. The thought of splitting someone's skull open gave me as much pleasure as the thought of me being thrown through a window—both made me salivate.

"I will tell you whatever the fuck I want," Pimp shot back.

"Fuck off, motherfucker. You worry about your own shit."

"Rolling!" an inmate yelled, which meant the COs were starting count. When COs begin count, inmates are prohibited from talking, making noises, or moving. Strict adherence to the rules of count is expected. But we continued our exchange. Surprisingly, the COs did not shut down this toxic situation. They went down the range, back, then out.

I went to my cell and sat in a chair at the far end, opposite the doorway. I was alone, my body shaking from an excess of adrenaline.

Only moments had passed when Pimp showed up in the doorway.

"Don't come in here," I warned.

But he stepped in. I was surprised by this brazen act. Walking into another inmate's cell uninvited is a violation of prison rules, the prison code, and the fourth commandment—thou shall not enter an inmate's cell for any reason without permission.

"Get the fuck out!" I snarled. My stance and gestures resembled an aggressive red-boned bloodhound.

Pimp said nothing but continued towards me, intent on bringing violence. I stood and met him, halfway to bring my own violence. My face became unrecognizable, distorted by a fever of profound anger and desire to harm. Any hope for a diplomatic and nonviolent outcome had disappeared.

"Kick my fucking ass and throw me through a fucking window, you fucking motherfucker!" I yelled, then rammed into Pimp.

Violent shoves quickly became intense grappling and wild swings. I struck Pimp in the throat with a forearm but did not strike squarely. He blocked my second attempt, then shoved me to the side, using my own momentum. My left foot crossed over my right and my body twisted to the right. Pimp moved in to topple me. But I threw my right elbow back in an unaimed, wild Hail Mary swing, angling upward, connecting with the right side of Pimp's face. I then quickly regained my balance and steadied my footing. Pimp then bull-rushed me, smashing me hard into the lockers; objects were sent flying and spilled out on the cell floor. Hitting the lockers prevented me from falling completely over but caused a gash to my left shoulder blade.

We grappled and butted heads, slamming bunks and objects within the tight quarters. Then we broke and began to bob and weave, looking for the next opportunity to strike. Pimp struck first with a stunning uppercut to my chin. My right leg buckled slightly. But I answered reactively, without contemplation, with a headbutt striking squarely Pimp on the nose, causing intense pain as his eyes watered profusely. Both of us had mild injuries, but nothing severe enough to declare dominance either way.

Suddenly, other inmates flooded into the cell to break up the fight. Fellow Irishman Bill O'Halloran jumped in between, facing me and pushed me back, urging me to stop fighting because of potential serious disciplinary repercussions. "Don't, Paul. It's not worth it. Let it go, let it go. They'll send you to the Hole. You'll lose good time. Let it go," Bill pleaded. After several seconds, I took a deep breath, focused on Bill, and stopped trying to advance.

I suddenly felt stunned, then quickly realized Pimp had sucker punched me on the right side of my face above the cheek bone. I pushed forward to answer in kind, but by that time, nearly a dozen inmates were in the cell and there was no room to move.

Frustrated, I shouted, "You cheap-shot bastard. Come on, you motherfucker. Kick my ass and throw me through a window, you cheap-shot bastard. I need my ass kicked. I'm pleading with you. Kick my ass. Come on, fucker."

The situation eventually deescalated. I remained charged up on my own chemistry for ninety minutes.

Later that evening, I reviewed the entire scene and wrote it down. I had one regret: I hesitated slightly when Pimp stood at my cell door. Rushing Pimp, throwing a chair or broom, then coming in with a barrage of kicks or punches should have been my first reaction. I gave him too much ground. Ted would have been disappointed in me.

I also felt a change, what felt like the death of a civil being. The rules and codes of civil society do not work in this harsh and rude environment. Most importantly, I knew Pimp would never challenge me again, and no one would fuck with me. Other inmates understood I was not meek or passive, nor easily dominated, and if I'm challenged, they should expect strong and somewhat crazy resistance.

One day after the fight, I was notified again I was being transferred to another facility, and I needed to quarantine for three weeks. *Here we go again*, I thought. I sent an email out to Leif and called my two oldest children to inform them I might not be able to contact them for at least three weeks. I gathered all my personal property and my mattress and moved into the quarantine unit.

I was assigned a bunk but there were many open ones, so I chose one about halfway down the range. There were twelve other inmates in quarantine. I knew about half well.

For the first two days, I stayed in my cell space and rarely interacted with others. I sensed I was in the middle of a transition, from civilian to prisoner. All inmates go through it. Just as they go through the transition from prisoner back to civilian. Sometimes the transition is not easy, especially in higher security situations like extended lockdowns, SHU, medium FCI, and US penitentiaries.

The civilian ways of everyday life do not work in prison. The rules, environment, culture, and people in prison are significantly different than those in civil society. There are prison rules and the prisoner code, some of which might seem like those in general society, but the ranking of severity, enforcement, and consequences are different. These rules and code are discouraged in society. The prison environment is defined by security checks, counts, restriction, and confinement. Prison inmates learn to be selfish, guarded, clannish, and distrusting; such qualities are adaptive. The opposite is true for civilians, where trust, openness, and sharing are encouraged. Inmates are characteristically different than civilians; inmates are more deviant, impulsive, and antisocial, and less intelligent, educated, and insightful than those in general society. I was learning to live differently.

I felt myself regressing back to the savage way of my younger years, but without the innocence. The savage code is like the prisoner code—both focus on survival and self-interest. The savage code—might makes right, satisfaction of self-interests, live according to basic needs, and protect your kind.

***

On September 1, 2020, the Camp administrator walked into the quarantine unit and called out, "Smith 039."

I responded, "Here."

"Come with me."

I followed. The administrator directed me to his office. Once in the office, he informed me that my court hearing for compassionate release was about to take place.

"Sit at the chair next to the phone," he instructed.

I sat in the chair, then picked up the phone. I recognized I was on a conference call. Leif, my attorney, was on the call as well, but there was no one else at that time.

"Leif, hey, we ready for this hearing?"

"Yes. The judge and prosecutor will sign on shortly. The judge will likely start with me. I will give an oral version of what I have written in your motion, highlighting the essential components of your argument. Then the prosecutor will have his to turn to argue against your motion. The judge might ask questions as well. After that, the judge could render a decision now or at some later date."

"Sounds good." I asked the camp administrator, "Are you going to give confidential space here?"

"No. I'm not leaving the office."

"What if I asked the judge to make it so?" I replied quickly.

"Then you'll have to reschedule your hearing, which might not happen in the next six months."

"You're having fun with this, aren't you? Is it a power thing? Or are you just nosy? I mean, this Camp—and you are the lead administrator—does not respect the client-attorney confidentiality I and all other inmates have. You are aware I have those rights, correct?" I asked angrily.

"Do you think I give a damn what your hearing is about? It means nothing to me. But I'm not leaving this office with you in it alone," the administrator rebutted.

Leif could hear me arguing so he intervened. "Paul, don't worry about him. You're not on speakerphone. Him listening or not doesn't matter to the outcome of this case. Focus on what we've got to do here."

"All right, all right."

The judge entered the conference call, then the prosecutor a minute later. The judge explained the hearing process and had everyone acknowledged their presence for the record. The hearing was being held via video conferencing because of Covid restrictions, except I was available by audio only. The judge asked Leif to begin.

Leif laid out the case very well, cited the law, covered each criterion, provided evidence of serious medical vulnerabilities and the BOP's inability to stop the spread and harm of the virus. "Based on the Center for Disease Control and Protection's relevant medical data and expert consensus, and his own primary care physician's expert opinion, Mr. Smith's medical vulnerabilities put him at an increased risk of death if he contracts COVID-19. The Terre Haute prison complex is experiencing a breakout of positive cases and two inmates have died despite the BOP protective measures. Mr. Smith does not pose a danger to his community. His security status is minimum and he has no history of violence. He has followed all rules starting with pretrial services, then post sentencing, and during imprisonment. He has zero infractions. This evidence shows Mr. Smith is capable and willing to follow all rules set for home confinement."

The judge called on the prosecutor to provide an argument to deny the motion. The prosecutor gave a summary of what was put in the written response to the motion, mainly the BOP has implemented an action plan to protect against the spread and harm of Covid, the medical vulnerabilities are not severe, and I do not have enough time in prison to serve justice or deter behavior.

The judge asked questions of both Leif and the prosecutor. Leif did an excellent job answering questions and countering the prosecutor's arguments. The judge even commented about how well he presented the case. "Your motion is one of the best I've seen. The case law, the information, the evidence—the way you layout this motion is excellent." The judge went on to make his decision. "Now, I believe Covid is causing great harm, and I believe Mr. Smith's situation is serious. But I deny the Motion because his medical conditions are not severe enough; in my judgment, they do not present an extraordinary and compelling reason for compassionate release. He is not suffering from a terminal illness or an advanced disease severely effecting his ability to function in a prison setting."

I did not remember much of what was said after the judge denied my motion. The judge seemed to focus on Circumstance A (Medical Condition of the Defendant, under Extraordinary and Compelling Reasons) instead of addressing Circumstance D (Other Reasons). Leif and I knew I would not meet criterion for A because I was not terminally ill. But Leif argued the case under the criterion for D, stating I had an increased chance of death. The judge did not explain why circumstances under D were not met. Therefore, it did not matter how medically vulnerable I was, even if I had a quadruple bypass heart surgery or removal of one of my lungs in the past month. If my current health was stable and treatable within prison, and my life expectancy was beyond a few months, the judge would deny the motion. The risk of death did not matter, even if those serious health conditions increased the risk twenty-five or fifty percent.

I was disappointed but prepared myself for this outcome. Leif's performance was so stellar that it eased my disappointment. I believed my case could not have been presented any better. I went back to my cell on the quarantine unit.

After two weeks, three quarantine inmates tested positive. The quarantine procedures were not working. This meant my transfer would be delayed once again. I was becoming increasingly worried about contracting Covid, especially because inmates testing positive were all around me sharing the same space. I could tell, along with many other inmates, the staff had given up on the COVID-19 Action Plan, though the BOP continued to post mostly meaningless data on its website.

After another three weeks, I was placed back out into general population, but this time I was told the transfer would resume within the next two or three weeks.

***

In mid-October 2020, the Complex warden sent out a Bulletin announcing additional death row executions in November, December, and January. This time, inmates from the Camp were told they would take their mattress to the UNICOR building, along with food and drinks. UNICOR is where inmates manufacture items for the BOP and branches of the military, such as clothes, towels, lockers, bunks. Inmate rumors indicated the administrator got in trouble because of the conditions he subjected inmates to during the last batch of executions. Apparently, he talked with a dozen inmates who filed complaints against him, trying to talk them out of it.

There were a total of six executions scheduled.

Orlando Cordia Hall, November 19: Hall, a forty-nine-year-old Black man, was sentenced to death for the rape, kidnapping, and murder of a sixteen-year-old girl. He and four accomplices kidnapped Lisa Renee from her home in Arlington, Texas, in September 1994, as revenge on her brother, who they believed had reneged on a $4,700 marijuana deal. Hall and his accomplices kidnapped her at gunpoint and Hall raped her in the car. She was repeatedly raped at a motel before being hit over the head with a shovel and buried alive in a park.

Brandon Bernard, December 10: Bernard, a forty-year-old white man, was scheduled to be executed for his role in the 1999 murder of Todd and Stacie Bagley. Bernard was an accomplice with Vialva, a previously executed inmate; they kidnapped the couple at gunpoint after Todd Bagley agreed to give them a ride. While parked on the Fort Hood military reservation, Vialva shot Todd Bagley in the head, killing him instantly, and shot Stacie in the face knocking her unconscious. Bernard set the car on fire, causing Stacie Bagley to die of smoke inhalation.

Alfred Bourgeois, December 11: Bourgeois, fifty-six, was being executed for abusing, torturing, and murdering his own daughter. He had taken his two-year-old daughter with him on a trucking route, where he abused her by punching her in the face, whipping her with an electrical cord, and burning the bottom of her foot with a cigarette lighter. He killed the girl in July 2002 by slamming her head against a truck window and dashboard after she knocked over a training potty.

Lisa Montgomery, December 8: Montgomery, fifty-two, was convicted of a federal kidnapping which resulted in death after fatally strangling pregnant Bobby Jost in 2007. Montgomery cut the fetus from Jost's womb and attempted to pass the child off as her own.

Corey Johnson, January 14: Johnson, fifty-two, was involved in a large drug trafficking conspiracy in Richmond, Virginia, between 1989 and 1992. In early 1992, Johnson killed seven people for perceived slights or rivalry in the drug trade.

Dustin John Higgs, January 15: Higgs, forty-eight, was sentenced to death for kidnapping and killing three women. Higgs had invited the women, aged between nineteen and twenty-three, to his apartment in Laurel, Maryland. In

January 1996, after one of the women rebuffed his advances, he offered them a ride to Washington, DC. But instead, he drove them to a secluded area where another man shot and killed the women.

As reported in the *New York Times* in December 2020, sometime during these executions, at least eight members on the execution team and at least fourteen death row inmates contracted Covid, including two with execution dates. Some in the media were arguing these executions were superspreader events of the virus. I was not surprised, as this provided additional evidence of what I already knew—the BOP had been utterly ineffective in combatting the spread and harm of COVID-19.

***

In early November 2020, for the third time, I was informed I was being transferred to another prison facility. I was ordered to pack up my stuff and move back into quarantine Unit S07. By this time, a second unit was set up for quarantine, Unit S09, as the demand for space expanded significantly. Unit S09 was a small space between the building for Units 1 and 2 and the building for Unit 3 and 4, which held a maximum of eight inmates. Quarantine spaces were used for inmates coming into and leaving the Camp, but most were being released to home confinement. Camp inmates who tested positive were now being sent to the SHU for a minimum of two weeks.

To date, I had done a total of eleven weeks lockdown just in quarantine, not including this third stint. I was also in lockdown for a week during the George Floyd riots. I spent five weeks in the medium-security SHU prior to my transfer into the Camp. I surrendered to prison eight months ago and had spent over four months in lockdown.

I sent out an email informing Leif of the transfer status, called my two eldest children, sent regular mail letters to my two youngest children, then gathered all my stuff and moved into Unit S07. I picked a cell at the far end of the range. Luckily, no other inmate was in the cell. I picked the bottom bunk furthest from the doorway, unpacked, and made the bunk.

In one of the lockers, I found a 2009 *Sports Illustrated Swimsuit Issue*. *A priceless item*, I thought. I looked through the images over and over for an hour, identifying the most desirable, which was nearly all of them, then tore out eight of the most insanely beautiful. I used magnets to hold these beautiful images to the bottom of the metal bunk above and other nearby places. Through fantasy, they became my girlfriends, always there when I needed comfort, companionship, and a beautiful contrast to the ugliness around me. The cover girl, Bar Refaeli, was my favorite.

Without doubt, I believed fantasy was a powerful and necessary mechanism to combat the many painful realities of prison. Broadly defined, I viewed fantasy as a spontaneous or semi-directed stream of consciousness, synonymous with daydreaming, rumination, tuning out, distractibility, disassociation, and wish fulfillment. Fantasy was used beyond sex and power, to include all important domains of life and living. Fantasy was especially important and necessary to protect against the "wasting of life," an experience many inmates encountered when subjected to extended periods of maximum confinement and restriction.

For some reason, while in the SHU the first time, I experienced spontaneous fantasy but was unable to utilize well-directed fantasy. I thought possibly the initial novelty of the experience may have been distracting, then the extended period of no new or fresh stimuli of any kind— no letters to read, no crossword puzzles, no books, no magazines of beautiful women—caused a failure to initiate or perpetuate a directed fantasy. But now my fantasies were becoming an elaborate and rich alternate existence. And over time, I had become much better at sustaining a fantasy trance, what seemed like a half-conscious state induced by self-hypnosis, where I was both director and subject of powerful imaginary and social interactions.

For example, when experiencing an intense wasting of life, I directed my mind to a recurring fantasy about a bizarre Kafkaesque justice system. The justice system combined traditional criminal law with mathematical equity algorithms. The system was designed to ensure, through equity algorithms, that justice was served accurately—as defined by those in power. This type of fantasy allowed me to escape or dissociate from the wasting of life, and deal with, through daydreaming and wish fulfillment, the perceived injustices and cruelties I experienced.

The extended restrictive measures continued to cause generalized stress, frustration, and behavioral reactions among the inmates. Through inmate rumor, I and the others in quarantine were updated regularly about inmate conflicts, infractions and sanctions, and contraband busts within the general population. The whole Camp was like a sociological experiment, which examined the effects of systematic oppression on the human condition. I concluded that there is an inherent drive to revolt against oppression. The stress and frustration also spilled over into quarantine.

During the evening of my fourth day, an altercation broke out between a Hispanic inmate and a Black inmate. Esteban (nickname *El Toro* or "The Bull"), a forty-four-year-old large and aggressive-looking Hispanic inmate, squared off with Otis (Dead Eye), a skinny, seventy-year-old Black inmate with one eye. Dead Eye was upset for some reason and began making comments publicly about El Toro, which he viewed as strongly offensive. Even after being confronted, Dead Eye continued his offensive comments but added some smack, including references to "kicking ass." El Toro put his face an inch from Dead Eye's, stared at him with an aggressive and intimidating look, then chest-bumped. Dead Eye stumbled back a step but foolishly continued with his comments and smack.

I felt an urged to intervene, to deescalate the situation, and I stood up to do so. But Yeej stopped me and said, "No, don't get involved."

Yeej "The Victorious" Tang, thirty-six-year-old Asian-Hmong, served sixteen months of a 120-month sentence for delivery of methamphetamine. Yeej was somewhat of a gangster, involved in some serious violence, possibly murder. I could tell he would go all the way and do whatever it would take.

"But El Toro will beat the shit out of that old man," I protested, stating the obvious.

The Victorious explained, "It doesn't matter—never get involved in a fight between two other inmates. Never. Dead Eye will either learn or suffer. If he talks shit, then he needs to back it up on his own. If he can't back it up, then he needs to be beat down. No fucker is going to talk that way to me and expect a free lunch. No, he's gonna pay for it."

"Man, it doesn't seem right," I replied.

El Toro stopped advancing, studied the situation about ten seconds, then calmed himself. He shook his head and said, "You're a crazy old fool." Then he walked away. Dead Eye shouted out a feeble attempt at smack, intended to finalize the situation in his favor.

"Teej, you're right. Interfering in a fight would have been violation of the prison code. I'm still not used to living by this code, but I am starting to understand the wisdom of it. Regardless, I need to respect it. I know that. In prison, it's wise to be selfish, self-serving, self-protective."

I walked away from the situation feeling something, but could not articulate it in words, other than I was transitioning further from civilian to prisoner.

Later that day, I played three-handed spades and euchre with The Victorious and another inmate, Harley Johnson.

The games were entertaining and at times straight-out crazy. There was wicked banter, and hilarious and sometimes raunchy stories shared.

Harley was a forty-four-year-old white man, who was down thirty-seven months on a sixty-month sentence for distribution of heroin. He was severely addicted to opiates and struggled to achieve long-term abstinence for years. He had tattoos all over his body, up on his neck, on his hands and legs. On the knuckles of both hands, he had the word "forgiven" spelt out. He talked often about riding his Harley-Davidson motorcycle. He was on Social Security disability due to mental issues and chronic pain.

"I'm sorry, gentlemen, but both of you are going to lose miserably. Remember, there is no crying while playing cards," I said playfully.

"Okay, white boy, let's see how you do," The Victorious sent back.

"Hey, Charlie Chan, you'd better brace yourself," I countered.

Harley added, "Take a look at this, you homos." He laid down the ace, king, and queen of spades. This gave him a commanding lead.

"What's the score?" I asked.

Harley replied, "17 Teej, 24 Dick Head, and terty-twee for me." Harley tweeted the number 33 because he did not have in his upper dentures.

"Say that again, what do you have?"

Harley responded, "I got terty-twee."

"What the hell is terty-twee? Are you fucking Tweety Bird?" The Victorious said, laughing hard.

I added, "All right, twee-twee-twee-Tweety Bird, throw the next card."

Harley threw down the ace of hearts. Jack answered with the 7 of spades. But The Victorious threw the 8 of spades and took the book.

As the games went on, Harley told random stories, some relevant to the general conversation but often not. "Standing in line to order a sandwich at a deli restaurant. There was a police officer standing right behind me. There was a girl taking orders. She was slow as fuck and kind of rude to customers. I was getting impatient... so I told her to pick up the pace. She told me to stop complaining, she would get to my order soon. I didn't like the way she talked to me, the snotty bitch. Well, now I was pissed off. Then I yelled, telling her, 'Why don't you order a cockmeat sandwich minus the bread?' The police officer cracked up laughing."

I and The Victorious laughed, not because the scenario was funny—it was, mildly—but because it was so damn odd. The story was tangential to the flow and course of conversation. But that was common for Harley. He tended to make off-the-wall comments.

Harley had a rough-and-tough biker look about him. I was certain he would do well in a fight but was lousy at keeping his cool. He often bantered way beyond acceptable limits. During one game, Harley and I got into an argument. He was rude, rough, and tended to make harsh jokes. I gave back smack. But Harley lost his composure and start threatening physical violence. I ended the game, told Harley to settle down or things would get physical. He backed down, maybe because he was being released soon and did not want to jeopardize his status and standing. But I was disappointed in myself because I jeopardized my own situation and became increasingly concerned about losing control of my temper and facing dangerous situations fearlessly and without caution.

I sensed Harley was unstable, that it was foolish to go back and forth with him. At first, I tolerated Harley's nonsense, but it got to me eventually. He got way too personal and threatening. The Victorious agreed with me, but he was better at avoiding conflict.

In addition to journaling prison experiences, I was taking notes on behavioral observations of certain inmates. Harley was one of those inmates. After enough interaction and observation, I could give an accurate psychological account of how and why a particular inmate committed a crime and ended up in prison. I made my own informal rating scales for certain factors: overall IQ, neurocognitive functioning, clinical and personality psychopathology. I noticed different clusters of factors that were distinctive enough to categorize inmates by type. Harley was the prototype of one type of prisoner, and probably the worst—below average IQ, poor executive functioning, emotional dysregulation, chronic substance abuse, entranced Cluster B personality traits (antisocial, narcissistic, borderline, histrionic).

After about two weeks in quarantine, I began to experience mild persistent symptoms including low fever, chills, and headaches one evening. By the following afternoon, I had a cough and body aches. Initially, I thought I might have the flu or a cold. But the following day, I lost the sense of smell, which had never happened before. On the third day, I was bedridden, miserable, and emotionally distressed. I had taken a Covid test three days prior and was a week away from my transfer.

But the next day, a CO came down the range with paper in hand. As he was walking, he referenced the paper and called out four names, including "Smith 039." I and the other inmates acknowledged our presence.

The CO ordered, "Leave all your belongings and meet me down at the front entrance."

I asked, "Why am I leaving the range? I'm supposed to be out of here in seven days."

"Well, there's been a change in plans... you got Covid and you're going to the USP for quarantine," he replied in a monotone.

"Shit!"

Once again, my transfer would be delayed. This was the third time. I left Duluth nearly eight months ago and still had not reached my destination. This delay meant there would be a delay in getting into an RDAP program and other training and program opportunities. These delays jeopardized my opportunity to get the hell out of prison early. I was rotting in this hellhole, a state worse than anything else. The rotting and waste of life underlined the prison experience; it was the source of the deepest agony.

Ninety-two other inmates and I, who all tested positive, were taken via bus to quarantine for two weeks minimum. Apparently, seventy-two inmates positive for Covid were sent to quarantine the week before. When an inmate is moved from one prison facility to another, even within the same complex, the receiving prison facility assumes responsibility. The transfer is recorded, and the new location is observable through inmate look up on the BOP website.

There were several inmates who had Covid symptoms but avoided testing if possible because they did not want to be subjected to intense confinement at any quarantine location. Some healthcare staff walked into a range and handed out testing swabs to all inmates. The inmates were then instructed to swap deep into their nasal cavity, then bring up the sample when completed. The healthcare staff matched the inmate's name to a list, placed the swab in a small bag, and put an identifying code on the bag.

But some inmates dipped the swab in water. Some didn't hand in a swab.

I observed half a dozen such inmates. The BOP either did not care or significantly underestimated the motivating power of lockdown and maximum security. Clearly, the numbers of positive Covid cases posted on the BOP website did not match the reality.

CHAPTER TEN: THE PUNISHMENT

It is said that no one truly knows a nation until one has been inside its jails. A nation should not be judged by how it treats its highest citizens, but its lowest ones.
Nelson Mandela

During my first three months in prison, I was constantly on guard—scanning my surroundings, ruminating about possible dangers, and bracing myself for anything. I suffered from severe and persistent anxiety and paranoia. Sleep was hard to come by. I developed compulsive habits—grinding my teeth, clenching my fists, and carrying an internal tension deep in my gut. I kept a sharpened pencil in my left hand, gripping it often just to reassure myself I had a weapon. I was hyper aware of everything around me and never allowed anyone to sit or stand behind me. If I entered a room or enclosed space, I immediately formed an exit strategy.

Before I surrendered in March 2020, I thought I had a clear idea about prison. I'd done time in a small rural county jail thirty years earlier. But that was nothing like this. Back then, I knew many of the inmates and jail staff personally. I had regular visits from family and friends. That experience gave me a glimpse into the pain of confinement and idleness. Like many people, I'd also seen countless fictionalized prison movies and shows, sensationalized stories in the news. I'd read books and talked to former inmates. All of that shaped my image of prison. I could imagine the physical environment, the characteristics of inmates and staff, violent situations, and the overall sense of being confined and deprived.

But now, every minute was intensely felt, and the pressure of each one added to the next. Each hour was unbearable. Every day felt like I was pinned down with a knee on the back of my head, bracing for fists to rain down. By the end of each day, despair crept in, along with a sense of a foreshortened future. After being introduced to metal doors, concrete cells, and chains, I began to feel something less than human. "If I live in a state of constant fear, can I remain human?" I asked myself, reciting Solzhenitsyn.

But the first few months passed, and nothing happened. The violence I expected never came. I experienced harsh things, including being chained, confined, restricted and deprived, separated from my family and loved ones, and many other consequences that are a part of the punishment of prison. But I didn't experience or witness rape, murder, shanking, or intentionally sadistic and harmful behavior by wardens and staff. These things did occur in prison, more so than in the general population, but they were not commonplace. This list does not include physical fighting, punching, slapping, or shoving due to some disagreement, unless an inmate was ganged up on and the outcome was serious harm or death. Nor does the list include being disrespected or subjected to rude behavior by staff, as that kind of behavior was expected and as common as the color orange in prison. I conceded there were some inmates who experienced severe violence, predominantly at a USP, but I concluded that most inmates within the BOP system serve their entire sentence without experiencing or witnessing firsthand any of those heinous acts.

For months, I was intensely vigilant and on guard due to faulty preconceived ideas of prison violence. Much of my fear was anticipatory and based on lies, not on reality. I understood well that most information I obtained about prison was exaggerated, sensationalized, or completely fictional—or, to use the terms of the time, what was referred to as misinformation and disinformation. But I thought many of the common themes across the various sources, including reports from former inmates, suggested a firm reality. They were not, in my opinion. These exaggerated, creative, and fictional stories of prison were consequently harmful, not only to inmates but also to the general civilian population. And in my view, the inmates were the most prevalent and pervasive source of exaggeration and lies about prison. There were inmates who could be trusted to provide objective and accurate information, but most were incapable. A close second in exaggeration was the prison staff (of all ranks). I felt like I was fooled.

Based on my experience, most civilians without any prison experience view prisoners as inherently violent, untrustworthy, and deviant animals to be feared, avoided, and shunned. That perception was true, but only for a small portion of the inmate population. But it was often generalized to include all inmates, even those who were not violent or truly psychopathic. This was harmful and unfortunate, especially in a country that has created a nation of prisoners through mandatory minimums, excessive punishments, and a judicial process that eliminates the defense. There's no wonder the United States has imprisoned more people than any other country in the history of the world. Yet, despite being a so-called nation of laws, the country has not achieved higher levels of liberty or become less disorderly, violent, or criminal.

I witnessed numerous examples of this misperception in the news media, during my personal social interactions out in society, and from other sources. Often, I heard politicians, news reporters, and other public figures talk about felons as if they were a monolithic group, seemingly overlooking the fact there are vast differences between types. Someone who commits murder and someone who commits federal tax evasion are both felons, but they are significantly different on many levels. To group them together is to tell a lie. Also, numerous times I heard family, friends, and others who had never been incarcerated before make comments or jokes about violence and rape, such as, "That guy is gonna be shanked and stomped for what he did." "He's gonna be somebody's bitch whether he likes it or not." "Bubba is going to turn him into a sex puppet." I reflected on my own misperceptions of prison just prior to surrender. They contributed to nearly half of my self-induced agony and suffering prior to entering prison.

I thought about the punishments of crime. How does the government define punishment? What are the types of punishments beyond prison? What are the common and "real" experiences of prison for most inmates? Are there secondary or collateral effects and consequences of prison? What's the worst thing about prison? When will the punishments end? How long will the effects of prison and punishments affect me?

I believe there's a distance all people fall after they commit and are indicted for a felony. That distance and fall are psychological, not physical, but painful all the same. For me, it was a fall from the point of my life just prior to indictment, all the way down to the prison cell floor where I stood. That distance was far and the fall crippling. For those who lived a chronic lifestyle of crime—the gang bangers or the drug-dealing prostitutes, for example—the point of their life prior to indictment may have been only a small step away from the prison floor. At most, the fall might result in a bruise or two. Not that career criminals didn't suffer— they did—and in ways, they suffered harshly throughout most of their lives for failure to assimilate an adequate level of civilization.

The cell floor I stood on was in the US penitentiary, in quarantine, under maximum security conditions, a long way away from the life I once knew. The quarantine unit was occupied by ninety-five Campers and thirty-one USP inmates, all sick from COVID-19. I was allowed out of my cell for ten minutes twice a week to shower only. I was given one piece of paper and a pencil, but had no access to books, TV, radio, mail, phone, email, or commissary.

During these extended periods of intense incapacitation, which might last from weeks to months, I sensed a "wasting" of life. That experience was terrible, cruel, and dehumanizing. The wasting was not a sharp or sudden pain or a sense of death or "the dying of the light." It was a torturous squelching of sensations, thought, and action. It was a place between life and death—the dimming of the light. When considering all the punishments of prison, in my view, the wasting of life was possibly the worst, and certainly up there with being separated from my children and family.

I experienced much milder degrees of wasting of life prior to prison. There were times when I went through periods of dull stagnation, lack of creativity, and unproductiveness— like the times I spent strung out on cocaine in my twenties, suffering through severe hangovers, or idling because of fear or indifference. But those were often self-induced and incomparable to what I experienced in prison.

Prior to being placed in quarantine at the USP, I spoke on multiple occasions with my cellmates and other inmates of what I knew about their experiences of punishment and prison. I often started the conversation with, "What's the punishment? Help me understand." By then, my cellmates and others had become used to—and even looked forward to—my structured interview-style conversations and occasional pontifications. Initially, it seemed odd to other inmates. But all of them were oddballs in their own unique ways, and most recognized that in themselves. Moreover, most inmates understood I brought up certain topics and used certain methods because I planned to write about the experiences of prison. Some requested I include them in the story or writings. Lightheartedly, inmates made comments like, "Oh no, there he goes again, trying to psychoanalyze us." But I sincerely wanted to know how others experienced prison.

"In all seriousness, what is the punishment?" I asked. "What I mean is this: while standing in front of the man, I was given my punishment of fifty-one months in prison, fines, and two years of probation. But that doesn't define or explain much of anything. What does it mean and what are the consequences of being locked up in prison for an extended period and completely separated from almost everything that was you and your life?"

Big Baby responded quickly, "I haven't seen my family. My dad's sick, real bad. He's got nobody but me, but I can't help him."

"Same here, and I think that's true for most inmates. Perhaps one of the most severe punishments is being separated from your family. Other forms, and closely related, are not being able to care for or support them, or fulfill one's duties as a husband, father, or family member," I said, making notes.

Flamethrower added, "Yeah, my wife takes care of everything, working full time as a nurse, paying the bills, and she is looking after two children. I'm useless. No... it's worse than that. I am unable to support my family and am a big stress to them. My punishment punishes them, and that makes me feel even worse."

Slick stepped into the cell and listened to the conversation. Closely behind him was a large Black inmate nicknamed Tommy Cat.

Tommy Cat was forty-eight years old, 5 feet 10 inches tall, and dressed out at about 370 pounds. I once saw him take down six bear claw pastries, stacked and devoured two at a time, as a mid-morning snack. He was sentenced for delivery of cocaine, second offense, and was serving a 120-month sentence. As usual, he was looking for food. But he also hung around and listened to the conversation.

"Well, I don't experience that 'cause my family is fine. I don't have a wife or any children that I know of," Machine Gun responded. Then he continued, "Man, the worst thing about this is I can't do what I want—like the simple things. Like having a whiskey and Coke while watching a ball game, smoking a cig or a good cigar, having my lady over, or, like, going down to the gun range and firing off a few rounds. I guess what I'm saying is I wanted to do what I wanted to do, but now I can't do what I want to do."

"Amen! You got a witness," I replied. "There were a million little things—like those kinds of things you mentioned—I was free to do and did do. Most of the things I took for granted, never thinking about whether or how much I valued them. If one or two of those things were suddenly taken away, I would feel the difference, for sure, but probably wouldn't grieve the loss severely. But if most are suddenly gone—which they are currently—then it's an extremely painful adjustment. The little things matter. Not being able to enjoy them is another form of punishment."

Flamethrower jumped in, "I was also thinking there are obvious consequences but not the ones people think of as punishment—like embarrassment and humiliation, loss of trust and respect. Also, there is the stigma that follows an ex-con for life."

"I agree to that," Big Baby added after he came up for air from attacking a peanut butter and jelly sandwich. "When I was arrested, I don't think I'd ever been more embarrassed in my life. I disappointed lots of people. Let them down. I could barely look at my dad in the eyes."

I nodded. "Very good point. I was and still am deeply ashamed of what I did... and all the harm I caused others. I still have difficulty looking at myself in the mirror. And someday I will face many people who know I committed a crime and spent time in prison. I dread that."

In the background, Tommy Cat was humming a gospel song. I recognized it and started humming along. Then I closed my eyes, took in a deep breath, and started singing, confidently and soulfully, "Oh happy day... Oh happy day when Jesus washed, oh when he washed..."

Tommy Cat joined in with background vocals, and Flamethrower and Slick followed my lead. "When Jesus washed... washed my sins away. Ohhhhh happy day...." Indian Joe, Hector, and Shorty joined in from out in the hallway. We let it all hang out—no inhibitions. This powerful, spontaneous group phenomenon was orchestrated by a common hardship and agony we all experienced. It was a message to the universe that our spirits endeavored to persevere.

Once we regained our composure, the conversation picked up where it left off.

Machine Gun said, "My experience of being arrested and convicted was different... The people I hang around know me and are not gonna look at me any different. That's the lifestyle I chose. I sold drugs to people who wanted them. I didn't sell to kids or handicapped people. The people I sold to were adults making adult choices. When I get out, I just may decide to sell drugs again. I don't know yet. The point is I know what I did was against the law, but I don't believe it's wrong. Maybe you guys feel ashamed because you did something you believed was wrong, or maybe you became ashamed as soon as others found out what you did."

"Excellent point at the end there," I commented. "When I was indicted, I felt like the whole world knew what I had done. I felt as if I had the word 'guilty' branded on my forehead for everyone to see. I wanted to hide—

desperately—from the people I knew. I couldn't face them. At one point, I was certain I was going to take my own life because I didn't want to face the hell in front of me and I didn't want to start all over again. However, I suppose if my long-term business plan was to live a lifestyle of crime by, say, healthcare insurance fraud, then the whole matter would settle differently in my mind. Shame and humiliation are powerful emotions that can break a man. Hell, O'Halloran— the dude at the end of the range in Cell 7—attempted suicide twice because he defrauded a nonprofit organization, got caught, and couldn't live with himself. His first attempt was by hanging, then he tried by overdose. That should leave no doubt he was sincere. He believed he had failed himself in the worst kind of way. But that doesn't make him weak. Not at all. That guy is as tough as nails. I'm not kidding. But we all have our limits."

Machine Gun took the conversation in a slightly different direction. "No doubt we're suffering a lot, and prison is a big part. But prison probably saved some of these guys' lives. Man, a lot of these guys were way strung out on drugs, drinking, partying... it's a fucked-up lifestyle. No shit! Now, they got routine, they're detoxed, more stable, feeling better, thinking better. Some are doing fucking exercise, which they probably hadn't done in years."

"That's true for me, man. I was smokin' and doin' meth every day," Big Baby confirmed.

Flamethrower criticized the point. "Yeah, it's true some of these inmates were initially better off in prison than running the streets high and wild; maybe prison saved some lives. But let's see those inmates after ten years in prison. I doubt any of them will believe they're better off."

"I agree, I don't think any of them will believe they're better off. But..." I paused for a moment, looking up toward the ceiling to gather my thoughts, "but I understand where Machine Gun is headed. Think about this: since I've been in prison, someone else has done my laundry and made my meals. I haven't had to pay for one damn thing—no food expenses, mortgage, car payments, gasoline, utility bills, healthcare insurance, internet, phone, all the shit that makes you run around like a chicken with its head cut off. Now I wake up and no longer have the dread that comes from having an overextended and unbalanced lifestyle. I can read every day for several hours, use the recreation area and religious services, hang out in the library, or play cards. I have more freedoms—well, no, maybe it's more accurate to say I have more time and less responsibilities— than I had before prison. I've felt relief since I've been in here. But none of that is worth it. None of that is worth the time I spend in this fucking shithole. No, I don't have to cook, clean the bathroom, take the trash out, or do my own laundry. No, I don't have bills to pay. But also, I can't visit with family and friends, attend my own church, sleep in my own bed, and make love to my wife. I can't kiss and hug my children, help them with homework, or parent them when they need it. The net outcome of prison is severe waste, loss, and agony. Doesn't matter how much lipstick you put on this pig… it's still an animal who loves to roll in shit. Fuck pork. I will eat it no longer."

Slick chimed in. "I hate the damn disrespect. I'm a man… I'm a human. That administrator was shoutin' at me for not havin' a belt on during work hours. He came off like I did some serious crime. I shouted back at da fool. I told him don't treat me like that, like some kid… I'm a man, damn it."

"Yeah, I saw that. There's something wrong with that administrator. He's like that with everyone," Machine Gun affirmed.

Tommy Cat added, "I's surprised he wasn't stomped on by some inmates at the USP. Some of those guys got life. They got nothin' to lose."

I went further. "Most of the staff and COs are assholes and probably have been their entire lives. But that guy is the rudest I've met. Prior to prison, I thought the staff and COs were rude because dealing with inmates was a tough job and that made them cranky. But that's not the case. Most staff and COs have deficits in certain social qualities… they have warped ideas about us and are just straight-up lazy. They see us as something less than human. They see us as things. When talking to other humans, they must at least attempt some level of respect, regard, and social finesse. If they don't, they suffer social consequences. My guess is, even when they sincerely try, most of them still suck at it."

Machine Gun interjected, "That's why most of these prison staff don't look like they've ever been laid. Simms looks like he's been blue-balling it for his entire life. And Ms. Hoggs looks like a sumo wrestler who can't say anything polite or nice. Maybe if she tried to smile or said something nice, I'd let her give me a hand job."

The group roared in laughter. Slick spit out his drink. Tommy Cat and Big Baby laughed themselves into coughing fits.

Eventually, I reclaimed my time and continued. "However, the staff don't have to do any of that with a less-than-human thing. Besides, it's easier for them to be rude. They've been practicing it for years; it's part of their temperament and nature now. They probably feel more comfortable being an asshole than being a nice person. Even the most enlightened and decent prison staff here view us as equivalent to a dog. That's as good as it gets here."

Flamethrower added, "I bet you that administrator owns a dog, and when his dog misbehaves, he beats the shit out of it. He probably gets pleasure from beatin' a dog. The worst he can do to us is shout and give unfair punishments, and that probably frustrates the hell out of him. But God knows that asshole wants to beat us down… the thought of it gives him a stiffy."

I offered a slightly different take. "You might be right on some of it. He seems sadistic at times. I think he gets off on ordering us around. But I don't think he gets off on punishing us. Although some could argue that him ordering us around is a form of punishment. Anyway, for him, I think it's about control. He's high strung... he can't handle stressful situations, and he's lousy at multitasking. He yells at inmates because it's easier than solving problems. And there's no doubt in my mind he's a lazy bastard. Probably been lazy most of his life. So, one day he's a CO over the USP, and someone on the executive team offers him the Camp Administrator position. That person probably flattered him, told him he was well-suited for the position given his 'experience' and 'natural strengths,' and offered to put more coin in his pocket. And the dumbass took it. Now he's overwhelmed with stress and headaches because he has real work, accountability, and responsibilities."

"What are his responsibilities?" Flamethrower asked. "It's hard to tell. Some days he looks overloaded, other days he's not doing anything... he sits in his office with a dull, stupid look on his face. I wonder how much he makes?"

"Unfortunately for him, the Camp admin position doesn't come with any real authority to delegate work. Did you know he has zero authority over other staff? CO Rainboltz told me the Camp administrator has no direct authority over COs, case managers, counselors, or other administrative staff. And most of the admin staff can't stand him. Rainboltz also said the warden offered him the position, but he declined because the pay increase was only ten percent more than his current salary and 'ten times the responsibility.'"

Slick brought up the effects of serving a long prison sentence. "You know what really bothers me about prison? When I see guys who've been down fifteen years or more, like Billy Boy on 5 Unit. He's been down eighteen years. You can see the wear and tear from living in prison. The way he talks, his movements... nothing seems to excite him. It's like prison took life right outta him."

"Yeah, I've seen that too. Billy's a real good guy though. He don't bother nobody. He just keeps going," Big Baby added.

Machine Gun offered, "He's what you'd call institutionalized."

"Slick, I was thinking the same thing," I reacted. "Billy Boy, Slim, Irish, and others have been in prison a long time, and I think they all show similar signs and characteristics—certain behaviors, vocabulary, slowed thinking. When they're not engaged in something, they just stare off with a dull zombie look. Some of the long timers who are getting ready to be released in the next six to nine months look slightly different, like they're waking up out of a coma but still disoriented. They're human beings who've become institutionalized. They've accepted, assimilated, and adapted to the prison culture and system for over fifteen years. This daily bullshit has become their first choice, reflex, habit, instinct, and way of life. The federal government even acknowledges that a long prison sentence disables, to a significant degree, a human being."

"Yeah, that's sad," Tommy Cat said. The group nodded in agreement.

Flamethrower changed things up when he said, "All that is sad and scary, no doubt. But what about just being accused, say, of rape? The accusation alone can destroy someone. Going through arrest, prosecution, trial—it's agonizing. I went through it with my fraud case. The process itself is punishment. Now, imagine the accused is found innocent and truly is innocent. That person's still destroyed by the system."

"Hell yeah, and what if he goes to prison and he's innocent?" Slick said.

"And that would be horrible," I responded. "And Flamethrower has a good case on appeal that will hopefully prove his innocence. But that's not me—and not ninety-nine percent of us here. We're guilty. We're being punished for what we did. But our argument is that the stated punishment we were given by the court—a prison sentence—is not the only punishment. It started long before sentencing and will continue long after we're released. Maybe for life. So, when have we paid enough? When have we paid our debt to society?"

The discussion continued another thirty minutes before the group thinned out. I eventually left with my notes, paper and pencil in hand, looking for a quiet place. The best I could do was a chair in the main hallway near the phones and email kiosk. Echoes bounced down the corridor, but I tried to tune them out as I reviewed the conversation.

One thought stuck in my mind: a consequence of crime, prison, and punishment I hadn't fully considered is a doubtful mind. After my indictment, I suffered from chronic extreme self-doubt. It wasn't just indecision; it was pathological. I once wrote a question on a piece of paper: *What do I need to change about myself?* And nothing came. No answers. Even after minutes of thought—nothing. Eventually, I concluded I was incapable of answering any serious question. I was doubtful about what to say, do, or feel about anything. I lost my sense of direction in life.

While pacing my narrow USP cell, I experienced a stretch of tireless energy and creative flight. It started with a sense of eagerness, then a rushing stream of ideas, images, and connections—all fueled by elation and pleasure. I could follow the flow, hold focus, and think clearly, like I was in a state of rapture. After forty minutes, the meal slot clanged open. The noise shattered my focus. I jolted, then crashed back into reality, filled with dread.

That evening, during a smaller creative wave, I began outlining a fictional fantasy about justice, crime, prison, and punishment. The ideas flowed fast. I felt productive and accomplished—more than I had in years. I didn't know why it came now, but I welcomed it. Then, like a snap, an inmate screamed something unintelligible. The shriek yanked me back to the present.

There, sick with COVID-19, locked in a maximum security USP cell, confined in a chaotic and cruel system, and possibly in a manic episode, I outlined my bizarre vision. That will be another book.

CHAPTER ELEVEN: THE TRANSFER

On January 24, 2021, the CO on duty told me I was being transferred the next morning and to have my personal belongings packed and ready by six a.m. I hoped I would be leaving Terre Haute for good. The transfer and release processes were unreliable, even more so due to the pandemic. I allowed myself to feel certain only later—once I was physically in transit.

"What's my destination?"

"You know I can't tell you that," the CO answered. "But if you look at the piece of paper in my hand while I am looking away, then that might be helpful."

I smiled and looked at the paper. It had itineraries for several inmates set to transfer over the next three to four days. I saw my name, then my destination: McKean Satellite Prison Camp. I took a deep breath and let it out slowly. The confirmation brought a feeling of cautious relief and a brief flicker of hope—like maybe I was finally being released from Hell. But I cut the thought off fast, shaking my head to check my thinking. My mind had become temporarily unguarded, undisciplined by hopeful desires and wishes. I knew those thoughts were useless—delusional. There were still more months ahead of me than behind, and I wasn't being released from suffering. The next place could be equal to or worse than anything I'd experienced. Within moments, my mental state shifted back to an anxious depression, and my hatred for life deepened.

"Thank you, CO," I said respectfully.

I'd spent ten months in that shithole—half of it in lockdown. Nearly all of it was dead time. A loss. A waste. There were no reliable opportunities to develop trade skills, earn certificates, complete First Step Act programming, or benefit from RDAP. I was no closer to my one enduring goal: spending the least number of days possible in prison.

Transfer was my only realistic chance at reducing my time. If I stayed out of trouble, I would receive a fifteen percent reduction for good time credit. My sentence was fifty-one months—fifty-one minus fifteen percent, or 7.65, equals 43.35 months. Terre Haute had no RDAP and clearly wasn't doing FSA programming. RDAP could reduce my sentence by another twelve months. That would drop it to 31.35 months. FSA programming might add another six to eight months off, but time was critical if I wanted to qualify. I hoped McKean had better Covid control and offered the programs I needed.

Still, I was disappointed. I had my mind set on Morgantown, West Virginia. I'd researched the place thoroughly—location, climate, facilities, resources, skill-building programs. I'd talked to inmates who'd been there and completed RDAP. I even knew the route, the holdovers, the days involved in getting there from Terre Haute. But I knew nothing about traveling to McKean. Morgantown might've taken two to three weeks. McKean? Could be months. Extra holdovers. More shackling, more deprivation, more lockdown. To me, the transfer process was the worst kind of punishment.

The next morning, I was loaded into a van with other inmates and taken from the Camp to the medium FCI. The sky was black as hell. A strong wind blew snow across the road. I began to feel uneasy, agitated, as I thought about how much I hated life. In my mind, I stretched out my arms, palms up, weighing the good and bad. In my right hand: pain, suffering, failures, destruction—whether from my own choices or just chance. In my left: joy, happiness, success, accomplishments. The right hand felt five times heavier. "So why should I continue this misery? I've weighed life—and it's not worth it." Then a bright response came: "Because you have a purpose. You must care for the children all the way into adulthood and independence." The thought didn't comfort me, but it focused me.

At the FCI, we were taken to the Receiving and Discharge area. I was surprised by how many inmates were there. The noise and commotion irritated me. We, the minimum-security inmates, were placed on benches in the hallway. The holding cells were packed with higher-security inmates. The hallways were jammed with movement and objects everywhere, large tubs full of mesh bags stuffed with inmate property. I figured this was the first major movement out of Terre Haute since last March.

While sitting on a bench, I heard an inmate in a nearby holding cell make a comment about "campers." That drew snickers. I looked over. A large white inmate was grinning at me. I recognized the situation—where higher-security guys looked down on us, thought we hadn't seen "real" prison and were weak, ripe for picking on. Already irritated, I stared back with a stone face, holding his gaze.

His smile faded. "Oh, you think you're tough, huh? You're not tough enough to look at me like that. You're just a fucking camper," the guy snarled, locking eyes.

His cellmates laughed, but kept it quiet, not wanting to draw CO attention. They were enjoying the show.

I wasn't startled or afraid. My stare shifted to curiosity. Coldly, without caring how it landed, I said, "I'm not just looking at you. I'm looking at you in a cage. That cage suits you—the kind made for an ignorant wild animal."

"Oooh," some of the cellmates reacted.

"Yeah, and if you were in here, I'd lay you out," he snapped.

Still locked in, I took a deep breath and replied on the exhale, "So, you'd risk SHU, your security level, your transfer, your good time—just because a camper stared and called you ignorant? My, my… aren't you a tender one." I stood up, moved benches, and ignored him.

It reminded me of my youth, learning how dogs react to eye contact. Locking eyes was a threat. Most dogs would look away. But sometimes a feral dog would charge—hair up, teeth bared, wild eyes, full snarl. I'd respond in kind—growl, bare my teeth, lock eyes like a madman. A human watching would see madness. And sometimes madness wins. Usually, the dog sensed danger and backed off. Sometimes, it didn't... which then might result in club versus tooth.

Staring down another person is risky. In prison, it can be savage. I knew I acted foolishly. I shouldn't have responded, especially not with a stare down. I had promised myself not to start or escalate conflict. But I broke that rule again.

Then it dawned on me. The danger wasn't out there—it was inside me. The root was this irrational, harsh environment and my deteriorating mental health. I was becoming a wild dog again—locking eyes, fighting for some primitive idea of dominance. But dominance over what?

I felt uncertain again—uncertain about myself and how to survive this place. This place is ruled by code, selfishness, and aggression. I could feel the barbarization in me, from a human ruled by law and principle to an animal led by impulse and rage. Was the barbaric better suited to prison life than the civilized? Since my surrender, I'd regressed—deeply. And I was afraid I wouldn't be able to recover, that I wouldn't re-civilize. That even if I survived, I'd be permanently changed. I kept asking myself, "How could this experience not change someone forever?"

My transfer was finally underway. Other inmates and I were transported by bus to an airport designated for inmate air flight. The flight schedules are kept secret from the public. From there, I would fly to the Federal Transfer Center in Oklahoma City, Oklahoma. After that, I was uncertain. Some fellow inmates told me about possible routes, holdover locations, and timeframes on my way to McKean.

Upon exiting the bus, we were restrained with handcuffs as well as ankle and waist chains, which were double locked. We were escorted about fifty yards from the bus to an area near the airplane. All inmates were patted down very thoroughly, then ordered to stand in line, side by side, facing away from the airplane.

Minutes later, an airplane taxied its way next to the parked plane, where I was standing. Apparently, this plane came from Atlanta, Georgia. The doors opened and several inmates exited, both female and male. The female inmates looked tough, bitter, and guarded, and exhibited little if any traditional feminine qualities. The male inmates looked hardened and heavily ladened, as if carrying a stone equal to their body weight. These inmates were already cuffed and chained, but some, who apparently posed additional danger, were forced to wear extra restraints, such as a device to restrict hand movement and a face mask that prevented biting and spitting. I looked at an inmate with a face mask, thinking I had never seen anything so ominous. They were patted down and frisked, then escorted to the airplane headed to Oklahoma City. The US Marshals demonstrated an impressive show of force with several officers holding shotguns lined up in place around the perimeter. I began to smirk. The entire scene seemed surreal, like out of a movie.

The plane was a Boeing 737, six seats per row, three seats on each side of the aisle, with an approximate 120 inmate capacity. Inmates were seated in no apparent order or security consideration, except for two, who were placed towards the back. I was placed in an aisle seat about midway, next to two white medium-security inmates. Directly across the aisle there were two Black inmates with extra wrist and waist restraints; one had a pitchfork tattoo on his neck. Directly in front of me was a Black man who appeared to be in his late sixties. In front to the left of me was a white inmate in his late thirties who was covered with tattoos and had a closely shaven head. Every age group, gender, race, and ethnicity were present, with a disproportionate presence of young Black males compared to the general society.

Several inmates were heavily tattooed on their arms, neck, head, and face, males more so than females. I tried not to stare, but I had never seen tattooing that extreme. Some inmates had tattoos on every square inch of exposed skin, over their entire arms, hands, neck, head, and face including eyelids, lips, and ears. Most tattoos were words, phrases, names, female faces and bodies, children's faces, animals, and skeletons. I also saw a lot of gang-related content. Most appeared to be symbolic of local or lesser-known affiliates, but I did see one or more of the following: shamrock with the initials AB, SS lightning bolts, black hand, six-pointed star, and crossed pitchforks.

About an hour into the flight, I felt a strange wet sensation on my feet. I looked down and noticed my shoes were wet and a liquid was dripping down from under the seat onto my shoes and the floor. I was confused at first as I studied the liquid. I then looked around the seat in front of me and discovered the elderly man had urinated on himself. He was standing up. The whole front of his pants was soaked in urine. US Marshals soon became aware of the matter but did nothing. He was not offered or given a change of clothes—maybe there were none to give. The old man sat back down in his seat. There was nothing he could do. This angered me, thinking the officers could have done something to help and not leave him saturated in piss. For a moment, I thought perhaps there was nothing the officers could do. But almost immediately I thought otherwise. This was a callous act.

When the plane landed and taxied to the place of arrival, an officer yelled out, "Those in 'drop out' should exit now." About twelve inmates got up and exited out of the back of the plane. These inmates were in protective custody, and most were former gang members who "dropped out" of the gang. When an inmate dropped out, they're placed in protective custody because their life was in danger. Dropping out does not necessarily mean the inmate became an informant for the government. There are gangs that will punish or kill members who attempt or even decide to leave a gang, especially while in prison.

The Federal Transfer Center in Oklahoma City is a facility designed to house holdover inmates who are in transit to other facilities. It's the main hub of the Justice Prisoner and Alien Transportation System (JPATS), known as Con Air. Upon entering the facility, I and about 120 other inmates went through a comprehensive health and safety screening process. I hated the recurrent assessments involved in the transfer process—they were burdensome—and I never saw any evidence they were used in any meaningful way.

The process began with metal detection and a strip search. Two inmates directly ahead of me set off the metal detector. Both appeared to have paperwork verifying metal in their bodies. The first inmate, a white man in his late fifties, had metal from a hip replacement. The second, a younger Hispanic guy, had shotgun pellets lodged in his back. He told me he was going to fail the test—as he had many times before—because he'd taken three rounds of buckshot in a street shootout. After failing the first time, he was ordered to take off his shirt and walk through the detector again. I could see the deep scarring on his back.

After passing through metal detection, inmates—twelve at a time—were directed to a long row of stalls for a strip search. Three correctional staff processed four nut sacks and four assholes at a time, then issued us new clothes. From there, we went through a brief orientation about prison rules and regulations, including information on sexual assault and abuse. Then came the medical and mental health screenings—unusual in my experience. They told me the housing units consisted of double-bunked cells with a toilet, sink, and a common shower area. The average stay at FTC was four to six weeks, but it could be as brief as a few days. Because of the Covid pandemic, the entire facility was on lockdown. Twice a week for forty-five minutes, we were allowed to shower, make phone calls, and check email.

Against all odds, I was placed on the sixth floor, in cell 620B—with Jason Ware, the very inmate I had stared down and insulted at Terre Haute. But Jason didn't seem to recognize me. That surprised me, but I was glad to go with it.

Jason had been at the Terre Haute FCI SHU as a holdover, in transit from USP Thompson (a high-security facility) to FCI Schuylkill (a medium-security). Technically, BOP policy doesn't allow inmates with different security levels to bunk together, and there's good reason for that—but from what I'd seen, that policy was often ignored.

Jason was serving a 120-month sentence for felony meth possession. He'd done thirty-four months in a USP and had become eligible for a medium designation. Now he was on the move.

Jason was a 6 foot 4 inch, 280-pound slab of anger. He looked like a cow carcass hanging from a meat hook—solid, pale, and powerful. His head was shaved, and he wore a well-groomed mustache and goatee. "Roxy" was tattooed on the left side of his neck. His upper arms were covered in skeleton-themed ink, and the top of his right hand bore a gang-affiliated tattoo between his thumb and index finger.

Jason often talked about his wife—he had sent her divorce papers after finding out she was with another man. Now, he was considering reconciliation because she'd broken it off with that man. He was obsessed with cleanliness, compulsively wiping down surfaces and floors. He also ruminated endlessly about relationships and felt compelled to share with anyone who'd listen. He had five kids with three different women, but none with his current wife. He'd served in the military in his teens and early twenties, and had done ten and a half years in prison before his current bid. He never said what that crime was. That omission told me he had something to hide. He worked in tree trimming and did some construction. His mother had been a military pilot for twenty-five years—he spoke of her with deep respect. And for whatever reason, he liked to brag about having a "big dick."

I was surprised he "qualified" for a lower-level security designation.

"I get the bottom bunk," he said, leaning over me. First words out of his mouth.

"Fine with me," I replied, trying to sound unfazed. But his entitlement irritated me. I knew that even if I'd called dibs or asked to split time, he would've insisted on it and made a scene. I didn't want conflict—but I hated the tension it caused. In my mind, I fantasized about kneeing him in the balls and slapping him across the face.

We were given bedrolls and told to grab hygiene items from a table nearby. We walked up the stairs to cell 620B. He immediately made his bed, spread out his towel, arranged his hygiene items. When he finished, I did the same. Within ten minutes, we were settled in and tired of each other. The cell was maybe twelve feet by six and a half feet. Bunk bed, toilet, sink, desk, chair. So small I felt claustrophobic.

Jason began pacing. Incessantly. "So, you're a camper?" he asked.

"Yeah."

"Where you going?"

"McKean, Pennsylvania."

"That a Camp?"

"Yeah."

"Why you going from one Camp to another?"

"For RDAP. Terre Haute didn't have it."

"I was supposed to do RDAP at Terre Haute FCI, but the lady in charge didn't put me in until too late. Wouldn't have helped with time off."

"That sucks."

"It is what it is. Can't do anything now."

Evening trays arrived. The CO opened the slot and handed them through. We were both hungry and ate in silence. I sat in a plastic chair by the window, leaving Jason room to pace—about three and a half fast steps in each direction. He started talking about his wife again, how she'd cheated on him. He kept repeating himself, weighing whether to take her back.

Then he stopped pacing and wiped down the toilet and sink. Then the floor.

"Look at this dust and dirt. Is this coming from you? Look at the crumbs—where you ate. You're a slob. Clean it up." He resumed pacing. "You think I should get back with my wife?"

I didn't answer.

"What do you think?"

"I don't know your situation."

He went on and on. "This guy she cheated on me with— he's fat, his breath smells like shit. My daughter—different mother—talked to her daughter, they're friends. She said the guy's breath smelled like a butthole." Then he got angry again. "I'm gonna beat his ass when I get out.

"What do you think I should do?"

I responded instinctively, like a therapist, "Can you forgive her?"

"I don't know."

"You talk to her since the divorce papers?"

"No. But I might call her. She's beautiful. If you saw her, you'd wonder how a guy like me landed her."

He kept pacing, ranting, repeating himself. When I didn't answer, he would snap—demanding I respond.

To change the subject, I asked him about USP Thompson.

He launched into a speech about "real" prison. Claimed twelve or thirteen deaths in the last two years at Thompson—mostly stabbings and stompings. I knew that couldn't be true. The BOP would have shut the place down. But prisoners lie.

"When you get to Thompson, you find a group—a 'car.' Race, gang, or where you're from. The leader's the shot caller."

I'd heard this before. I wrote a few notes.

"You writing down what I'm saying?" he asked loudly.

"Yeah, just some prison slang."

"That's weird... Why are you doing that? That's weird," he said louder. "You better not do that anywhere else. Someone's going to get angry... You shouldn't be doing that, man."

"Okay, I'll tear it up. Flush it," I said to deescalate.

He started pacing again. "You better lay low. Someone's gonna fuck you up." He repeated this multiple times.

Panic shot through me. This man is dangerous. My life could be in danger. I tried to appear calm. Discreetly, I assessed the cell—how I might defend myself. Jason was eighty pounds heavier, four inches taller, stronger. If it came to a fight, I couldn't go toe to toe. I'd have to strike first—maybe stab with a pencil, kick the scrotum, punch the throat, strangle. I felt my hands tremble. My face twitched. I must strike first. I will, or he'll harm or kill me. I won't survive another day in this cell.

But I wasn't ready. I'd been deeply depressed for months. Panic could only take me so far.

That night, I fell into a fitful sleep. I dreamt of my children crying, reaching for me, but I couldn't get to them—I was trapped in a dark place. I woke up early, more depressed than the day before. Their faces haunted me. I missed them. I needed contact. I needed strength—but I had none.

Then Jason stirred and coughed. I tried to focus—be ready—but couldn't find the will. Until a thought crept in—bold and mad.

I reached under the mattress and grabbed a screw I'd found two days earlier. In desperation, I drove it into my thigh. Pain exploded. I thrashed, clamped my hand over my mouth to muffle the moan. It shocked me how much it hurt—but that pain cracked the spell of depression. I started breathing heavily. Rage and hatred flooded me.

I did not know this method would work prior to trying it. As a backup, I thought about jamming my finger on a sharp end of the metal bunk or punching the concrete wall. But all other options disappeared in my mind. The pain I was experiencing was adequate.

How dare this fucker threaten me. Fuck him! I was ready for blood.

"What are you doing up there?" Jason asked.

I didn't answer.

He slapped the mattress. "Hey! I said, what are you doing?"

"Get your hands off my bunk," I said, cold and firm.

"All I'm asking is what you're doing."

I stayed silent.

"What's with you? Were you writing more shit down?"

"What the fuck are you talking about?"

"You… writing stuff about someone. You're gonna get fucked up."

"Is that right? Who's gonna fuck me up?"

"Maybe me," he said, like it meant nothing.

Suddenly, the door flap opened. Meal trays were sent through the slot. I grabbed the trays and gave one to Jason.

He sat at the table, as he did each meal, and I placed my tray on my lap while sitting down on the chair.

I was ready. I had the strike plan. This was the time. I would toss my spork over to the left side of Jason, drawing his attention in that direction, then come from the right side and kick him in the throat as hard as I could. Then I'd immediately rush in with a harsh barrage of blows to the scrotum, throat, jaw, and face. I knew if I miscalculated or wasn't accurate with my violence, the odds of taking Jason down afterward would drop significantly. I had to knock him unconscious—or at the very least, make him too weak to defend himself. Once Jason was down, I'd hit the emergency button next to the cell door and explain to the CO that I had no choice, that I believed my life was in danger.

Jason took in a big bite of food. Then I pitched the spork over to his left side, and his eyes and head turned that way. I brought a roundhouse with force into his neck. His reflexes were quick, and he managed to reduce the lethality of the blow. I came again, bringing my tray in a right uppercut motion to his jaw, then a left hook to the side of his head, and again the tray in a slam down to his scrotum. Then I stepped back toward the cell door as Jason reached for me. I didn't want to grapple. I knew he'd overpower me.

Jason was clearly stunned and injured, but not down. He lunged at me. I dove over and across the bottom bunk to get behind him, then picked up the plastic chair and pushed it in jabbing motions toward him. He reached down and grabbed a sheet from the bottom bunk. I drove the chair legs into his side, then stepped back quickly. He winced from pain, then started kicking toward me and began to twist part of the sheet into a rope. I lunged in with a chair jab. He stepped back, then swung the twisted sheet repeatedly, trying to snag the chair, then pushed forward with violent kicks. Taking two steps back, I was now against the far wall.

We were both breathing hard. We rested for a moment. I thought, *This is it. The cell is too small to maneuver, and there are no other weapons from my position. There's nothing I can do but face it.* Taking in a breath, I moved forward and gave it my all. I threw fists wildly, bobbing and weaving. I felt exhilarated and insane. I don't remember how many times my punches connected, if at all. But within minutes, Jason drew back, discouraged.

Both of us were breathing hard, sweat draining, small spackles of blood on the floor. I was bleeding from a minor gash on my temple and had deep red welts on the left of my chest and shoulder. Jason's nose and jaw were red. I must have connected a couple of times. Neither of us yelled or said a word—until that point.

Jason was the first to speak. "Why did you come at me?"

I replied between breaths, "You were upset... and threatening... because I was writing stuff down. And there was the story... of you beating your cellmate. You sucker punched him. And when... he fell with his arms... up over his head, he was... reflexing from a serious blow. You could kill somebody... with one punch. But you gave that guy... a punch, a knee, and a punch. That might kill someone like me who is older."

Suddenly, a male CO rapped on the cell door and called, "Smith 039!" Both of us were startled.

"Here," I said, grabbing a towel and wiping the blood off my face. Jason started doing the same.

"You're being moved. You have fifteen minutes to get your stuff together."

"I don't have anything. You can take me now," I said.

"I'll be back in two minutes," the CO replied.

Still breathing hard, Jason asked several questions without pausing, "Why are you being moved? Did you say something... to staff during shower time? Did you tell him... I was threatening you? Why are you moving?"

I responded, clearly irritated, "No. What? No. You know they don't tell us anything before we get moved." We paused. Still breathing hard. Then I said, "You scare me. You and I stared each other down and shared some tough talk at Terre Haute just before getting bussed to Con Air. Yes, that was me. I'm very depressed and hate life, and I don't know how to communicate with you without unintentionally offending you sometimes. I came at you because I wasn't going to be sucker punched and suffer a serious and potentially fatal injury."

I didn't have anything to pack. I gathered some shampoo and two coffee packages, then sat in the plastic chair near the cell door looking down at the floor.

"So, what do you think I should do about my wife and marriage?" Jason asked.

Just then, the CO opened the door. I stood up, looked back at Jason, and said, "You're high-strung, hyper, and impulsive—and you think like a criminal. Leave her alone. You shouldn't bring any more pain to that woman or anyone else. You've got some work to do. But I'm nobody—it doesn't really matter what I think."

The CO, who overheard the exchange, chuckled as I walked out of the cell. He said, "We made a mistake. You and three others are going to be placed in E Block, Top Tier, with other minimum-security inmates."

"Well, thank God. That guy I was with is out of his mind and dangerous," I said sincerely.

"Sorry you had to go through that. Like I said, it was a mistake," the CO said, surprisingly apologetic. Since my surrender, I'd only heard one other BOP staff apologize for anything.

I was escorted to E Block on the second level. The CO stopped at a distance from the first cell, had me stand back, then walked over and opened the door. A Black inmate, mid-thirties, with long cornrows sat on the bottom bunk looking back at the CO.

"Are you all right with this inmate?" the CO asked. What he really meant was: are you okay with a white cellmate?

The inmate leaned over, looked at him, then said, "As long as he's no chomo."

The CO quickly answered, "No, he's minimum security."

"All right then."

The CO came over to me and asked, "You got any problems with the cell arrangement?"

I looked at the inmate, then said, "No."

I walked into the cell and the door locked behind me. We introduced ourselves. Through the rest of that day, at a casual pace, we exchanged questions and information typical of new cellmates. His name was Darnell Gordon, thirty-eight years old, slender, serving sixty months of a 120-month sentence for robbery. He was about 5'8" with thirty-inch cornrows. Well spoken, intelligent, and had completed some college. He was an active member of the Crips. He was in-transit from the low security FCI in Seagoville, Texas, to a minimum security FPC in Yankton, South Dakota. Darnell talked about crimes, including gun violence, like talking about the weather.

"I'm from Omaha, Nebraska. Most of my family lives there now," he said.

"Is there a significant Black community in Omaha?" I asked.

"Oh yes. It's about thirteen percent Black. My grandma is still alive... she's ninety-two. Been there since she was young. Her and I are very close."

"What do you plan on doing when you're released and go back?"

"I'm thinking about buying some land outside of Omaha and building housing for ex sex offenders."

"Really? Sex offenders? Explain," I said, surprised but intrigued.

"Hispanics all do homosexual things. The clickers don't like the touchers. Very few SO [sex offender] homo inmates are in steady relationships. Most SOs have sex with multiple partners. A lot of them have HIV/AIDS, Hep C, and they receive treatments... but they still sleep with multiple partners. There was a Black inmate named Mad Dog, high on K2, and he tried to tear his dick off his body. He also had sex with an inmate suspected of having AIDS. Mad Dog had never had sex with another man before prison. His cellmate said he tried to tear his penis off because he did a homosexual act, and after that, he didn't like himself."

"I think you would have to screen people coming into your housing project. And maybe you require that they continue with certain treatments. I don't know, but it's a very interesting idea. Those inmates need a place to live upon release from prison, regardless of what a person thinks about them."

Darnell went on for a while about what he observed at the SOMP (Sexual Offender Management Program). Then the conversation turned to violence he had witnessed directly while in prison. He told me an inmate was killed with a chicken bone. Apparently, there was strong animus between two inmates, and one of them "lost his shit." The inmate perpetrator took a chicken meal from the kitchen, ate the chicken quarter, then used the bone of a leg with a broken end and stabbed the victim in the eyes. Another incident involved an inmate killing a CO. Apparently, the CO was picking on the inmate. So, the inmate taped blades to the palms of his hands, then went up to the CO and sliced him on both sides of his neck. In another incident, a female CO was raped, then murdered. The inmate, who believed he was unfairly targeted, pushed the female CO into his cell and secured the door. The inmate punched her in the head several times, then raped her. When other COs came to save her, the inmate slit her throat.

I thought these stories might be exaggerations. I didn't bother to question the veracity. I didn't care. Darnell seemed like a serious man, and the stories seemed believable. I also believed Darnell was a tough man, someone who had seen and brought on a lot of violence. But I had learned not to put complete faith in the stories told by inmates. Inmates were the biggest source of exaggeration and lies about prison.

***

After nearly two months of lockdown in the FTC Oklahoma City, I was woken at three in the morning by the CO on duty and told, "Get your things ready... you're leaving this morning."

Through staff and other inmates, I determined that I was destined for Atlanta, Georgia. I was disappointed. According to several inmates who had direct experience, it was one of the most inhumane prison environments in the entire system. I was already living in hell but seemed to be descending further to the lower rings where the prisoners and punishments were proportionate to the worst sins. I would not be staying there long, so maybe God was showing me what could be.

While going through Receiving and Discharge, I was placed in a holding cell with five other inmates: two high security, three medium security. No one was handcuffed or chained. Once again, I found myself surrounded by inmates with higher security levels. A Black inmate, high security, was serving twenty-five years for second-degree murder. He had spent twelve years in prison but was soon to be reclassified to medium security. A Hispanic inmate, also high security, was sentenced to thirty-five years for distributing over five hundred kilos of methamphetamine—about 1,100 pounds. That weight triggers mandatory sentence minimums and certain enhancement statuses, such as kingpin. He explained his case to anyone who would listen. I didn't ask questions but listened as he explained to the other inmates.

There was something he said that hit me hard. He stated, "When I was sentenced to thirty-five years, I was absolutely blown away. I had no idea what thirty-five years meant because I was only thirty-three years old at the time I was sentenced. There is no future. I've only done three so far, so how do I do the rest? I don't know."

"I don't know what to say. I... I can't... imagine it," I replied sincerely.

For several months, I had observed a phenomenon I called borrowed time. I noticed inmates serving less than ten years talked about life, family, and the future differently than inmates serving twenty or more years. I, who was sentenced to four and a half years, could easily imagine what my life would be like once I was released. I could plan and prepare for my life after prison. When I spoke with my children, I could focus on the present—what they were learning in school and their friends—but also on the future: what we would do together once I was released. I could borrow time from my future and use it in the present. Thinking about what I would and could do when I got out made me feel better, more focused, more able to cope with the present realities of prison. Borrowed time gave an inmate the power of hope.

But that man—sentenced to thirty-five years with twenty-nine more to go—he couldn't borrow time from his future. There were no vivid or realistic ideas about life after prison. He likely had no conversations with his children or wife about things they would do once he was free. His out date was 2050—*after* good time credit. Because of the type and nature of his crimes, he wasn't eligible to benefit from First Step Act (FSA) programming or the Residential Drug Abuse Program (RDAP) in terms of sentence reduction. The authorities who made the sentencing rules—mainly Congress—ensured he would never be allowed hope. By the time he was released, his wife would be in her sixties, his kids in their early forties. He would spend most of his thirties, all of his forties and fifties, and most of his sixties in one of the worst environments imaginable.

An inmate who serves a long sentence can never borrow time. After several years, his life, involvement, and influence in the world fade to nothing. It's much like a death. He never again feels like—if he ever did—a member of society.

The six of us spent four agonizing hours and ate sack meals for breakfast and lunch in the holding cell before boarding the airplane. The departure process was just like the arrival—same staff, same chain of confusion. The flight to Atlanta took nearly five hours. I was tired enough to sleep through some of it, even sitting upright.

After arriving in Atlanta, I was unchained at the ankles and escorted in single file into a building and down a long hallway. After what seemed like seventy yards, we stopped at the edge of a narrow platform in the middle of the hallway. On one side, several officers stood with chains in hand. Groups of about fifteen inmates at a time were brought up onto the platform and shackled around the ankles. Some inmates were escorted down the hallway through a set of doors. The rest of us—including me—were led out of the building toward another airplane.

I asked a seasoned-looking inmate next to me, "Do you know where we're headed?"

"Harrisburg, Pennsylvania."

"Thank God," I said. "I feel like I dodged a bullet. I thought for sure I was being placed here as a holdover."

"It's good you didn't get placed here. This is the dirtiest, most racist, and worst organized prison I've ever been at—and I've been at seventeen different ones."

"Well, I'd say that makes you an expert on prison shitholes."

We both laughed.

More than one hundred of us boarded the plane to Harrisburg. It sat on the tarmac for nearly three hours before taking off. Since three that morning when I was rousted out of my bunk to start the day, I hadn't seen one process run smoothly or on time. Everything was chaos. But the plane finally took off around one p.m. Flight time to Harrisburg was nearly two hours—around a three o'clock arrival.

I did some quick math in my head. If a bus picked us up and drove straight to McKean with no stops, it'd take about three hours. That would work. But if it took any longer, I'd likely be placed in another facility first.

We landed in Harrisburg. Some inmates were taken off quickly. I wasn't. I waited in my seat for nearly two hours before finally being escorted off. The stairway was dangerously steep. As I reached ground level and approached the bus, I heard shouting behind me.

An elderly inmate—late sixties or early seventies— was about a quarter of the way down, clutching the rail and frozen in fear. Officers shouted at him, telling him to move. He didn't. They threatened sanctions. "I got bad legs! I can't do it!" he yelled. The officers kept threatening. Finally, the man turned around, hugged the railing, and descended one step at a time.

I looked up at the sky and said, "Those callous bastards."

It was now four-thirty. I had no idea where the bus was headed, but I had a gut feeling I wouldn't reach McKean that day. That meant I'd be held over again. Officers wouldn't answer questions. One inmate said the first stop was Schuylkill, where he'd be dropped off. Beyond that, he didn't know.

The bus held sixteen inmates, all cuffed at the wrists and chained at the waist. I rarely talked with other inmates during transport. Usually, I tried to sleep or plan for the future. But sometimes, when the conversation was strange or compelling, I listened in.

The inmate next to me, a Black man in his mid-sixties, had completed twenty-nine years of a thirty-five-year sentence for attempted murder-for-hire. Apparently, he was finally preparing for release within the next twelve months.

He was being transferred down from a USP to an FCI. Without being prompted, this inmate started recounting his crime and certain periods of his imprisonment, and the wisdom he gained over time. The social interaction started between him and another inmate but quickly grew to include several others. He came off to me as boastful, with an old gangster vibe, like he believed he deserved respect because of the dues he'd paid—twenty-nine years in prison. And honestly, I agreed. Spending that time in a USP earned a man some kind of reverence.

"I's supposed to be paid $150,000 to do the job. I got $75,000 down, then I get $75,000 when it done," he claimed.

"Damn, I'd do it today for $25,000!" a younger Black inmate said.

Another Black inmate in his thirties jumped in. "Shit, I do it for $10,000."

A Hispanic inmate with a finely groomed goatee asked, "So what happened? You got $75,000 down but didn't get the other $75,000?"

"I got the seventy-five K, then the guy who ordered the hit got caught. Then he turned on me," the inmate said.

"So you didn't commit the crime?" the Hispanic guy followed up.

"Nah, I didn't murder no one. I agreed to it. Took the seventy-five K. But I didn't even set up a plan."

"Man, that's like not attempted, but more like conspiracy," the younger Black inmate said.

"No, not conspiracy because he took the money. It was already moving forward," said the guy in his thirties.

"I shouldn't have gotten thirty-five years, but I's a Black man in the early '80s."

After we left Schuylkill, I overheard the officer driving the bus tell an inmate that the next and final stop for the day was Lewisburg. So, finally, I knew my fate for the next several days—or possibly weeks. I knew nothing about Lewisburg and didn't ask. I figured I'd let it all unfold on its own. I estimated we'd arrive sometime between seven and eight o'clock. That was unusually late to process inmates through Receiving, but I didn't give a damn anymore.

The sky was dark as we approached the prison at Lewisburg. The outer edge of the property had a rural feel—open fields, scattered outbuildings. Then in the distance, I saw it: a massive brick wall, at least fifteen feet high, stretching three to four hundred yards in length. From behind it, a faint orange glow from the floodlights painted the sky. *That must be the penitentiary*, I thought.

I started orienting myself. North, then approximate size of the property, trying to count buildings and structures. I figured the whole place was over a square mile—maybe 640 acres or more. Inside the wall looked like twenty-five to twenty-eight acres, if each side was roughly the same. As we pulled in closer, I noticed the Gothic architecture.

The guy sitting next to me nodded toward the wall. "Behind that wall is the Big House."

"It looks like a medieval castle," I said.

"Yeah, it's kind of mean looking. I was there five years ago... behind the wall. There's a Camp outside it too."

"How many inmates does this place hold?"

"About 1,100 in the USP, three hundred in the Camp. The USP's been around since the 1930s. Some famous gangsters did time here—Whitey Bulger, John Gotti, Henry Hill. You know, Hill, from *Goodfellas*—Ray Liotta played him. And I think Jimmy Hoffa was here too." Later, I'd find out Wilhelm Reich, the eccentric psychoanalyst, was also once locked up here.

The bus passed through a metal gate, then into the main compound. We were escorted off into a building where everyone got screened for Covid. After that, they split us up. The guys designated to Lewisburg were taken one way. Us holdovers, we were ushered into another room.

High anxiety shot through me as I looked around. Along the outer wall were narrow cages lined up side by side. It looked like something out of a movie—an exaggerated scene meant to shock. But it was real. Each cage was about thirty inches wide, thirty inches deep, and maybe six and a half feet tall. *These cannot be for human use*, I thought. They looked like they were built for animals—maybe wild ones. But there I was, being put inside one.

Once we were locked in, conversation started up fast. Some inmates knew each other from other joints. The place quickly turned loud—laughing, animated storytelling, tough-guy prison talk echoing off the concrete.

Across from me, a big Black guy—thirties, armed robbery—was recounting brutal stories to a small crowd. Murders, assaults. His voice was steady, almost casual, like he was reading the news. He loved talking about his dirt.

To my right, a Hispanic inmate in his early forties, doing three hundred months for drugs and guns, was preaching Christ and quoting scripture. He told his story—violence, gang life, redemption through faith. He had charisma, no doubt, maybe even leadership potential. But I noticed he didn't listen well. He rarely let the conversation breathe. That kind of blind zeal, even when it came from a good place, still lacked insight.

What really got me was how comfortable most of these men seemed. Like being stuffed in a standing cage was just another Tuesday.

Most of us couldn't sit. When we got tired, we'd lock our knees and lean back. After about an hour, the groans started. But as usual, complaints went nowhere.

Strip searches were done right there, one man at a time, in front of everyone. They started with the first cage by the door and moved clockwise. I noticed nearly everyone looked away when it was someone else's turn. It was a small courtesy, a nod of respect. Everyone knew the searches were for security. Stories always circulated about guys smuggling in contraband through creative orifices, but in over twenty strip searches, I never saw it happen. Still, the threat of it probably kept some guys in check. That made sense. But what I couldn't shake was the feeling that we were treated like animals. The strip search wasn't about safety. It was about control. A performance. A sideshow in a grand human zoo.

When we were finally processed, we were taken to the second floor and locked in cells. I was alone. Security was maxed out. We only left the cell twice a week to shower. No phones, no email. Even the count was lazy—no standing, no orders, just silence.

The cell was ancient. Cramped. Less than sixty-five square feet. The bunk was inches from the toilet, too close to sit straight. I had to angle my knees to the side. The walls were filthy. Paint chipped and cracked everywhere. In the corner, a steam pipe ran from floor to ceiling. It was either scorching hot or completely cold. No in-between. Just thirty minutes of comfort, if I was lucky. It was the heart of winter. A dark corner of Hell.

The next morning, they gave me a pencil, some paper, envelopes. I slept a lot the first couple days, then spent the rest writing letters—to my kids, family, friends. It'd been nearly two months since I'd been able to reach out to anyone.

On the third night, I passed my tray out and spotted a book cart. I asked the CO if I could grab one. He slid the cart close enough for me to reach, and I snagged *Tarzan of the Apes* by Edgar Rice Burroughs. I started reading immediately, desperate to escape.

Within minutes I was engrossed in the content. But after the first couple of chapters, I began to have memories of my youth and the feeling of something old and familiar. I set the book down and allowed myself to go back to the hills, forest, and swamps of my youth, when I lived in almost perfect freedom. I believed I was at my best from ages ten to twelve. At no other time had I felt more significant, powerful, or happy.

My reminiscence went on for hours. I remembered sitting down with the family watching old black-and-white movies from the 1930s, 40s, and 50s. Occasionally, a Tarzan movie or a Western was on, and everybody stopped what they were doing to watch. By far, I favored the Tarzan movies, especially those starring Johnny Weissmuller. There was something about the character and the story that resonated with me deeply. I was not just entertained, fascinated, and intrigued by the character, but also related to and understood certain elements and situations in the story. My understanding was not cognitive; it felt something like empathy. After watching a Tarzan movie, I often headed for the forests and swamps with a knife or spear in hand. I felt a strong urge to be in a place where I was strong, sure, and capable, where I could become Tarzan. Within thirty minutes, I would build a lean-to or some crude structure for a dwelling. Not far away, there would be a water supply and an option to spear fish out of the creek or set traps for squirrels or rabbits. Depending on the season, I would pick mushrooms, wild berries, and other food. If I could not find enough food in the wild, I went to the neighbor's garden and dug up potatoes and carrots or went to a nearby orchard and picked apples, cherries, and other fruit, whatever was ripe at the time.

Without exception, I would cross paths with imaginary wild animals, like black panthers, tigers, giant snakes, and rhinoceroses. I would face these fierce animals without fear and, after a long epic battle, kill them. To make the battle more realistic, I might choose a bale of hay or a sumac tree to beat on and destroy. Occasionally, I would tie up one of the dogs, pretending to burn it at the stake. Upon defeating my foe, I beat my chest and let out a thunderous Tarzan call.

As I recalled these adventures, I smiled and occasionally laughed out loud in my cell. I didn't care if anybody heard or thought I was strange. I was far past anything like that.

My remembrances were not guided. Whatever came to my mind was spontaneous, often associated with prior thoughts. Then I had a memory I had forgotten, not recalled for decades. I, eight years old at the time, fell in love with a girl named Jane Bahr. It happened when I was in a second-grade classroom, sitting on the floor in a circle with my fellow classmates. The teacher was reading a story. I sat next to Jane. Jane had big eyes, long hair, and was wearing a yellow sundress. Without understanding why, I stared at her long golden hair and simply could not look away; it was shiny and magical. Then, without realizing until it was already happening, I reached for her hair and began to run my hand slowly from top to the end, repeatedly. I felt an instant rush of excitement and bliss, then numbness, and soon started to feel dizzy. I thought I was under a spell, cast by Jane through her lovely hair. Then, my spirit awakened to the beauty of a girl, and to love. And yes, I loved her, with all my heart. Though the romance only lasted until the end of class, I was forever changed. I even thought about her that evening and the next day.

Lying in my prison bunk with my eyes shut, I smiled, and let out a slight chuckle, as I imagined myself at eight years old staring at Jane and her divine, touchable rays of golden sunshine.

My attention was suddenly interrupted by an inmate howling down the range. The noise echoed for moments, then was gone. Then my attention became divided by two competing images: a scarred old prison cell and a pickaxe. These images burned into my memory, even as of today. The scarred cell was my present, the here and now, trying to hijack my attention, but the pickaxe was from long ago and drew my curiosity. Then suddenly I had an elaborate recall of an incident that occurred when, again, I was eight years old. I had recalled the incident numerous times in the past.

On a summer afternoon, eight-year-old me was playing outside in a large field. From a distance, Father called me.

"Paul, I need your help. Over here." Father was standing outside the red barn, waving me over. I headed to him. Still at some distance, Father put his hand up to motion me to stop, then told me, "I need you to go to the house first… ask Mother for a sharp knife and a cleaver, then bring them to me."

I acknowledged with a nod, then turned and walked towards the house. I didn't ponder why Father needed those tools, and I didn't care. I did as I was told. I went to the house and asked Mother for a knife and cleaver, explaining Father wanted them. She handed the tools to me and I walked back to the barn.

When I entered, the procedure had already begun. The first thing I saw was my father's deer rifle leaning against a nearby wall and thought, *Something is going to die.* Then I turned my head and saw Father with a pickaxe in hand standing next to a cow. There was a rope tied around the cow's neck and around a supporting wooden post. There was no briefing or explanation of what happened next, it just happened. Father raised the pickaxe up high and with all his strength, slammed it down into the top of the cow's head, breaching the skull. The cow's front legs gave out, but not the hind legs. The cow made no sharp movements; it seemed stunned. Father raised the pickaxe up high, then came down on the cow's head again. This time it made a loud cracking sound, like the noise made when splitting wood with a heavy axe. Surprisingly, the cow was still alive and now thrashing about. Father waited a few moments, but little changed. The cow was still moving and breathing. Father grabbed the lower end of the pickaxe handle firmly with both hands, then swung up, then down, up, then down, repeatedly in a continuous motion, unleashing heavy vicious blows to the cow's head. Father eventually stopped, not because the cow stopped moving or breathing, but because he was exhausted. Sweat began to drain down his forehead and his shirt became saturated. Although the head was clearly split wide open, the damn beast still lived. Frustrated, Father grabbed the .32 Marlin deer rifle, racked in a round, and pulled the trigger.

During this barbaric incident, little me stood in a state of horror with eyes wide open, breath rapid and shallow, and heart racing. I never saw anything like that. My mind was not developed enough to understand fully what happened and why. The blood, broken bone, and mangled flesh, and the methods used communicated barbaric violence.

CHAPTER TWELVE: THE ENEMY

For several days, the images of the slaughtered cow—its blood and mangled flesh—remained stuck in my mind. I'd recalled the incident many times in my life, but now that memory tore deeper, evoking an intense mixture of anger and sadness. I had seen many animals slaughtered before that, both farm and wild. The process was the same: kill the animal, clean and butcher the meat, wrap it, and place it in the freezer. But this slaughter was different. It was brutal. Cruel.

I wanted to go back in time, to pick up and hold myself—eight-year-old me—and not let go. I wanted to ease that boy's suffering and protect him from seeing or being part of any act of cruelty. I thought about my children and how badly I wanted to protect them too. But I knew I couldn't always be there. Life would inevitably show them cruelty.

The sadness deepened.

A thought rose to the top of my mind. *I'm subjected to cruelty... this prison experience. That slaughtered cow has become a symbol of cruelty in my mind. But how are these two incidents the same?* I focused in. *What is cruelty?* I looked around for my dictionary. It was on the floor just under the bunk, next to the Bible.

I opened the dictionary. The definition: Callous indifference to or pleasure in causing pain and suffering; behavior that causes pain or suffering to a person or animal.

So, how are the prison experience and the slaughtered cow alike? How are they the same?

My father wasn't concerned about the cow's physical pain, nor the negative impact such brutality had on me, his eight-year-old son. He didn't gain pleasure from it. No. He was slaughtering an animal, just like any other farmer or slaughterhouse. He was not intending to be cruel, but he was careless and callous, and his actions were brutal. As a result, I suffered, and no doubt the cow suffered greatly.

In prison, sympathy, concern, and care for an inmate don't exist at any level that could be considered humane. Callous indifference causing pain and suffering is the norm. Inmates are being punished, and pain and suffering are part of the experience.

Some acts of cruelty in life are necessary. A soldier's actions—to kill the enemy—are needed to protect life and freedom. My father's actions were needed to feed his family. The BOP's actions, authorized by DOJ, are needed to feed society—to satiate, maybe even to give pleasure—by the punishments and the inflicted pain. Prison is punishment, and nothing else. The prison punishment is cruel.

I am not complaining about the cruelty. I just want us to acknowledge it for what it is.

***

It was early afternoon when I arrived at the medium-security prison facility in McKean along with several other inmates. A double barbed-wire electric fence surrounded the place. Beyond the fence were rolling hills filled with maple and black cherry trees, tall grasses and wildflowers, swamps, and small ponds. I saw signs of wilderness: squirrels, groundhogs, and birds darting across the sky.

The landscape stirred something faintly positive in me— something tied to freedom and my youth. For a moment, I imagined myself flying above it all like a hawk. The view, the smell, the breeze—it felt like Northern Michigan. I was home. I was above everything.

Then the shackles around my wrists and waist tugged at me when I moved to scratch my chin. I was pulled back to the harsh here and now. The dread hit harder because of the contrast.

Then it hit me. I hadn't seen a tree, a pond, or any natural life inside any high- or medium-security prison compound before. The land was usually flat, sterile—nothing but concrete, gravel, and sparse patches of grass. Godless, artificial design.

In medium-security, you could at least see a natural landscape beyond the fence—if it was there. But in high-security, nothing. Solid walls blocked everything. That was another form of punishment. And not a minor one. No—this one hurt.

We went through intake: strip search, PREA[1] screening, new clothes, standard policies. Then they told us we'd be in mandatory fourteen-day quarantine lockdown. Everyone knew it wouldn't actually stop the spread of Covid, but the BOP could check their "protective measures" box. Quarantine units operated like max lockdown.

Eventually, I landed in a single cell—twenty-four-hour confinement, except for three twenty-minute outings a week to shower, use the phone or email, or walk around an old recreation space. Twenty minutes wasn't enough to do more than one or two of those things. If I showered, I had to skip calling home. Some inmates gave up showering just to hear their loved ones' voices.

There were TVs, but you had to stand at your cell door and crane your neck to catch a glimpse through a narrow window. For a fee, some inmates got remotes snuck in by trustees. Those guys picked what we all watched—

---

1. Prison Rape Elimination Act

Ridiculousness, Tyler Perry, *Street Outlaws*, *Price is Right*, sports. Rarely the news, which is what I wanted.

A sudden tapping sound came from the ventilation cover above my toilet. I froze. Someone in the adjacent cell?

"Yeah, I'm here," I said.

"Where you coming from?" a voice asked.

I climbed onto the toilet. Through the thick mesh in the vent, I could barely make out the face of a guy with a goatee. He was smiling.

"It's… complicated," I said.

"Well, I got all day," he replied.

So, I told him. I started in Duluth, Minnesota—second day in, bumped into a staff psychologist I'd gone to school with. Warden called it a conflict of interest and ordered a transfer. Eight days later, I was on the road. But transfers aren't direct. I bounced from Duluth to Sandstone, then to Terre Haute. I was supposed to go to Morgantown, but then the pandemic hit. Federal movement froze. Everything stopped. I got sent to McKean instead—for the RDAP program.

"Wow," the guy replied. "I've been in transfer eight months. Milan to Ohio to Lewisburg, now here. Been down seven years. Those eight months were the worst. I'm Jake, by the way."

Jake was fifty-three, doing twelve years for theft. He stole copper wire from his job in the RV industry—twenty thousand dollars per spool—sold it to fund his meth addiction and gambling. He'd binge for a week straight, no food, no sleep. Then he'd blow tens of thousands in a weekend at the casino.

I kept going. "From Terre Haute, I got Covid, ended up in the penitentiary there with over one hundred other guys. After nine months bouncing around Terre Haute, I flew on Con Air to Oklahoma City. Then Atlanta. Then Harrisburg. Then a bus to Lewisburg. Now here. Thirteen months of misery. Most of it locked in a cell."

I felt a little embarrassed after saying so much. I'd overshared. That's not smart in prison. Names are rarely even given early on. I was surprised Jake shared his.

"Hi, I'm Hank," came a faint voice behind Jake.

"Oh, right—Hank's my celly," Jake said, remembering his manners. But seven years inside had chipped those away. You don't share info like that in prison—not unless you trust someone.

"So, have the transfers been terrible, Hank?" I asked.

"It's been hell of the worst kind. Not a journey. An enduring nightmare." Hank was sixty-two, doing twelve years for embezzlement and fraud. Had his MBA. Accused of stealing from clients. Five years in, still appealing. "I'm not entering RDAP right away," Hank said, "but I was considering it. I've been trying to get info on First Step Act programs, but nothing's running."

"Yeah," I said, "they blame the pandemic for everything."

"Exactly," Jake chimed in.

Dinner was being passed out. A CO and a trustee—a guy with crude devil horns tattooed on his forehead—pushed the cart. The ink looked like a child used crayons. I figured the guy wasn't all there.

"Hey, CO, when do we get Rec?" I asked.

"Monday, Wednesday, Friday after last chow. Might extend it today."

"Thank you."

On the evening of the first night, it was rumored an inmate defecated in the shower because he did not have enough time to wash, use the toilet, and call his wife. The strong urge to defecate happened while he was in the shower. The inmate quickly weighed his choices, believing that if he took time to leave the shower, use the toilet, then go back to the shower, he would not have time to make a phone call. So, he "dropped the deuce" and jumped into another shower to clean up. He became known as the "Shitting Bandit."

I, and many other inmates, had not communicated with family members in weeks, if not months, because of the unpredictable, often unorganized, and erratic schedules of the BOP. I was certain I would do the same as the Bandit if I was in that situation. *Sometimes, you gotta do what you gotta do*, I thought, while wincing and shaking my head.

Jake, Hank, and I talked every day through the vent. Sometimes during out-of-cell time, we'd catch each other at our doors. COs discouraged it, so we kept it lowkey. I always started with questions—what to expect, how to handle things.

***

Wednesday. Doors opened one by one. I hit the shower first, then rushed to call my attorney. No answer. I checked my email—nothing. I wandered the pod.

Then three lieutenants entered—two men and a woman. Inmates were expected to stand at attention in their cells. I stood still where I was. The pudgy male lieutenant, mean-looking, stopped at the third cell. "I know you. You were an asshole. Expect a tough time here." Then he moved on.

The female lieutenant said something, but her mask muffled it. I didn't catch it.

"Pull up your fucking mask, inmate!" the pudgy one barked.

I flared. My impulse control is weak on a good day. My heart pounded. Heat shot through me. Fight or flight. No flight. I wanted to fight. I stepped forward and pointed to my mask. "Is this good enough for you?" I asked, dripping sarcasm.

He lost it. "Who the fuck do you think you are? You're just a fucking inmate. Nothing. Where you from?"

"Terre Haute."

"You think that was hard? Wait 'til you see this place."

"I came from the Camp."

"Oh, so you're a fucking camper? You don't even know what hard time is. Get against the wall."

They frisked me. I took off my socks and shoes. He kept ranting. "I'll come here every day. I'll have you searched. I'll throw you in the SHU. You're nothing. Less than nothing. You're an enemy of society, you piece of shit."

I said nothing. I stared at the floor. This wasn't my first time dealing with a power-tripping CO. But it was the first time I was called the enemy.

That word echoed in my mind for hours.

Later, I called through the vent. "Hank, you up? I got something I've been thinking about."

"Absolutely. Beats rotting. What's up?"

I took in a breath, then on the exhale started, "We are not prisoners, Hank. No. We are the enemy. That is clear to me now. We are placed in some kid of a Civil War situation by our own federal government. We are viewed and treated like an enemy, and there are no laws to protect us. Consequently, the actions, intentionally and unintentionally, carried out by the authorities—BOP, DOJ, etc.—against us, the convicted, are tolerated, even when those actions are well within the realm of harsh cruelty."

Hank responded, "Yeah, it is hard to miss that. The idea of making prisoners out to be society's enemies goes way back. J. Edgar Hoover pushed the idea with his Public Enemy Number 1 campaign starting way back in the 1930s. When someone received that title, they were the ultimate villain, someone the government and the people were united against."

"Oh yeah, that label elevated criminals like John Dillinger and Al Capone into symbols of all that was wrong with society. They were no longer dangerous citizens who caused harm and broke the law. They became enemies with no rights. This has become generalized to all lawbreakers, felons, prisoners."

"Exactly," Hank interjected with emotion. "Yes, that mentality has carried over into how we think about prisoners. It's like society believes prisoners, no matter what they were convicted of, are the enemies of society. Once someone is labeled a criminal or felon, it's like their humanity is erased."

"That's such a dangerous way to think," I said seriously. "When you're labeled as the enemy, the focus shifts from justice to control."

"I think a lot of the more recent rhetoric started in the 1970s with the War on Drugs. The way politicians talked about drug offenders back then was extreme. They weren't just criminals—they were enemies of society, like a cancer that needed to be cut out."

"Exactly! They were and still are demonized. And it wasn't just politicians; it was the media too. They amplified that narrative. Remember the 'super predator' stuff in the '90s? They basically said those offenders were beyond redemption."

"Right, and that led to all those mandatory minimum sentences. Instead of looking at the circumstances, they slapped everyone with these long, fixed sentences. It's like they decided that once you're in the system, you're not really a person anymore, just something that needs to be locked away."

Jake surprised Hank and me, adding, "The whole 'enemies don't have rights' mentality must go. People in prison are still human beings, and if society is serious about justice, they need to stop treating us, prisoners, like we are beyond help and change. The war on crime and drugs has gotten us nothing but an endless cycle of punishment and mass incarceration."

There was a pause. Two minutes passed. I broke the silence. "We are human beings and citizens who broke the law and caused harm. We should be punished but not be treated as less than or worse... the enemy." Then I paused.

I thought about what if one of my children were in prison. I thought about the pain, suffering, and the waste of life. I could not linger on this thought; it was too unbearable. I left the conversation without another word.

The following morning, I heard a rap on my cell door. "Yes?" I responded as he walked up the door.

"Get ready to be transferred to the minimum-security Camp," the CO on duty stated.

"Yes." After seventeen days in quarantine, I was transferred to the Camp facility.

CHAPTER THIRTEEN: THE RESIDENTIAL DRUG ABUSE PROGRAM (RDAP)

*Life, as we find it, is too hard for us; it brings us too
many pains, disappointments and impossible tasks.
In order to bear it we cannot dispense with palliative
measures... There are perhaps three such measures:
powerful deflections, which cause us to make light of our
misery; substitutive satisfactions, which diminish it; and
intoxicating substances, which make us insensible to it.*
Sigmund Freud, *Civilization and Its Discontents*

"Good morning, community. My name is Paul Smith. I'm
fifty-six, from Michigan, married but separated, with four
kids. My substance of choice is alcohol. I was convicted
of healthcare fraud and money laundering and sentenced to
fifty-one months." I delivered my introduction mechanically,
standing at a podium before a crowd of inmates seated in
six rows, three on each side of the center aisle. At the back
sat three Drug Treatment Specialists (DTS)—Hart, Fields,
and Baker—observing quietly.

This was the morning meeting of the Residential Drug
Abuse Program (RDAP), held in a corner of the prison

warehouse. COVID-19 had displaced it from the chapel to this makeshift, taped-off space, marked for social distancing. Chairs, neatly spaced, were stacked in the corner on weekends.

Before speaking, I had been prepped on the mandatory format for new inmates: name, hometown, personal details, substance of choice, crime, and sentence length. Now I'd completed my first RDAP obligation and took a seat to await the next introduction.

"Good morning, community. My name is Lance Harrison. I'm married with two kids from Ohio, near Cleveland. My substance of choice is alcohol. I was convicted of illegal gambling and tax evasion and sentenced to twenty-four months. Thank you, community." Harrison, a stocky, muscular man of forty-two with a confident demeanor, seemed eager to make an impression. A former wrestler, he had never faced incarceration before, and prison promised to test his mettle.

Then came John Jay Washington, his voice trembling. "M-my name is John J-Jay Washington. Good ma-ma-morning, c-c-community. I from Detroit, M-M-Michigan. Got three kids. Drugs of choice—c-c-cocaine and marijuana. I caught a drug c-c-charge and got thirty-six months. Th-thank you, c-c-community." Washington—forty-nine, from the inner streets of Detroit, and on his third prison stint—struggled through his stutter, a manifestation of severe social anxiety. I winced in sympathy, recognizing the courage it took for Washington to push through his terror. We all start from different places. We all have unique struggles.

On the marker board behind the podium, the date—April 5, 2021—was listed in the top right corner. This was the first RDAP community meeting since the Covid pandemic had shut the program down for nearly a year. The entire RDAP community, consisting of sixty inmates, was a diverse mix of ages, crimes, and sentences, but all members shared a singular goal: reducing their time behind bars. Successful completion could trim sentences by up to twelve months, though some inmates who were ineligible for this reduction still pursued early release credits. Freedom was the driving motivator, far outweighing any interest in personal growth or mental health. For many, this program was a calculated strategy, not a commitment to change.

After the community morning meeting, the new cohort of eighteen inmates—designated as Modified Treatment Community (MTC) 55—gathered in a circle for orientation. Mr. Hart, our primary DTS, addressed us.

"Welcome to RDAP. As I mentioned when we met individually, this treatment will include a number of activities, the community meeting, small group education, small and large group presentations, and journaling. You are all required to continue your institutional work assignments, and you may enroll in other programs, but RDAP has priority. Let's start with the basics. Inside the folder I've given you, there is important program information we will cover today. In the left sleeve, there is a document titled 'Eligibility Criteria.' Will one of you please read the criteria?"

Lance Harrison volunteered to read. "Eligibility for RDAP: An inmate must meet the following criteria: One, be in BOP custody; two, have a documented substance abuse disorder; three, sign the agreement to participate; four, reside in a BOP facility; five, have enough time left on their sentence to complete the program; and six, be willing to participate fully. Successful completion may result in up to twelve months off the sentence, financial incentives, and privileges. Inmates convicted of serious violent offenses are ineligible for sentence reduction."

Hart then explained, "All inmates in the RDAP are housed together in the same range or unit. Inmates who are not enrolled in the RDAP are prohibited from entering this space and will face sanctions for being out of bounds.

Similarly, RDAP inmates are not allowed to enter any housing areas except Unit A."

He continued for several minutes, outlining the basic rules and policies specific to RDAP. It quickly became clear to me that while RDAP aimed to create a therapeutic environment, its operations were ultimately subordinate to the prison's overarching security protocols. This prioritization made sense in the context of a prison but raised concerns about confidentiality, informed consent, trust, and other critical aspects of treatment.

As Hart spoke, I was reminded of my own experience as a clinical psychologist and the standard limits of confidentiality in professional practice. Typically, confidentiality could be breached only when a client posed an imminent risk of suicide (with thoughts, a plan, and intent), a danger to others (with similar criteria), or in compliance with a court order. The Bureau of Prisons followed these same guidelines but added one vague and troubling exception: when there is a security risk.

I raised my hand. "What exactly does 'security risk' mean?" I posed the question deliberately in front of the group, knowing that Hart was aware of my professional background and expertise. I had long felt that terms like "security risk" or "security concerns" were deliberately ambiguous, often used to justify overreach or obscure deeper issues.

Hart hesitated, his tone betraying a trace of nervousness. "Well, you're in prison… that's the first and foremost thing to remember," he replied. "If an inmate in this program says or does something that violates institutional security, then that information will be shared with the security office. Security is, of course, the BOP's highest priority."

The response didn't satisfy me, but it was predictable. To me, the word "security" was less a specific principle and more a broad justification—an excuse that could be wielded without definition or accountability.

After thirty minutes of reviewing RDAP policies, Hart described in detail the treatment strategies and modalities. This was followed by a series of videos explaining the program's history, development, and core strategies. "The RDAP was modified to work within the BOP system," he explained. "That is why your group was named 'Modified Treatment Community—55.'"

I was impressed to learn that the program was rooted in over fifty years of rigorous research by a prominent psychosocial expert. The videos showcased its foundational principles and demonstrated effective strategies designed to address not only substance abuse and criminal behavior but all critical domains of a person's life. The ultimate goal was transformative: to enact deep, structural personality change. However, I couldn't ignore the caveat that this was a "modified" version of the program depicted in the videos. While the concepts seemed sound, I was skeptical about their implementation. *All good ideas and philosophical ideals become perverted when put into practice*, I thought. It was a harsh truth I had seen play out time and time again in institutional settings.

I questioned the delicate balance between confidentiality and the institution's overarching focus on security. Hart's response was measured but unconvincing. "This is a prison, first and foremost," he said. "If there's a security risk, we have to act."

Back on the range after orientation, I sought advice from DeAndre Michaels, an experienced RDAP participant. DeAndre explained the intricacies of the program, emphasizing the tension between the RDAP philosophy and the entrenched prison code. "RDAP is about building trust and community—you'll hear the word 'community' a lot," he said. "But for guys who've lived by the code their whole lives, it's a struggle. You'll see it—some people fake it just to get their time cut."

I nodded, thinking of my own doubts. Could a program like this truly thrive in an environment dominated by mistrust and survival instincts?

DeAndre laid out the core principles of RDAP, beginning with its foundational strategies. This was mostly a repeat of Hart's presentation. "In this program, you'll go through a mix of activities—large group sessions, small group therapy, one-on-one treatment plan meetings with your DTS, and self-help exercises. You already got a taste of the morning meeting, which happens at the start of every weekday. That's when the entire treatment community gathers—including inmates, DTS staff, and occasionally the program director, Dr. Sanchez. He's got a PhD in clinical psychology."

I listened intently as DeAndre continued. "After the morning meeting, inmates move on to different activities based on their progress in the program. Since you and the others in MTC 55 are new, you'll spend a lot of time together in small treatment groups. You'll figure that out soon enough. You'll also have one-on-one meetings with your DTS to discuss treatment progress. Yours is Mr. Hart— same as mine, but I'm in MTC 54. A huge part of RDAP is journaling. Every inmate has to complete a series of nine self-help books. Each one builds on the last, covering the program's key concepts. I'm on book eight now."

I nodded. "We haven't gotten any books yet. I guess they'll hand them out soon?"

"Yeah. You'll get one at a time, about one per month."

I exhaled. "Good."

DeAndre leaned in. "Now, one of the most important tools in RDAP is Confront and Level. This is where you call out another inmate when they're not following the program's expectations—whether it's breaking rules, being disrespectful, or slacking on responsibilities. It's not just encouraged—it's required."

My eyebrows lifted.

"If you see someone failing to keep their space clean, for example, you have to confront them, explain how their behavior affects the community, and offer a solution. That's a one-on-one confrontation. But if that doesn't work, or if the issue is serious enough, you file a Pull-Up—a written form documenting the behavior and recommending a fix. That form needs to be signed by another inmate and a DTS before it's presented in the morning meeting."

I shook my head. "I saw that this morning. It looked intense."

"Oh, it can be," DeAndre admitted. "But if you don't confront others and submit Pull-Ups, you risk being held back in the program. It's a requirement. Everyone has to submit a certain number of Pull-Ups each week or month. If you don't, the staff sees it as you not engaging with the program."

I leaned forward. "So if you write a Pull-Up on someone, you have to call them out in front of the entire group?"

DeAndre nodded. "That's right. When it's time for Pull-Ups in the morning meeting, you stand up and say, 'I'm pulling up so-and-so.' That inmate has to walk up to a microphone across from the podium. Then, you deliver the Pull-Up in a structured format—clearly stating the problem behavior, explaining how it affects you and the community, and recommending how they should have acted instead. The inmate on the receiving end has to respond in a specific way—either asking for feedback from the community, accepting responsibility, and committing to the recommendation, or challenging by providing evidence or a witness. Few inmates challenge a Pull-Up successfully."

I stroked my chin whiskers. "This whole process sounds like the complete opposite of the prison code."

"Oh, absolutely," DeAndre said. "RDAP is about open, healthy confrontation to create a positive community. The prison code is about survival, keeping your head."

Our conversation was suddenly interrupted by a commotion. Two inmates, Tyrone Chapman and Jean Pierre, were squaring off, their voices rising. Chapman, a seasoned street fighter and gang member, exuded raw menace. Pierre, younger and inexperienced, tried to hold his ground but faltered. The tension escalated until one of Pierre's allies intervened. Chapman, undeterred, invited them all to step forward. "It doesn't matter to me," he said, his tone cold and steady. The confrontation fizzled, but the underlying volatility remained.

I observed silently, my mind racing. Prison creates wolves and sheep. How could a program built on trust and mutual accountability coexist with this pervasive undercurrent of mistrust, selfishness, and fear? Would RDAP's ideals be enough to counteract the deeply ingrained survival mechanisms of prison life?

The days grew longer as early spring became summer, and more sunlight brought warmer temperatures. Though COVID-19 continued to pose a significant threat, inmates were gradually allowed brief outdoor recreation time in staggered shifts.

For several weeks, I took advantage of this opportunity, walking and jogging around a track encircling the baseball field—a loop measuring roughly one-fifth of a mile. At first, I could barely run 150 yards before I had to stop and rest. But within a month, my endurance improved dramatically; I was soon running twelve laps without stopping. Over time, I began incorporating strength exercises into my routine: after each lap, I would do twenty push-ups, fifteen dips, and ten burpees. This consistent effort yielded significant improvements in my physical and mental health. I felt stronger, slept better, and experienced less frustration and depression. I even lost weight without altering my diet.

Then, without warning, the prison went into lockdown. The reasons varied: localized security concerns, systemwide lockdowns in response to outside violence, or vague justifications unknown even to the prison staff. Lockdowns could last anywhere from a few days to weeks. During these periods, inmates were confined to their cells or ranges, with little to no interaction with others. Recreation time was suspended entirely.

For me, these lockdowns were devastating. My physical health declined rapidly, and my motivation to exercise vanished. Although I dutifully completed my RDAP assignments, which required forty-five minutes to an hour of daily work, my efforts were half-hearted. The pervasive sense of wasting away returned, leaving me overwhelmed by the feeling of stagnation and rot.

Eventually, the lockdown would be lifted just as abruptly as it began, and normal activities would resume. I returned to outdoor exercise, but my enthusiasm and motivation were inconsistent. I never quite regained the drive or focus I had felt during those first weeks.

***

Two months passed. MTC-55 were becoming valuable participants in the RDAP process. At the morning meeting, the date on the front marker board was June 3, 2021.

"Good morning, community," Jean Pierre announced from the front podium during the RDAP community morning meeting. "I would like to pull up Mr. Harrison."

Harrison froze, unsure of the reason for the Pull-Up. Hesitant, he stood up and walked to the microphone at the other end of the aisle. His mind raced through recent events, but he couldn't pinpoint what he'd done wrong.

Pierre continued, "I am pulling you up because you urinated outside the door of the recreation building. Urinating in public goes against not only our community standards but also institutional rules. That kind of behavior affects me and the community in the following ways: it's disgusting and offensive. No one wants to see you expose, intentionally or not, your body parts. I strongly recommend that you stop this inappropriate behavior."

The morning meeting group stirred uneasily. Some inmates chuckled, while others shook their heads in disbelief. Sitting near the back of the room, I thought the Pull-Up was bold—and risky. Physically exposing himself, even unintentionally, could be blown out of proportion by Fields, the female DTS. She was notorious for her disgust toward anything she perceived as violent or abusive toward women. In her eyes, every male inmate was a potential predator.

Before I finished this thought, Fields' voice cut sharply through the room. "This is not a minor offense or a simple failure to follow rules," she said, glaring at Harrison. "You could be charged with indecent exposure, a sexual offense."

The chuckles and smirks vanished. The room fell dead silent. Her statement was a chilling reminder to the inmates: no one could be trusted—not even RDAP staff. These kinds of remarks only pushed inmates deeper into secrecy and cover-ups. Pull-Ups were supposed to address petty behavior like leaving trash on the floor or talking too loudly after lights out—not potential crimes like using cell phones, drinking, or a male inmate whipping out his dick to piss. Fields, with her hardline stance, only reinforced the importance of sticking to the prison code: never snitch.

Harrison, required to follow protocol, cleared his throat and asked, "May I have some feedback from the community, please?"

Four inmates approached the microphone, one by one, each offering feedback. Their comments were repetitive and lacked depth.

"When you urinate outside, people don't want to see that," one said. "I recommend you do better."

"Yeah, same," another added. "Be more mindful."

After they finished, Harrison responded. "Good morning, community. Mr. Pierre is correct. The recreation building doesn't have a bathroom, and I had a strong urge to urinate. Instead of going back to the range, I went behind the door, trying to be discreet. But that's no excuse. I shouldn't have done it, and I won't do it again."

The remainder of the morning meeting was unremarkable, except for the very end. Dr. Sanchez, the program director, addressed the group from the podium. His tone was calm but commanding. "Last week, two RDAP inmates were caught using cell phones. Another was caught trying to smuggle in alcohol, tobacco, and cell phones. These are serious problems. Those inmates are no longer in the program and will be transferred to higher-security prisons. You... all of you... are not serious about your treatment and not ready to advance. As a community, you are responsible for correcting this behavior... but you haven't. Therefore, I am extending everyone's treatment by nine weeks. You will all receive new release dates. I will take only a few questions."

The room erupted in barely contained outrage, though no one dared fully voice their anger.

I leaned toward Harrison, my voice low but seething, "Why the hell am I being held responsible for somebody else's goddamn behavior?"

Several inmates raised their hands.

"I've been clean since I joined the program," one inmate said. "I follow the rules. I don't have contraband. And yet I'm being set back too. Why?"

Dr. Sanchez remained stoic. "Because you are not holding the violators accountable. That is part of the treatment."

"How can I stop someone who doesn't care about treatment?" the inmate asked.

"This is your community," Sanchez replied. "Don't tell me you're unaware of others using cell phones, tobacco, being out of bounds, or committing other violations. All of you need to confront and Pull-Up those who are not following the rules."

"If I pull someone up for a cell phone, will they get kicked out of the program?" another inmate asked.

"Not necessarily," Sanchez replied without hesitation.

Another inmate stated what was on the minds of several. "I was supposed to be released in late December or early January. Now my release will be March or April. That's completely unfair. So, if I don't tell on other inmates, I'm being punished?"

"This isn't punishment," Sanchez said, his tone sharp and deliberate. "You need more treatment."

I leaned back toward Harrison, my frustration boiling over. "That bastard is playing word games. He won't call it punishment—probably knows it's unethical—but that's exactly what it is. Sanchez doesn't give a damn about us. This isn't about treatment or rehabilitation. It's about his ego. When an inmate gets caught with contraband—like a cell phone—it's not just a rule violation to him. It's personal. It's a direct challenge to his authority. He doesn't assume the role of healer; he sees himself as a man in control—that his orders shall be obeyed. And if we don't acknowledge that control, if we don't bow to it, he'll make sure we pay. He acts like an extra month or two in here is nothing, like it's just a minor consequence. But that's because he's not the one serving the time. He and the rest of the staff don't live in this hell. They don't count the days like we do. And mark my words—this is going to backfire on all of us."

Back on the range, I finally snapped. My voice echoed down the range. "If any of you use a damn phone or bring in contraband in a careless manner such that I see it, without looking for it, I'll pull your ass up. I don't give a fuck. I'm not doing more time just because you rather use a cell phone instead of the institutional phone and email."

An older inmate shook his head. "If all inmates stop snitching, no one gets busted. Snitches need to quit."

"I hear you," I shot back, "but I strongly disagree. Yeah, some people snitch to the DTSes and CO staff, but others are just careless—using cell phones out in the open, drinking, making noise. We've all seen people get busted not because of a snitch, but because they were reckless. So don't put this on me. I'm not doing extra time for anyone's bullshit."

Several inmates began to gather in the RDAP unit, the air thick with unspoken tension.

I continued, "Sanchez made it clear. If you don't hold each other accountable—if you don't confront and level your peers when they violate the program's rules—then you are not participating in treatment. And if you're not participating in treatment, you're not progressing. If you're not progressing, you're not getting out on time. Call out your fellow inmates or risk your release date being pushed back. That is some fucking bullshit!"

I inhaled deeply, held my breath for a few moments. Then exhaled. For men who had spent years living by the prison code—mind your business, don't snitch, handle problems yourself—this was a nightmare scenario. The director of RDAP is now requiring us to do the very thing that could get us in trouble or harmed. But if we refuse, we stay locked up longer. That afternoon, the dilemma became real.

I went over to my bunk and pondered the situation further. This was a version of the Prisoner's Dilemma, a classic social psychological phenomenon. The Dilemma is a tension between self-interest and cooperation. Two individuals face a choice—work together or act in their own best interest. If both cooperate, they both win. If one betrays while the other stays loyal, the betrayer walks away with the better deal while the other gets burned. Since the risk of trusting the other person is very high, the rational move is to look out for yourself.

But in this RDAP situation, if inmates cooperate with each other by not snitching (adherence to the prison code), then they don't secure a win but the risk of getting busted decreases. There are many stupid inmates who lack foresight and are impulsive and careless. They get busted—not from snitching—and cause the rest to suffer. They cancel out an almost certain win-win outcome by introducing risk. If one inmate betrays—snitches via a Pull-Up—while the other stays loyal to the code, the betrayer walks away with the best deal while the other gets burned. The risk of trusting each other is very high. The rational move is to look out for yourself, confront and Pull-Up the violator, to avoid further release delays.

Looking through the window outside, I thought, *You can call me a snitch all you want. I will respond with a big "fuck off." I value freedom over so-called prison honor.*

The next afternoon I walked the outdoor track alone, lost in heavy thoughts. The afternoon heat pressed down on me; the temperature was well into the eighties and there wasn't even a hint of wind.

"May I join you?" a soft voice interrupted my reverie, startling me. I turned to see Jozsef Farkas, an older inmate with a faint foreign accent.

"Yes, of course, Jozsef," I replied with a small smile.

Jozsef Farkas was a sixty-two-year-old Hungarian-American inmate, serving a twelve-year sentence for healthcare fraud. Before his conviction, Farkas had been a neurologist and surgeon, holding prestigious positions at two hospitals and a university. I regarded him as a genius, someone with a seemingly infinite knowledge of medicine and the human mind.

For a few minutes, we walked in silence, our footsteps crunching against the dry gravel of the track.

"Prison is a waste of life," I muttered, more to myself than to my companion. It wasn't something I had meant to say out loud. It was just a thought I'd been carrying—a thought so heavy that it slipped free of my control.

Farkas responded immediately, as though the sentiment were obvious. "Prison has no soul."

I nodded. "You're right. It's soulless." I paused before adding, "How could there be a soul in a place that warehouses burdensome, costly things?"

We continued walking, the silence between us settling back in for several minutes. Finally, I spoke again, my voice carrying a weight that matched the heat of the day. "When I was at Terre Haute," I began, "I read this book about the psychology of decision making. I think it was called *Your Brain is Almost Perfect* by Read Montague. There was a chapter in it—'Sharks Don't Go on Hunger Strikes,' or something like that."

Farkas glanced at me, his interest apparently piqued but said nothing. I continued. "That chapter talked about how humans, unlike other animals, have the ability to override their deepest instincts because of powerful ideas. It's like this mental superpower we have. For example, Mahatma Gandhi went on several hunger strikes, politically motivated ones. He denied his body's hunger instinct for weeks at a time—sometimes as long as twenty-one days—all for an idea." My voice grew more animated. "When the human body is deprived of food for that long, it starts shutting down. It's programmed to survive, but Gandhi chose not to listen to that programming. How is it possible for a human being to starve themselves to death for a cause? For an idea?"

"Yes," Farkas replied thoughtfully, his voice measured. "Humans can override their instincts. It is one of the few things that makes us truly unique. But those extreme examples—like Gandhi's—are rare. Most people don't possess that level of control or dedication."

I nodded. "It's rare, yes. But it happens. And sometimes, it's not noble. Sometimes, it's savage and selfish. Like

Jim Jones in the 1970s." My expression darkened. "He convinced his followers in Jonestown to kill their children and themselves by drinking poison. Over nine hundred people died that day. How does someone override their instinct to protect their children? How do they override their own will to live—all for an idea? The power of an idea can be… extreme."

Farkas was silent for a moment, his face contemplative. Finally, he said, "Yes, but sharks don't go on hunger strikes. When a shark is hungry, it eats. There is no idea powerful enough to derail that instinct—except perhaps the instinct to mate."

I chuckled softly, though there was little humor in my voice. "Exactly. Humans are different. And that difference can be dangerous."

We walked on in silence again, but my thoughts refused to stay quiet.

"I grew up in a lower-middle-class family," I said suddenly. "We went through periods of real poverty. My parents worked themselves to the bone trying to support six kids. I saw how hard they worked, but sometimes, it just wasn't enough. There was this one time when my parents and their coworkers went on strike with their union. It lasted four months. Four months of living off welfare, government aid, and food stamps.

"That poverty left a hunger in me," I continued, my voice tinged with a mix of bitterness and reflection. "Not just physical hunger, but something deeper. It planted this idea in my head that financial success was the only way to escape that pain. That idea became my driving force as I grew up. It was more important than anything—more important than relationships, personal health and safety, peace and comfort. It became a superpower. Then years later, after I achieved long-term legitimate success, I faced a serious threat—something that would potentially destroy all I built. But the superpower idea of financial success compromised my moral judgment. So, I committed fraud. This was not an easy decision. I was tormented by the situation, and in some ways, I still am. That superpower hijacked everything."

***

I sensed trouble was coming the moment I stepped out from the Recreation building alone at night. The sky was black as hell, the wind howling. The three Hispanic inmates—Hernandez, Ramirez, and Gutierrez—had been watching me for days, whispering among themselves. I had heard rumors: they thought I was snitching, tipping off the DTSes and guards about their contraband operation. Booze, cell phones, drugs—big money moved through those trades, and a snitch could shut it all down. I had barely made it past the Recreation building when they cornered me near a dumpster, blocking any escape.

"You running your mouth?" Hernandez sneered as he clenched his fists.

Ramirez stepped forward. "We hear you been talking about our business."

I kept my hands at my sides, trying to stay calm. "I don't snitch, but I will Pull-Up someone during the meetings for careless behavior that will cause me more time. I don't know anything about what you guys do," I said evenly.

"Then why the fuck are the guards cracking down?"

Gutierrez barked, "They know what's going on."

I barely had time to react before the first punch landed—Gutierrez's fist connected with my right upper jaw, sending a jolt of pain through my skull. I staggered but didn't go down.

Another hit came, this time from Ramirez, slamming into my ribs like a fucking hammer. Then quickly followed by a hard jab to the left side of my face.

I threw a wild punch, catching Ramirez in the eye, slightly splitting the skin open. Blood ran down the side of his face, but it only made him angrier. I barely had time to brace before Hernandez caught me again, this time a brutal right hook, again to my right upper jaw, that knocked a tooth clean out of my mouth.

Spitting blood, I raised my hands. "Listen!" I shouted, my voice hoarse. "I never went behind anyone's back!"

Ramirez wiped the blood from his face, glaring. "Bullshit. You fucking lie."

I held up a hand. "I talk in the RDAP morning meetings. That's it. Out in the open, where everyone hears. I don't whisper to COs. I don't drop notes."

For a moment, silence stretched between us, thick with tension. Then Hernandez frowned. "Wait... the meetings?"

I nodded, panting. "Yeah. If I got something to say, I say it in the open. I don't snake people."

The three men exchanged looks. I thought they were gonna come back at me. But they weren't stupid—if I was a snitch, why would I talk about things publicly in the morning meetings where everyone could hear?

Ramirez exhaled sharply, wiping at the blood dripping from his eye. "Shit," he muttered, shaking his head.

I spat out another mouthful of blood. "We good?" I was hoping we were. My blood pressure was up, ready for fighting, but there was no way I was going to win.

Ramirez rolled his shoulders, still watching me warily. "For now."

Hernandez scoffed but backed off. Gutierrez was the last to move, his eyes still burning with suspicion. But eventually, he nodded.

I didn't trust them, not completely. They probably didn't trust me. I knew prison politics could change in an instant. But for now, the fight was over.

I sat on the edge of my bunk, rolling my sore jaw with my fingers. My missing tooth was a constant reminder of how close I had come to real trouble. The fight with Hernandez, Ramirez, and Gutierrez had settled things for the moment, but in prison, peace was always temporary.

Late that night, just as the tier had quieted down, a low voice came from the bunk next to mine. "Hey," the voice whispered. It was Darnell Johnson, a solidly built Black inmate who had been down for over a decade. He kept to himself, but he and I had an unspoken respect for each other.

I turned slightly. "What's up?"

Darnell leaned in, keeping his voice low. "Word is, some dudes are trying to set you up. Plant a phone in your bunk, then tip off the COs."

I tensed. I already knew the accusations about snitching weren't going away, but this? This was worse. Getting caught with a cell phone meant time in the Hole—maybe even a transfer to a higher-security yard. And if the wrong people believed I had really turned rat, my life wouldn't be worth much in here.

"Who?" I asked, keeping my voice steady.

Darnell shook his head. "Don't know exactly who's behind it, but it's spreading. They want you out, man. RDAP put a target on your back."

I exhaled slowly. I had seen this kind of setup before—how the drug program turned inmates against each other. RDAP wasn't just about getting clean; it was about following their rules, their way of thinking. They encouraged inmates to confront each other, to hold each other accountable, but in a place like this, that just meant turning people into informants. And if you got labeled a snitch, even unfairly, you were done.

I knew I had to act fast.

The next morning, I sat at the metal table in the unit, carefully writing a letter to my attorney. My handwriting was slow, deliberate, every word chosen carefully.

Dear Leif:

I am writing to formally document my concerns regarding my safety. Since entering the Residential Drug Abuse Program (RDAP), I have seen firsthand how this system pits inmates against each other under the guise of "accountability." The result is a dangerous environment where accusations—true or false—carry dangerous consequences.

Recently, I was confronted by multiple inmates who believed I had been informing on them. I was physically assaulted, lost a tooth, and barely managed to deescalate the situation. Now, I have received information that another group is planning to plant contraband—a cell phone—inside my living area and report it to the correctional officers. This is a clear attempt to remove me from the program and prison facility.

I fear that if something happens to me, it will be because of these false accusations and the hostile environment RDAP has created. I am requesting that this letter be kept on record in case I need to seek legal action for failure to protect my safety.

Respectfully,

Paul

I folded the letter carefully and sealed it in an envelope. I'd get it out through legal confidential mail, the only way to ensure it wouldn't be intercepted.

As I set the pencil down, I glanced over at Darnell, who gave me a slight nod.

"Appreciate you looking out," I muttered.

Darnell just shrugged. "This place don't need any more bullshit, man. Watch your back."

I already knew I would.

***

On February 15, 2022, I received notice of my release date—March 6, 2022. I was scheduled to finish all RDAP requirements the week before. I felt mixed emotions because I did not trust the system. Sometimes release dates changed. I had seen it happen before—cellmates packed and ready to go, only to be told at the last minute that a clerical error, a paperwork delay, or some bureaucratic technicality had postponed their freedom.

I refused to let myself feel excitement or relief. Not yet. Not until I was physically on the road, miles away from this place.

For now, all I could do was wait. I kept my head down, avoided trouble, and stayed out of any last-minute conflicts that could derail everything. Each night, I marked another day off my calendar, forcing myself not to hope too much. Hope was dangerous.

Still, as March 6 crept closer, I couldn't ignore the way my heart pounded a little harder. The way my mind wandered to thoughts of fresh air, real food, and life beyond this hell. Freedom was within reach—so close I could almost taste it. But I would not believe it until I processed out of Discharge and walked through the prison gates.

CHAPTER FOURTEEN:
THE RELEASE

On July 7, 2022, at the age of fifty-seven, I was released from federal custody after serving twenty-eight months. My incarceration included a month stay in a halfway house in Grand Rapids, Michigan, which helped prisoners transition from prison to back into society. I noticed the length of stay in the halfway house correlated with the length of a prison's sentence. Those with long sentences, say twenty years, often needed more time to transition back into society than those with a two-year sentence.

During incarceration, I suffered onset of high cholesterol, hypertension, sleep apnea, and borderline obesity (gaining fifty pounds), all disorders I did not have prior to prison. Additionally, my mental health had significantly worsened, becoming more pervasive and chronic and unlikely to remit significantly because of freedom. No. I was far into a deep depression caused by profound losses and traumatic stress. I saw other ex-prisoners suffering severe disability well after release, some for several years, others permanently.

During the last year of my incarceration, I was denied contact with my two youngest children by their mother. I discovered she, who was a native German, took the children out of the country permanently without my consent or knowledge and hid their whereabouts. This caused me extreme anxiety and distress; and it deeply frustrated me because I had no way to make inquiries while in prison.

This summary of my overall physical, mental, and family/social state upon release was my starting point. This was how I would begin life after prison.

At the halfway house, I was restricted to the building during the first week for orientation and initial adjustment. I was fitted with a GPS monitoring ankle bracelet and given a cellular phone with no access to the internet. The phone had Bluetooth connection to the ankle bracelet. An alarm would go off on the ankle bracelet and phone when I was out of bounds—a factor of location and time of day. If the ankle bracelet alarm triggered, I had to use my phone to call security. Randomly, I received notice on my phone to take a picture of myself. Once the picture was taken, it was automatically sent to security for processing.

Having a phone seemed strange at first because I had not held one in over two years. The phone was subject to random monitoring and inspection where I was required to hand it over to staff. No one was allowed to use any other cellular phone or communication device. The contact list and call log were reviewed.

When permitted to leave the building, I had to submit a weekly schedule in advance for any activities that occurred outside of the halfway house structure. The schedule would include times, places, and description of activities.

Within weeks, I was able to secure employment with a construction contractor, living arrangements, a down payment on an old truck, and health insurance. I also made video contact with my family and children, except my two youngest. In-person contact at the halfway building was not allowed.

While in prison, I agonized over my predicament, the deficits and the disadvantages, the wasting of life, the loss of agency and self-determination. But now, action was needed. It was "do or die." I was no longer rotting in prison, receiving the minimum three hots and a cot. I would have to care for myself—physical and mental health, my massive debts and financial obligations, and the responsibilities and duties as a father.

***

It was early morning on Tuesday when I received the official BOP release notice.

"It's done," I whispered to myself as I peered into the sky and raised a clenched fist slowly upward. The wind was forceful coming out of the west. The broad sky was mostly clear, deep blue, with some dramatic looking clouds. I paused, lowered my arm, closed my eyes and stood for a minute, before walking to my vehicle.

I left Grand Rapids heading north, back to the sacred hills and swamps of my youth, to Arcadia.

"Things are always better in the north," I said aloud as if I was speaking to someone.

I knew there were no rational reasons for life to be better in the north, but it was a strong belief I once held as a child. The north was relatively untouched, cold, harsh, and wild with dramatic scenery, the perfect place to get away from people for a while and contemplate the future.

Besides, Arcadia was my home. Since 1970, the Smith family lived and/or owned property there. I went to school at Arcadia Elementary and the nearby consolidated school system. I kissed a girl for the first time on Arcadia Beach off Lake Michigan. As a teenager, I worked hauling hay and picking fruit for the Miller family farm. I made love to a beautiful woman, my first wife, while camping on a piece of property I owned in Arcadia. From that love, we conceived my oldest child. My father and older brother were buried in a cemetery nearby. Yes, this was my home.

I was set to live in a camper trailer located on my son's property. The camper was in good condition and connected to water and sewer. The land was beautiful, consisted of eighteen acres of wooded swamp and twelve acres of open field.

Although excited about my release, I knew both myself and life out in the world had dramatically changed. I understood most parts of my life, including work, recreation, family, financial, and social network were disrupted or destroyed, and I would have to start all over in many ways.

For weeks, I went through profound adjustments. I often woke up feeling dread, thinking I was still in prison. The feeling often lingered for an hour or more. I had recurrent nightmares of being locked up for life and never seeing my family or children again. These nightmares would disrupt my sleep significantly.

When I looked into a mirror, which was infrequent, I did not recognize myself for a split second, causing me to squint and tilt my head. The image in the mirror and the image in my mind, what I expected, did not match. It was as if I were looking at someone else. As I stared for more than a few seconds, I recognized myself, but of a different version.

Socially, I was distant and detached. I was not fearful or intentionally avoidant. Rather, I was deeply apathetic, not caring or needing to be around people. Except family, I received no energy from others.

I worked every day, even holidays. When I wasn't directly working, I was in the wild, identifying timber to be logged, areas for land development, and thinking how I would live out the rest of my life.

I went to bed only when I was going to pass out from exhaustion. I took no breaks. There was no recreation, leisure, or hobbies. I would not waste a moment of life. Everything I did had to advance my life or the lives of my children, with priority always given to my children.

I knew prison had changed me. Prison had numbed my feelings. I was significantly more callous and less reactive, startled, and fearful. I no longer cared what my neighbors thought, what the community or the broader society thought. Their judgments and opinions about me no longer mattered. My sensitivity to social rejection was gone long ago. I knew rumors would come, as they always do in small towns, but viewed them as insignificant and not worthy of attention.

This hardened and callous state of mind endured since before I left prison and was not some mental defense to protect my ego, like numbing, blocking, or splitting. I simply viewed society as it viewed me, as nothing significant, no one cared, no one paid attention.

It was Friday afternoon when my oldest child, Erik, pulled into the property for an extended weekend visit. Erik was in frequent contact with me through text, phone, and Skype. I looked forward to spending time with my son; the first visit by a family member since my release two months earlier. I had intentionally isolated for a while because in prison there was no privacy, no time alone, without the noise of others.

Erik, now twenty years old, lived with his mother in Macomb County, Michigan, and was attending college. I was proud of his accomplishments, knowing he had to navigate through the last years of adolescence without his father. Erik was highly intelligent, insightful and deep, and gifted musically. He was physically perfect, stunning—a lean symmetrical, proportional, and toned body, with taut flawless skin.

Erik also had valuable skills and talents, and importantly the grit and tenacity necessary for independent life. I knew if he had to face life alone, he would survive and thrive well. Such thoughts gave me deep comfort.

I embraced my son and held on for a while. With teary eyes I said, "You and your siblings are most important in my life. You give me purpose… and strength." I paused for a moment, then went on. "I want to know what's going on in your life. What is important to you? What do you need and how can I help?"

"Dad, I'm okay. I don't need anything right now," he assured me.

We walked up to the trailer. I told my son to sit down while I took luggage into the trailer. I returned with iced tea.

There was silence for about three minutes. Both of us were comfortable with silence, neither felt an urgency to say something.

I then began, "You can ask me anything... about me being in prison or you can just start talking."

Erik replied cautiously, "I just want to be sure you're okay. I know you suffered... you were dragged through hell. That whole thing was hard on all of us."

"I know, and it was my fault..." I replied quietly.

"I will say, um, a lot of stuff happened... I mean, it was a long process. It began before prison... there was... it was... I mean... I think the whole experience weighed on everyone. I saw not just you suffering in prison, but all those months beforehand. It's not easy for a child to see a parent in such unrelenting pain and suffering."

"That makes me sad. What do you see now?" I asked.

"I think you are wiser, certainly, but I think you struggle to be as prideful as you were, prior to your indictment. I've noticed a significant shift in you from a healthy self to only others... to an extent where you put all your effort into other people. You don't think of your own well-being. You don't trust yourself and don't believe in your own value as a person." Erik looked away, paused for a few moments, then continued. "You focus all your time and energy on your children mostly while you're in prison and since you've been out. You told me in a letter we were your redemption. We are your only value. That is too narrow, too myopic. And it's hard to watch."

"Erik, you will never understand. How could you? It was a vow I made to God—" I caught myself, then repeated but louder "—to God." I paused. "...so I could survive. My vow... I meant it more than anything else in my life to that point. It became my power, my purpose. It gave me certainty and direction. Without that vow, I might not be here today. It is hard to go through a harsh experience like that without some kind of conviction or promise."

Erik began to tear up. He replied emotionally, "Dad, I'll never know what you went through. I do know you suffered horribly. I mean I have seen people in pain before... but because you were in my life, my father, I saw the suffering up close. I never saw anyone suffer that intensely and for that long before... nothing even comes close. I know—I know common sense tells me people suffer all the time, and some suffer very much, maybe more than you. But me seeing you suffering was real and immediate."

"I am sorry you had to see all that. I am sorry," I said in a near whisper.

"It is noble you want to take care of your children, bring us together as a family, and right the wrongs. But you might not succeed completely, or in the ways you imagine."

"What do you mean?" I probed, slightly shaking my head.

"When you went to prison, we were all punished, severely. It was catastrophic. Do you know I have not been able to communicate with my two younger siblings in over three years? Do you know their mother, my ex-stepmother, has denied me and your side of the family access to them completely? And there's nothing I can do about it. I looked it up—the relationship between siblings is not protected by law. Neither is the relationship between grandparents and grandchildren. I not only lost you, Dad, but I lost a brother and a sister. I may never see them again. I lost a sense of family, home, stability. Holidays have never been the same.

We all suffered and will continue to for a long time. We were all sentenced."

There was a slight pause in the conversation. Then I looked straight into his eyes and said, "Yes, it's been devastating... for all of us. So, here's the deal: I am doing what I need to do now, truly. I went to prison. I lost nearly everything, including my family. God knows I paid severely. That is enough! No more! I will not allow my past decisions, crime, and conviction, continue to perpetuate harm and destruction. Enough."

I paused for a moment and looked downward. I knew I could not control life and therefore the ongoing outcomes and consequences. More than anything, what I said was a hope and prayer. Moments passed, then I continued, more seriously, "I will not be remembered for the good things I did in life. I will be remembered as either an ex-convict who faded away like a coward or a man, once beaten down, who rose up again and moved his life forward. The odds are against me. I have maybe a one-in-five chance."

"What do you mean, one-in-five chance?"

"That's based on everything I know about mental health and stressful life events, trauma."

***

I spent four days with my son. Conversation between us was infrequent but flowed comfortably. Randomly, I embraced my son and expressed words of affection. We walked the property several times and talked about plans for development.

On the last day, when Erik was about to leave, I hugged my son and told him, "I love you as much as I know how."

Erik got into his vehicle and drove off.

After a few minutes, I experienced an imperative, a strong irresistible urge to go somewhere immediately. I headed straight toward the dense wilderness, the trees, animals, and all the small and creepy things. As I approached the tree line at the edge of the field, I began to feel a powerful tension flooding my body. I entered the dense woods, heading in a straight line to the deepest, wildest area. Flowing water, deep mucky patches, dense brush, downed trees, nothing would stop me. The tension within me began to build and expand quickly. I sensed my body could not hold the tension much longer, that there would be an eruption. How it would be expressed, I did not know. Seconds later, my will and body were overtaken.

Then I suddenly stopped, drew in a deep breath and on the exhale, let out all that was in me in a loud and extended roaring cry.

Again, I drew in a deep breath and let it out.

And then again.

The last cry was as powerful as the first.

Though initially uncertain, I now knew what it all meant—the imperative, the wilderness, the tension, the loud cry. I needed to hear from God.

"What do you want from me? How should I be? How should I go forward?" I asked in a pressured voice.

I paused. "What do you want from me?"

I needed an answer. My life was destroyed and would never be the same. My family was scattered and disconnected. I had no money. I lost friendships, career, health, and confidence. There was no assistance, no encouragement, no prescribed plans. I was deep into a dark and unknown situation. I was not beginning at zero. No. I was beginning at far less than zero, with profoundly serious deficits in most life domains.

I knelt on the ground in a comfortable position. I took in a deep breath and let it out slowly and repeated for several minutes until I entered a state of calm alertness. I waited for a response, an answer, some kind of sign, anything.

My mind became flooded with childhood memories. The themes varied. I remembered fighting the family dog, falling in love with a girl's smile, waging war against sumac trees and beehives, building a lean-to and camp in the deep woods, play boys' league baseball, navigating the wilderness like Tarzan. The memories kept flowing, and in them, collectively, came the answers I needed. I remained in that holy place, in a state of revelation, until early next morning.

For More News About Paul Smith,
Signup For Our Newsletter:

http://wbp.bz/newsletter

Word-of-mouth is critical to an author's long-
term success. If you appreciated this book please
leave a review on the Amazon sales page:

https://wbp.bz/cruelunusualr

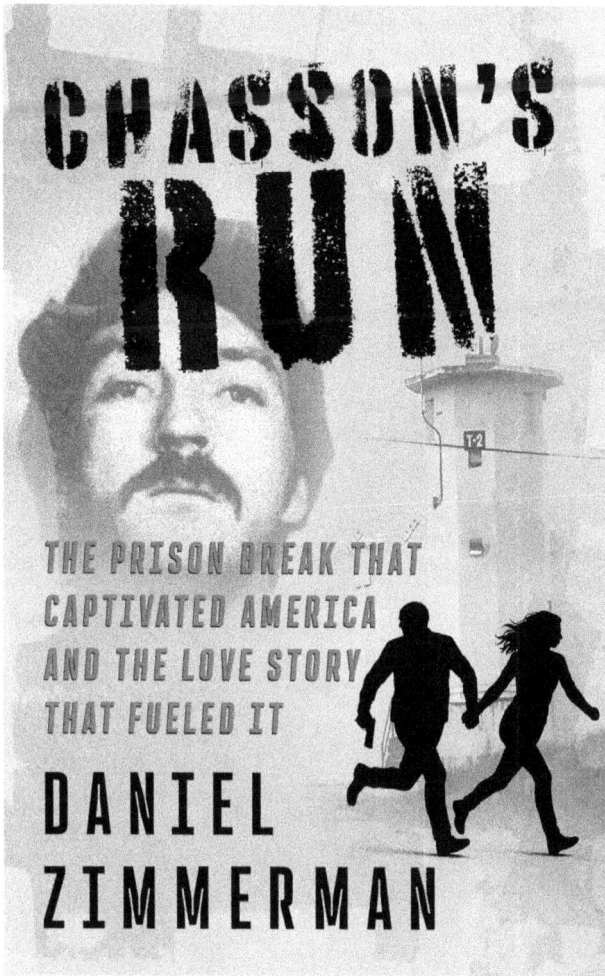

CHASSON'S RUN by DANIEL ZIMMERMAN

http://wbp.bz/chassonsrun